The Rise of the Imperial Self

Front cover: A picture of a bronze executed by Paul Manship in 1925, of the figure of Actaeon. According to myth, Actaeon was a celebrated huntsman who, after offending the goddess Diana, was turned into a stag and remorselessly pursued by his own dogs. The sculpture of which this photograph was taken is in the collection at the Carnegie Museum of Art in Pittsburgh.

The Rise of the Imperial Self

America's Culture Wars
in Augustinian Perspective

Ronald William Dworkin

Rowman & Littlefield Publishers, Inc.

ROWMAN & LITTLEFIELD PUBLISHERS, INC.

Published in the United States of America
by Rowman & Littlefield Publishers, Inc.
4720 Boston Way, Lanham, Maryland 20706

3 Henrietta Street
London WC2E 8LU, England

British Cataloging in Publication Information Available

Library of Congress Cataloging-in-Publication Data

Dworkin, Ronald William.
The rise of the imperial self : America's culture wars in
Augustinian perspective / by Ronald William Dworkin.
p.   cm.
Includes bibliographical references and index.
1. Social values—United States.   2. Individualism—United States.
3. Tocqueville, Alexis de, 1805–1859. De la démocratie in Amérique.
4. Augustine, Saint, Bishop of Hippo. De civitate Del.   I. Title.
HN59.2.D86   1996   306'.0973—dc20   96-2178   CIP

ISBN 0–8476–8218–8 (cloth : alk. paper)
ISBN 0–8476–8219–6 (pbk. : alk. paper)

Printed in the United States of America

∞™ The paper used in this publication meets the minimum requirements of
American National Standard for Information Sciences—Permanence of
Paper for Printed Library Materials, ANSI Z39.48–1984.

To Sandy

Contents

Acknowledgments

In 1980, my life's path was deflected when I took a course in political science at Swarthmore College taught by Professor James R. Kurth. Professor Kurth is one of the most interesting people I have ever met and can best be described as someone who sees far. Perhaps it is a combination of great intelligence, practical sense, and true religiosity that enables him to do so. Whatever may be the exact formula, it was Professor Kurth who placed my feet on the path of knowledge that I tread to this day, and I owe him great thanks.

Another person who provided invaluable assistance during this project was Professor Benjamin Ginsberg of The Johns Hopkins University. As my faculty advisor in the Department of Political Science, Professor Ginsberg asked exactly the right questions, thereby shaping the course of much of this book. I would also like to thank Professor Francis Rourke who advised me on the project when it was still only a small bud.

Professor Peter Berkowitz of Harvard University is both a good friend and a very smart person, which made it convenient when I needed to call someone late at night for help in deciphering confusing passages in philosophy texts. Many thanks, Peter.

Other people whom I would like to thank are Father Thomas Halton, who introduced me to some important writings of Saint Augustine, Steve Leavitt, another good college friend and one with an excellent knowledge of computers, Stephen Wrinn, my editor at Rowman & Littlefield, who was both very helpful and very patient during the writing of this manuscript, Matthew Roller, Steve Bundy, Dr. John Gable, Professor Matthew Crenson, and the entire faculty and staff of the Department of Political Science at The Johns Hopkins University. I am also indebted to Drs. William Zitzmann, Matthew Brennan, and Pedro Garcia, and the doctors, nurses, and staff of Physician Anesthesia Associates.

Finally, and most important, I would like to thank my parents. My mother, Alyse, taught me early on how wonderful reading and learning could be, and she gave me great encouragement during the years I grew up in Lakewood. And a special thanks to my wife, Sandy, who has a noble soul and who believed in me from the beginning.

Introduction

In writing *Democracy in America*, Alexis de Tocqueville believed that America was very different from the world that came before it. The difference between America and the Old World was not really one of wealth or cultivation, but rather of spirit. For centuries, philosophers had warned that a taste for anarchy was synonymous with democratic practice, that the more the great mass of men were raised high, the more society would sink low. The Americans showed the error of this rule as they succeeded in joining a love of freedom and equality to strong religious belief, a respect for the fortunes and rights of others, and a strict code of morality. The Old World built its greatness on the superior position of the few, and the spirit of human motivation attached to this practice radiated extremes of arrogance and envy, domination and servility, and refinement and squalor. The America observed by Tocqueville eased the distance between those extremes, and achieved greatness by lifting up the souls of all who labored and relying on the intelligence, optimism, and piety of its citizens to scale the peaks. In the history of the world, this spirit of human motivation was unprecedented, which is why the birth of America signified a radical break with the past.

Yet in looking at the American present, one gets a sense that America's break with the past was not so radical after all. Certain Old World ideas presumed absent from the psyche of the American have now become apparent, albeit in new forms. The ideology of expressive individualism has come to dominate the worldview of many Americans, and within the American experience, this represents something new. But ironically, it is this change that has ushered in opinions and attitudes held by citizens of an earlier age. While the Old World principle of inequality has not made inroads, the line Tocqueville drew between America and the Old World has nevertheless blurred. With the rise of expressive individualism, America has not shifted further down a continuum, but rather come full circle.

If there is a specific moment in the history of the Old World that the American present brings to mind, it is the period of late antiquity in which Saint Augustine lived. This is because the circumstances of late antiquity and contemporary America are strikingly similar. In both, one world set on the horizon of time as a new one approached its zenith.

Augustine, with his own eyes, witnessed the death of a world—the sack of Rome and the collapse of Roman Africa. Like a supernova that heralds the death of a star, the world of late antiquity radiated an enormous spectrum of energy. During that period, Augustine, the Catholic, was forced to wrestle intellectually with a strong and diverse opposition, including the Manicheans, the Pelagians, the Donatists, the Platonists, and the pagan aristocrats. At times, perhaps, it seemed as if the cultural struggle would yield no clear victor, but with the triumph of the Augustinian position, the world was set forth on a new path. The triumph in Christian beliefs and values is what the philosopher Nietzsche correctly saw as one of the great transformative events in world culture.

Americans in the latter part of the twentieth century are also witnessing the death of a world—that of Tocqueville's America. They are living in the midst of a second cultural supernova, in which different ideologies and value systems are competing energetically for support among the populace. The competition is not a battle of interests but, as in late antiquity, a battle of worldviews. In the fight between the premoderns, the moderns, and the postmoderns, what is at stake is not simply how much wealth is to be redistributed or who is to get the larger share of government contracts, but all of the values and beliefs of a culture. With the answers to such basic questions as "what is just?" "what is good?" and "what is evil?" now a matter of debate, the term "culture wars" has appropriately been used to describe the scene in contemporary American politics. And just as pagan Rome died and gave way to the new culture of Augustinian Christianity, so is Tocqueville's America dying and giving way to the new culture of expressive individualism.

Tocqueville's American as an Augustinian Figure

That there is so much debate over what life was like in the American past suggests that some kind of break with tradition has already occurred. When tremendous energy and scholarship are needed to gain insight into the simplest motives of even the most average minds of a past age then one world has gone by and another come to be. For the purpose of this speculation on the American present, the America of the past to be used for comparison is based on observations made by Alexis de Tocqueville during his travels through this country in the nineteenth century. Historians may argue whether "Tocqueville's America" provides an accurate picture of nineteenth-century America, but Tocqueville's insightful study has endured because it provides a first-hand account of the animating spirit of the nineteenth-century American. His analysis remains as valuable as that of twentieth-century scholars who use more sophisticated research methods but do so with hindsight.

The composite of the nineteenth-century American painted by Tocqueville shares much with that of the contemporary American expressive individualist. In both figures can be found a love of novelty, a feeling of smallness and insignificance that comes from living among the democratic multitude, a love of gossip about the private lives of the rich and powerful, and a tenseness and restlessness despite living in the midst of prosperity.[1] Still, certain behavioral traits in Tocqueville's American make that person a unique character type, set apart from the contemporary expressive individualist.

Tocqueville's American was an individualist not because he or she was selfish and acquisitive, but because that person imagined himself to be completely detached from others.[2] In this way, Tocqueville saw that individualism was a new imagined experience of being and not simply an intensification of the age-old tendency towards ambition and desire for personal glory. Contemporary expressive individualists share this imagined experience of detachment and join such natural impulses as self-centeredness and lust for personal gain with the special belief that one travels through life alone, separate from others. Yet Tocqueville's American, unlike the expressive individualist, combined with the feeling of detachment a willingness to submit to a higher power. He would yield some freedom to conform to a predetermined order. Whether it was bowing before the altar of the Christian God he worshipped, placing his neck under the yoke of public opinion, or adhering meticulously to the rules of democratic procedure, Tocqueville's American added to the well-known aggressiveness, confidence, and definiteness of the individualist character type a tincture of reverence for something beyond the self.

The experience of Augustine in late antiquity is relevant to the condition of Tocqueville's America, for Augustinian theology also preached a love of something beyond the self, over and above a love of self. In this way, Tocqueville's American individualist stands at the mortal limits of Augustinian thought. No character type has come closer to transcending the rivalries of the Old World and distancing himself from the worldly concerns that consume the lives of most people. Tocqueville's American lived and worked in the City of Man, filled as it is with human glory and achievement, with passion, joy, and hatred, but his interior sense possessed a certain degree of calmness and imperturbability of the kind that Augustine envisioned in the City of God. Tocqueville's American strived in a world where each man loves himself most of all, yet through the particular way in which religion and democratic principles were interpreted in that figure's mind, he escaped complete absorption. The animating spirit of the City of Man is the love of self, and it was by resisting the pull of that worldly draw that Tocqueville's American came to be an Augustinian figure and thus something markedly different from the contemporary expressive individualist.

The Contemporary Expressive Individualist as a Synthesis of Anti-Augustinian Ideas

What distinguishes the contemporary American expressive individualist as a unique character type, and very different from Tocqueville's American, is precisely his or her intense love of self. The expressive individualist feels detached from others, and therefore is an individualist in the Tocquevillian sense, but combines the experience of detachment with a tremendous pride even during moments of charity and self-sacrifice. The ambition of the contemporary Wall Street businessman who aspires to be a "master of the universe"[3] is different from the ambition of Tocqueville's American capitalist. The former hoards glory for himself. The latter worked and persevered in his duty towards God. But even less cold and calculating expressive individualists such as those who commit to sacrificing themselves by working in a "calling," who find meaning and purpose in building "communities," or who "save the environment" out of "mission," display an intense love of self hardly differing from that of the aggressive businessman. As will be shown, these pursuits are also associated with a religious fervor that tries to catapult man into a higher stratum of being.

The love of self is an old theme in world history, and it is by revisiting this theme that the America of the present brings to mind the experience of the Old World. In particular, the expressive individualist outlook contains within it some of the prejudices and opinions of late antiquity. This time, however, it is not Augustinian theology that has been reanimated in American culture. Rather, it is the coalition of ideologies Augustine fought against— Manicheism, Platonism, Donatism, Pelagianism, and pagan aristocracy— that has resurfaced. Those ideologies were subscribed to by people who had little in common with one another except, as Augustine noted, an extreme love of self.

In his work, Augustine criticizes the tremendous vanity and presumption of superiority demonstrated by the members of these sects. The Donatists "do not put their trust in God, but in men, such as the great Donatus," and their break with the Church was "the fruit of pride."[4] The Manicheans claimed to possess elements of the Divine within them, those parts of the Kingdom of Light that had been siphoned off from God, and Augustine says of them, "They become vain in their thoughts and 'profess themselves to be wise,' by attributing to themselves the things that are yours [God's]."[5] The Platonists were men of wisdom who "revolted from His wholesome humility" in the pride of vain science, whose heads had swelled so that they could no longer see the Truth.[6] The Roman aristocrats gave more honor to Romulus than to the Olympian gods, and did so in the spirit of vanity, not reason.[7]

Expressive individualism shares with these now-defunct ideologies a similar presumption of superiority. Unlike Tocqueville's American, the expressive individualist will not bow his head before an altar unless doing so feeds his own pride, and he will not conform to any predetermined order unless his autonomy and individuality are preserved. More importantly, the very basis for the great vanity of the anti-Augustinian sects of late antiquity has found its way into the ideas and beliefs of modern expressive individualists. The actual principles of Manicheism, Platonism, Pelagianism, Donatism, and pagan aristocracy can be detected in the worldview of contemporary Americans. In a way, the culture wars in America are a replay of the culture wars of late antiquity. They represent a struggle between Augustinian theology and a field that is united by an opposition to that theology. The same actors are present under new guise.

A Genealogy of Aristocracy

Of the various anti-Augustinian groups, one survived the period of late antiquity and continued to flourish—aristocracy. The impact of aristocracy on the politics and culture of the Old World remained so powerful that, in some ways, it rendered the triumph of Christian beliefs and values incomplete. Of modern aristocracy, Tocqueville and Nietzsche are keen observers. In both *Democracy in America* and *The Old Regime and the French Revolution*, Tocqueville, who was himself an aristocrat, provides a glimpse into the mind-set of Old World aristocracy. Nietzsche is almost the philosopher of aristocracy, and his discussions comparing the life-affirming instincts of the aristocrat with the life-denying and vengeful thought patterns of the slave capture in an even more vigorous way the aristocratic mentality. I suggest that there is a link between the modern aristocrat described by Tocqueville and Nietzsche and the pagan aristocrat whom Augustine criticized in the first five books of *The City of God* and that a genealogy of aristocracy can be traced. While the status, economic position, and behavior of aristocrats have changed tremendously over the centuries, something constant remains in the spark of life that animates them. That constant leads me to place the aristocrats described by Tocqueville, Nietzsche, and Augustine under a single heading—the aristocrat in the City of Man.

Two recent studies of aristocracy, *Kings or People: Power and the Mandate to Rule* by Reinhard Bendix and *The Politics of Aristocratic Empires* by John Kautsky, find something enduring in the aristocratic experience over many centuries and around different regions of the globe. In Western Europe and Asia, from as far back as the eleventh century to the modern era, aristocrats have exhibited an extreme status-consciousness, a contempt for manual labor and moneymaking, a tremendous respect for blood, rank, and tradition, a system of manners and dress that distinguishes them from others, and a regard for honor, nobility, and superior position. While the aristocrats of the thirteenth century may have prized martial valor in comparison with the court aristocrat of the seventeenth century and may have been more impulsive and physically aggressive, something within the aristocratic experience nevertheless endures.[8] This is what Kautsky notes when he says that "behavioral and ideological patterns can be perceived among aristocracies across different cultures and periods of history," and that the concept of a general aristocratic culture is a logical one.[9]

The same characteristics observed among aristocrats of the modern era can be found among the Roman aristocrats of late antiquity whom Augustine criticized. In *The City of God*, Augustine describes their "love of esteem," their love of power and domination, their "desire of human praise," and their obsession with honor, which Augustine scorned as merely "smoke which had no weight."[10] The Roman aristocrats, who looked "for glory from one another,"[11] who desired all eyes to be directed on them, and who performed great deeds for their own reputations and not to serve God, share common ground with the feudal aristocrats described by Bendix, for whom "fighting vigor" supplanted all thoughts on the hereafter.[12] Like the modern aristocrats, the Roman aristocrats suppressed their desire for wealth by loving honor and glory even more, and their obsession with high rank and domination recalls the aristocrats of the modern era who "commonly assert their own superiority over all others" and place supreme importance on titles.[13] Even Kautsky notes the similarities between the Roman aristocrats of late antiquity and those of the modern era, and how the Roman aristocrats "looked down in scorn on trade in any form" and believed a posture of religious humility was incompatible with "honor."[14]

What endures in the aristocratic experience can be summed up as an extreme love of self. While the love of self can take various forms, it is in general terms what establishes the link between the aristocrat of late antiquity and the generations of aristocrats to follow. From an Augustinian perspective, both the Roman aristocrat of late antiquity and the European aristocrat of the modern era are aristocrats in the City of Man. Their interior senses are enmeshed in the shifting currents of earthly existence—in honor, rank, prestige, and glory. All of the institutions of aristocratic society are arranged to serve this tremendous self-love. By investing certain jobs with more honor than others, by catapulting one group of people into the highest stratum, by following strict codes of conduct that separate them from commoners, or by praising military glory, aristocratic society appeased, rewarded, and honored that self-love. In the language of social science, these arrangements are given the formal and seemingly neutral title of "aristocratic institutions," but from an Augustinian perspective they are nothing more than tributes to self-love.

In the long timeline of aristocracy, Tocqueville's American represents the first great interruption. This is because Tocqueville's American, although a democrat, ushered in a new age of aristocracy—not aristocracy in the City of Man but in the City of God. His interior sense was enmeshed in that which transcended the visible world—in Christian faith, in public opinion, and in the order of republican principle. It was not the love of self so much as it was a love of those ideals, and the order spawned by those ideals, that quickened the early American's spirit. Investing all jobs with the same degree of honor, adhering to the rules of democracy (even if they were enforced by a "petty" magistrate), deferring to the will of the majority, and persevering in God were activities that demonstrated a love of order paid at the expense of self-love. The institutions and social arrangements of Tocqueville's America represented a new experience in democracy. But from an Augustinian perspective, they are special because they formed the basis of a new society, one that for the first time in history paid tribute to the love of something distant and immemorial and not just self-love.

In this way, Tocqueville's American stands at the nexus of the three great philosophical traditions founded by Tocqueville, Nietzsche, and Augustine. He is the synthesis that combines Tocqueville's praise of the American democrat and contempt for the aristocrat in the City of Man, Nietzsche's contempt for the modern democrat and praise of the aristocrat in the City of Man, and Augustine's contempt for the aristocrat in the City of Man and fervent belief in an otherworldly experience in the City of God. As an aristocrat in the City of God, Tocqueville's American is the one figure who combines democracy, aristocracy, and Augustinian theology and thus can draw support from all three philosophers.

The rise of expressive individualism in America represents the second great interruption in the long timeline of aristocracy. It signals a return of the interior sense of the American to the City of Man. The movement of expressive individualism is filled with Manichean, Pelagian, Donatist, and Platonist elements, but it is the tendency towards conventional aristocratic behavior within the movement that provides some of the most glaring examples of self-love. In expressive individualist America can be found the opinions and prejudices of the aristocrats observed by Augustine, Tocqueville, and Nietzsche. In this way, by returning to the City of Man and its theme of self-love, America has come full circle.

Part One

America and the City of Man

1

Expressive Individualism, Manicheism, and the "Higher Self"

How Manicheism and Expressive Individualism Share Common Ground in a Belief in the "Higher Self"

Manicheism was one of the three great religious systems of late antiquity, the other two being Catholicism and Neoplatonism. In their practical organization, the Manicheans had the "aura of a secret society,"[1] and Augustine was a devout member of the sect for nine years. The Manichees espoused a dualist theology that divided the world into a Kingdom of Light and a Kingdom of Darkness. The Kingdom of Light was composed of all that was good—in other words, God—and set against a force of evil no less real and substantial, called the Kingdom of Darkness. The two kingdoms were co-eternal and hostile, and the history of the world was believed to be a history of a titanic struggle between these two powers, with bits of Light coming to be trapped in Darkness (of good becoming trapped in evil). For example, the divine substance that was an animal's spirit was believed to be contained within a fleshly mortal coil; light (or spirit) could become trapped in darkness (or matter). The Manichean worked towards a unity of all the bits of Light because each piece represented an element of the divine that had been broken off from God.

This struggle in the external world was believed to mirror the struggle in a man's soul, between one nature that was good and another that was evil.[2] The two souls were yoked together, with the good soul longing to be set free, to divorce itself from the rage, passion, and tension spawned by one's evil nature. The good soul desired to approach unity with the Kingdom of Light and to retrieve that "untroubled, original state of perfection."[3]

Through this dualist system, the Manichees were able to preserve the

3

purity of God's goodness. They argued that evil did not come from God but from an invasion by an independent force. The power of evil cornered and enveloped small crumbs of divine substance and thus represented a completely different nature. The Manichee who was "illuminated," who was "filled with light,"[4] came to realize that he had a "good soul," or a "higher self," trapped inside something evil or lower. This true knowledge, or *gnosis*, of his real condition was sent to liberate him from the power of demons. The Manichee came to understand that it was not he who sinned when committing a base act, but rather the evil nature within him. The identity, or the "I," was split apart in Manichean dualism, causing one part of the soul to remain untouched and unaffected while another part received all the blame.

In contemporary expressive individualism, a dualist system is espoused that is similar to Manicheism, one that confers spiritual benefits such as revelation and salvation. It can assume different forms, such as psychotherapy, Dianetics, empowerment training, and self-improvement, but each form has within it a belief in the "higher self." There are no Kingdoms of Light and Darkness in the expressive individualist adaptation of the Manichean system, but the concept of a higher self forms a core principle, and the sects associated with it preach, almost like the Manicheans, the way of the true *gnosis*. In self-help books, in consciousness-raising seminars, on the therapist's couch, and in the office of the counselor, the believer is helped to struggle free of entanglements impeding or dragging down his or her higher self. Expressive individualists may disagree over what constitutes the higher self, and they may seek advice from different sources, but they have in common a belief that one can be healed by stripping away one's lower nature.

The Manichean fought against the Kingdom of Darkness in the effort to realize this hidden greatness. He fought against lusts, snares, and passions so that the baser nature of his person would be "split off and shoved away."[5] In the same way, the expressive individualist fights against illusions, dreams, memories of trauma, neuroses, fears, and self-deception. He accuses them and says they prevent him from passing from worse to better. He calls them "obstacles" just as if they had real substance and were somehow separate from his person. For both the expressive individualist and the Manichee, the higher self is imprisoned in another substance, one composed of painful memories, emotional demons, and imagined phantoms. The two part ways only over the exact definition of evil.

The Manichee lusted after someone and committed a sexual act and afterwards believed that evil had been done. He attributed the sin, however, not to himself but to some other nature within. Similarly, the expressive individualist may have difficulty forming intimate relationships, which the culture of expressive individualism recognizes to be abnormal. Yet like the

Manichee, the expressive individualist attributes the sin not to himself but to some other nature within. It is, for example, the memories of a cold and impersonal mother, of a harsh father, or a malevolent teacher that impinge on his consciousness and deflect his life's path. Such obstacles restrain from functioning properly the other nature within that is good and loving and higher. The therapist in contemporary America actually encourages this idea, suggesting that the afflicted person is a "victim" of certain childhood experiences, that the memories of those experiences form "obstacles" in the mind, and that they form another nature within the person lying beyond the person's control.

A few examples from the literally hundreds of book titles on the subject of mental wellness in America should help to illustrate this point. In *Reclaiming the Inner Child*, edited by Jeremiah Abrams, it is argued that virtually every adult has experienced an anxious and stressful childhood, with the abused "inner child" needing to be healed in order to resolve old traumas. In *Healing the Shame That Binds You* by John Bradshaw, the addictions, compulsive behavior, and character disorders in people are understood as the result of "toxic shame," the nature of which the author tries to characterize. "Toxic shame" colors the entire identity of a person and is presumed by the author to have its origins in the negative experiences of infancy. In *A New Guide to Practical Living* by Albert Ellis and Robert Harper, irrational beliefs are believed to impinge on the way people think about themselves and their world, causing psychological problems. Therapy is advocated as a way to erase fears and conquer anxiety. In *Unlimited Power* by Anthony Robbins, the higher self is achieved through the power of conscious thought, with all mental energy directed towards building images and habits that support one's higher goals. In *Anger: How to Live With and Without It* by Albert Ellis, rational emotive therapy is designed to help people rearrange and organize their anger. In *Passion, Profit, and Power* by Marshall Sylver, the effort is made to reprogram the subconscious by pinpointing target areas that impinge on well-being.

What is unique and striking about each of these books is not simply their tendency to "scientize" feelings and emotions by placing them in rational conceptual frameworks, but that each divides the self into two natures. "Toxic shame" is like a dark and mysterious cloud that rolls in from nowhere and "surrounds" the person. Irrational beliefs "impinge" on one's healthy psyche. Mental energy is used to "overcome" bad or unhealthy images and help good ones take their place. Anger is "shunted aside" within the psyche, beaten back into the corner of the brain where it can do less harm. In each case, there is a rigid division between those mental processes that are pathological and the idea of the higher self, with the higher self emerging once mental evils have been controlled or defeated. Words like "impinge," "overcome," and "surround" heighten the sense of struggle between the two opposing forces, and between the two different natures.

In this way, the Manichean understanding of the good as being "singularly passive and ineffective"[6] is perpetuated in the imagined experience of the expressive individualist. The Manicheans argued that the good is "essentially passive, impinged upon by the violent activity of the bad."[7] The Kingdom of Darkness was the active force—"it impinged, it violated, it was driven in upon the 'Land of Light'."[8] For the expressive individualist, that which is pure and good in a person—the higher self—is invaded, dragged down, and violated by a force of evil. The force of evil has substance. It is composed of memories, fears, anxieties, mental ruts and traps, habits, cravings, and lusts. It is this force that both the expressive individualist and his therapist imagine bearing down on him, limiting his freedom and autonomy and forcing upon him a life of pain and tension. This is how evil is disowned by both the expressive individualist and the therapist, and the expressive individualist, like Augustine when he was a Manichee, is allowed to excuse himself and accuse some other nature within him, but which is alien to his being.[9]

The Manichean ideal was a corporeal fantasy that gave Augustine hope and pleasure, one on which he was fed and nourished. He describes how the Manicheans filled his ears with the melody of a sweet truth and how the idea of a higher self bolstered his pride and gave him joy and gladness. But he gradually came to reject their philosophy, and of the Manichean vision he wrote, "Food in dreams is very like the food of waking men, but sleepers are not fed by it: they merely sleep."[10] Still, Augustine tread the path of enlightenment with great difficulty. The Manichees, wrote Augustine, "boomed forth your name [God] at me so many times and in so many ways, by the voice alone and by books many and huge."[11] Manicheism was embraced by the cultured and sophisticated of the day.[12] It offered a rational account of the universe, one that did not impose its will on believers through the simple demand of faith or by terrifying one with fables, but instead by appealing to reason and inviting the believer to join after he had been given an understandable account of its truths.[13]

The situation in contemporary America is analogous. The ideology of expressive individualism is dominant in America. Its voice is heard in film, on television, and in song, and the scientific literature supporting the idea of a higher self fills hundreds of shelves in the library. Like Augustine when he was a Manichee, the soul of the expressive individualist is "borne about and turned around, bent this way and bent that" by the blasts blowing "out of the breasts of men who think they know."[14] Expressive individualism is embraced by the cultured and sophisticated of the day, and it appeals to people not by demanding faith before reason, as, for example, do some of the established conservative churches, but by inviting a person to join in a rational dialogue about his or her problems.

Augustine argued against the Manichean conception of evil, saying that evil was not a force or a substance but rather the privation of good.[15] When evil is committed, it is not a separate and evil nature that is responsible but the whole person who has fallen away from good. It is the self that sins and not some other nature within the self. Evil can not be all wrapped up in a big lump and pushed away. Instead, it has to be admitted as an integral part of our single nature.[16] Augustine conveys the pleasure his earlier delusion had given him, saying "It gave joy to my pride to be above all guilt, and when I did an evil deed, not to confess that I myself had done it. . . . I loved to excuse myself, and to accuse I know not what other being that was present with me but yet was not I."[17]

Augustine's criticism of the Manichean understanding of evil is relevant to expressive individualism. Just as Augustine the Manichee was comforted in his belief that inside he was being thwarted or constrained, so is the modern expressive individualist comforted in believing that beyond one's destructive impulses, one's painful memories, and one's neurotic behavior stands something greater, higher, unique, and unalloyed. The expressive individualist who pours through self-help books, consults a therapist, or claims to be a "victim" of psychic trauma finds joy in believing that his or her encumbrances are alien ones to be gotten rid of. The expressive individualist imagines them dissociated from the self, away from the body, and leaving a residue more noble and pure. It would be catastrophic for such a person, and an insult to his or her pride, if he or she discovered that lying within was nothing higher, that the higher self is a figment formed out of personal misery, that there is nothing within the self that exists separate from personal frailties, and that the idea of a higher self is merely food in dreams.

Augustine criticized the Manichean effort to rest the division between good and evil on a division between spirit and matter. In *Against the Epistle of Manicheus Called Fundamental*, he says to the Manicheans, "How could you be so blinded in mind as to say that only the region of darkness was material, and that the so-called region of light was immaterial and spiritual? . . . two regions cannot be joined at their sides unless both are material."[18] Spirit and matter can not have an interface unless they are all one or all the other.

Both the Manichee and the expressive individualist materialize that which is psychologically painful and oppressive by placing it adjacent to the joyful, the loving, and the higher. As a Manichee, Augustine pondered good and evil and "postulated two masses opposed to one another, each of them infinite, but the evil one on a narrower scale, the good one larger."[19] He imagined an interface (and a struggle) between the higher self and the lower self, between the good and the evil, stating, "I believed you [God] to be infinite in other parts, even though I was forced to admit that you are finite in that part where the evil mass stands in opposition to you."[20] This same understanding of the division between the higher and lower natures of the soul can be found in expressive individualism. In both Manicheism and expressive individualism, the realms of good and evil are imagined to be limited on one side by an interface and unbounded on the other. In expressive individualism, the higher self and the lower self grapple with each other, both aspiring to the prize of one's identity.

But this belief in the two realms is contradicted by the existence of the interface, for if there is an interface (and a struggle) between realms, both realms must be of the same nature. The higher and the lower already have the same configuration (bounded on one side, infinite on the other), and if they are bounded on one side, they must be so by a nature that is fundamentally the same, one that tests and limits the expansion of the other.[21] Otherwise, no common border or struggle could exist. (There can be no interface or struggle between light and water because they are not of the same nature. Two liquids can have an interface and limit each other's expansion, but only because they are of the same nature.)

Haunting memories, oppressive guilt, and overwhelming fear consist of the same substance as joy, peace of mind, and moments of confidence, and such phenomena combine to form a single unity called the psychological experience of the self. While they are qualitatively different, they cannot be used to separate a person into two radically independent selves. Making such a distinction is like dividing two sections of water and calling them fundamentally different types of water. If there is struggle at an interface, the nature and power of the two realms divided by the interface must be the same, in which case the idea of the interface separating two radically different phenomena is a fantasy. The two realms are really one, composed of the same substance. In this way there is only one self, or one will, not two independent natures. Moods and emotions swim in and out of consciousness, but "good" and "bad" mental experiences cannot provide a basis for two different selves. They are of the same substance.

Augustine criticized the self-deception propagated in the Manichean division between the higher and the lower. The Manichean, Faustus, spoke not of two Gods but of God and *Hyle*, and Augustine noted how absurd it was for Faustus to deny the name of God to that which the Manicheans admitted had the power of God ("In reality, it is absurd to call the one *Hyle*, as it is to call the other God.")[22] It was a rhetorical device meant to conceal the

Manichee's embarrassment at having to assign the name "God" to a "lower" nature that, in truth, had the same nature and substance as the Manichean God. The expressive individualist uses a similar device. The expressive individualist puts painful memories, fears, and bad habits in a category separate from the higher self and calls them the lower self. Yet these dark thoughts have all the power of one's positive and joyful thoughts; they are of the same nature as feelings associated with the higher self. It is absurd to deny the name "higher self" to that which the expressive individualist admits has all the power and energy of that self. It is absurd to call the one "lower" and the other "higher," just as it was absurd for Faustus to call the "lower," *Hyle*, and the "higher," God. The Manichean Faustus was too embarrassed to link certain phenomena to his God and so he concealed the link by giving them different names. In the same way, the expressive individualist is too ashamed to link certain psychological experiences to his or her person or admit they form essential elements of his or her identity, and so he or she imagines them apart from the self and gives them different names.[23]

The Augustinian attack on the expressive individualist division between the lower self and the higher self can be heard emanating from quarters identified with the nineteenth-century (Tocquevillian) tradition, especially the conservative churches. Their lectures on guilt, sin, blame, and individual responsibility are derived from an Augustinian conception of the human will—that the will does not house two natures but one, and that it is the self that sins and commits evil and not some evil nature separate from the self.

In this belief, one cannot be a victim of an independent psychological experience because the self cannot be separated into two independent natures. There is no higher self independent of evil and capable of standing on its own, but only a single identity (a single will) that errs and sins and commits evil. Evil is caused by a defective self, not by something beyond the self. Evil is not active substance; it does not rival, impinge, violate, or victimize. It is merely a negation of the good. In this way, traumatic memories, harmful neuroses, conflicting passions, and great tensions signal conflict within the self, but not between two different natures (or wills) within the self.

Augustine was not insensitive to the pain of troubled souls. On the contrary, from personal experience, he knew well how burdens can weigh one down, how habits can hold one fast, how memories can distress, and how moments of life are often spent in quiet despair, and he eloquently describes such emotional states in his *Confessions*. The cravings, the losses, and the great tensions longing to be resolved are felt intensely in each person, and it is the yearning for perfection that Augustine said "makes the heart deep."[24] But this is why Augustine criticized the idea of the higher self and the belief that purity could be achieved through wisdom, training, and practice. His criticism applies equally to the philosophy of expressive individualism. He wrote,

> Let them deal harshly with you, who do not know with what effort truth is found and with what difficulty errors are avoided; let them deal harshly with you, who do not know how rare and how exacting it is to overcome imaginations from the flesh in the serenity of a pious intellect, let them deal harshly with you, who do not know with what pain the inner eye of man is healed, that he may glimpse his Sun.[25]

Augustine knew full well how a person could be tormented from within. But he rejected simple models of human behavior that promised perfection and salvation. Such models, he believed, were deceitful and ensnared a person by appealing to his or her vanity. From an Augustinian perspective, the expressive individualist belief in the higher self follows in the Manichean tradition as simply one more attachment imagined by the mind, of the same corporeal substance as the Manichean God who was an "immense shining body,"[26] inspired by the same boastful pride, and leading to the same useless effect.

How Manichees and Expressive Individualists Share Certain Customs

The similarities between Manicheism and expressive individualism are not confined to the debate over whether the human psyche contains one or two natures. They extend further. After Augustine left the Manicheans to became a Catholic, he wrote an essay titled "The Catholic and Manichean Ways of Life" in which he criticized the religious customs of the Manicheans. There are some very interesting similarities between the customs of the Manichees and certain practices found among expressive individualists.

The Manichees preached abstinence from meat and wine. They argued that animals possessed a mixture of evil and the divine (of darkness and light) and that when the animal was killed, the divine part escaped, leaving only filth. This is why the Manichean believed the souls of those who consumed meat were defiled. In the society of expressive individualism, the purchase of food is shrouded in similar mystery. Americans are very particular about the food they purchase, and their abstinence from certain foods suggests a high degree of religious fervor. When the expressive individualist counts calories in the supermarket, refrains from sugar or caffeine, or trims the fat, he or she feels more noble and more worthy and that he or she has demonstrated stamina, honor, and perseverance. For the expressive individualist, the purchase of food represents a conscious milestone on the way to the higher self.

Slicing off fat, substituting margarine for butter, and consuming more fruits and vegetables are practices the benefits of which have a scientific basis. The result is often lower cholesterol levels and an improved intake of vitamins and minerals. But the spirit in which expressive individualists inspect their food, recoil at the sight of fat, cringe if they smell grease, and demonstrate an almost instinctive revulsion towards any artificial ingredients represents something still more complicated. Augustine criticized the extreme zealotry of the Manicheans in their practice of abstinence, and the term "Manichean" became a byword for anyone who failed to enjoy the simple pleasures of life. [27] The "pale and gaunt"[28] Manichean with his obsessive perfectionism has a kindred spirit in the fat-avoiding, caffeine-dodging, calorie-cutting expressive individualist who looks tired and haggard after his ten-mile jog. An element of the extreme is present in the dietary habits of expressive individualists that is not found among Tocqueville's Americans.

The Manichean feature in expressive individualist dietary habits can perhaps best be demonstrated by applying a modification of Augustine's criticism of Manicheism to the experience of the expressive individualist. [29] Imagine a person who is so frugal and abstemious that he refrains from any food other than an occasional piece of bacon fat and a morsel of cheese and who occasionally wets his lips with beer and whole milk so as not to suffer dehydration. Now compare that person with someone who lusts and salivates over heaps of fruits and vegetables and countless loaves of bread, who sups all night on that pile, consuming it voraciously, who experiences a kind of orgasmic delight with each swallow, and who thinks halfway through the meal that the festival should be repeated the following night. Which of these two persons is leading a more abstemious life, asks Augustine. The Manichee, if he is to be true to his principles, must prefer the glutton. The expressive individualist, who recoils at the idea of fat and cautiously approaches any new calorie, would probably also prefer the glutton. This is because the expressive individualist, like the Manichean, believes it is not a person's intent when consuming a meal that is potentially sinful but rather the content of the meal itself. The Manichee thought that he would burn in hell if he ate small bits of Darkness and merged them with his soul. In the same spirit, the expressive individualist feels tremendous guilt when allowing his lips to be violated by a drop of fat.

For the American individualist, this represents nothing less than a complete redefinition of sin and evil. The nineteenth-century American Christian believed that gluttony, not the content of the food, was the vice. This idea was supported in scriptural passage, that "what goes into the mouth does not defile a man; but that which comes out of the mouth, that defiles a man,"[30] and Augustine quotes this passage in his attack on the Manicheans. For the nineteenth-century American Christian, all food is clean, and the only evil is in the offense given while eating it. The person who is greedy, who is unable to contain himself, is the one who is sinful.

For the contemporary expressive individualist, the divine is not in the intent but rather in the substance of the food, and the expressive individualist can consume ten plates of delicately seasoned vegetables, feel free to eat as much as he wants, and wash them down with so many bottles of fruit juice that he is ready to explode because the good (or the divine) is believed to reside in the material, not in the intent. He is virtuous because he has refrained from eating fat, butter, grease, and oil, even if he has conducted himself in a repulsive manner. Like the Manichee, the expressive individualist can only defile himself by mixing Light with Darkness, by eating certain foods. Both the Manichee and the expressive individualist are extremely discriminating in the food they eat, for when they pick through various delicacies, they are searching not for pleasure but for God, with "nose and palate."[31]

This is the new meaning of the Americanism "you are what you eat," and it abuts the expressive individualist notion of the higher self. The new American abstinence rests partly on health concerns but partly on a belief that the division between the various food groups mirrors the division between the higher and lower natures within the soul. Fruits, vegetables, and breads are interpreted as being another form of substance that comprises the higher nature within the soul. The golden melons and the shining berries are like crumbs of Light, of divine substance, and they are consumed to replenish one's higher nature.

The Manichean system treated the visible world with an extreme literalism, as if it were an externalization of some inner, spiritual conflict. The link between the Manichean system and the ideology of expressive individualism can also be observed in some of the latter movement's extreme environmentalist views. Again, the criticism that Augustine directed towards the Manicheans can be applied to expressive individualism.[32]

Most contemporary environmentalists are not classic pagans. They do not believe, as the Manicheans did, that a fig plucked from a tree will cry or that chopping a plant in two causes a leakage of divine substance. But there is a definite Manichean component to their beliefs. For example, the idea of building an amusement park in the middle of forest is hateful to them, but why? They argue that it is because the forest is natural, while the amusement park is only man-made. Yet resonating within this argument is the special Manichean belief that some aspects of the external world contain more of the divine substance (the Light) than others. The environmentalists almost argue, like the Manichean, that "in grain, beans, herbs, flowers, and fruits some part of God is present,"[33] the evidence for this being in their brightness of color, their pleasantness of odor, and their sweetness of taste. For the environmentalist, more treasure lies in natural substances than in those made by man; the former possess a higher order of goodness. It is the same line of argument that Augustine attacked fifteen centuries ago.[34]

In criticizing the idea of an amusement park in the forest, the environmentalist judges the colors in the park too bright compared with those in the forest.[35] Yet are not the colors of flowers blooming in a field brighter and more varied? The environmentalist finds the park too noisy. Yet are not thunderstorms and rushing waterfalls noisier? The environmentalist says the smells in the park are bad. Yet is not the smell of animal waste left on the ground more putrid? The environmentalist finds the park cramped and uncomfortable. Yet cannot dense clumps of brush engender an even greater sense of confinement? For the environmentalist, the goodness in nature can be demonstrated through color, sound, and smell. But why does the whiteness of a flower speak to him and not the whiteness of painted metal? Why does the blue ocean speak to him as one of God's treasures, and yet a sea of blue cars is despised?

The environmentalist, like the Manichean, finds the senses qualified to judge the presence of the divine in material things; on this basis he discriminates between the forest and the amusement park. But as just shown, the eyes, nose, and ears cannot discriminate between natural goods and artificial evils on the basis of color, smell, or sound. Many artificial evils have the same physical characteristics as natural goods. The whole thing, Augustine writes, is "absurd,"[36] which is precisely the attitude voiced by conservatives in America who write from a nineteenth-century point of view.

In Tocqueville's America, there was no such movement as environmentalism, and even the conservation movement arising at the turn of the century was designed to aid farmers and businessmen in their quest to conquer nature; it did not arise because the divine had suddenly been uncovered in nature.[37] Crop rotation, the replanting of timber forests, and bans on strip mining were designed to help the individualist in his business ventures and prevent him from exhausting his resources. Absent completely is the contemporary American romance with nature, the belief that nature is somehow holy, and the idea that progress has been achieved when one part of the earth is made off-limits to man. As an Augustinian, the old Tocquevillian individualist could not discriminate theologically between the brown trunks of trees that were going to make him rich in lumber and the brown mill that was going to carve the wood, or between the yellow ore that would make him rich in gold and the yellow equipment that would help him extract it. Unlike the contemporary expressive individualist, his senses could not discern in the visible world the presence of the divine.

How the Consumption of Goods in the Society of Expressive Individualism Recalls the Experience of the Aristocrat in the City of Man

Contemporary America exhibits a rhythm of life that is in some ways the opposite of what Tocqueville observed in nineteenth-century America. In nineteenth-century America, the sphere of work was chaotic while life at home was ordered. Now, however, the situation is almost the exact reverse. Security and order are desired at work to allow for more choice at home. Americans are willing to give up tremendous freedom at work or in public life if they are allowed to gratify themselves in private life. Work may be constricting and ordered but as long as home life is experimental and liberating, the terms are acceptable. Robert Bellah describes the incredible diversity in habits and lifestyles among the Americans that has come into being under these new terms, and Lawrence Friedman has attached a name to the new state of affairs—he calls America the "republic of choice."[38]

The private life of the contemporary expressive individualist differs considerably from that of the nineteenth-century American. Tocqueville describes the domestic situation of the early American, writing, "But when the American retires from the turmoil of public life to the bosom of his family, he finds in it the image of order and peace. There his pleasures are simple and natural, his joys are innocent and calm."[39] Men in Tocqueville's America curbed the range of their desires. The "taste for excesses, a restlessness of heart, and fluctuating desires"[40] faded into the regularity of domestic life, and men found more simple paths to happiness.[41] Tocqueville writes,

> All men who live in democratic times more or less contract the ways of thinking of the manufacturing and trading classes; their minds take a serious and deliberate turn; they are apt to relinquish the ideal in order to pursue some visible and proximate object which appears to be the natural and necessary aim of their desires. Thus the principle of equality does not destroy the imagination, but lowers its flight to the level of the earth.[42]

Tocqueville notes that while the nineteenth-century American individualist was quite "addicted to reverie,"[43] the pleasures he enjoyed were orderly. Activities that "constituted the charm and safeguard of life"[44] were avidly pursued while "the more violent and capricious sources of excitement"[45] were avoided. The imagination was bridled and its horizon lowered as the American's taste for order colored his every impulse.[46] Tocqueville notes the effect of these new limits on the human imagination, writing that "society may be more tranquil and better regulated, but domestic life has fewer charms."[47]

Tocqueville noticed a similar contraction in the desires of women in early America. He says that women sacrificed a "spirit of levity and independence"[48] to preserve domestic happiness and strengthen the family's resolve during periods of economic privation. Tocqueville writes, "American women support these vicissitudes with calm and unquenchable energy: it would seem that their desires contract as easily as they expand with their fortunes."[49] It was domestic order, according to Tocqueville, that enabled the family to endure the disorder surrounding it, and the strong conjugal tie helped families persevere in a world of "countless perils and privations."[50]

Yet if the rhythm of life for many contemporary Americans is virtually the opposite of what Tocqueville observed in nineteenth-century America, with more energy now devoted to leisure time and "lifestyle," it is not fair to say that the new expressive individualists are more hedonistic than Tocqueville's Americans. Tocqueville says that the early American enjoyed his or her pleasures with relish and zest,[51] and while those pleasures were limited in scope compared to those of some contemporary expressive individualists, the two figures apparently place about the same emphasis on the importance of physical pleasure. No evidence suggests that the obsession with physical gratification in the United States is greater now than it was when Tocqueville commented on it over a century ago.

But there is a difference between the pleasure experience of the contemporary expressive individualist and that of Tocqueville's American, one suggesting not tremendous hedonism but a belief in a higher self. Many products are purchased by expressive individualists not merely to bring a little joy and satisfaction to their lives, but to adorn their higher nature. In this respect, the pleasure experience of the old aristocrat comes to mind.

The special aristocratic attitude towards objects of consumption was observed by both Tocqueville and Augustine among the respective aristocrats of their day. Tocqueville observes of the aristocrats,

> Such men are not satisfied with the pursuit of comfort; they require sumptuous depravity and splendid corruption. The worship they pay the senses is a gorgeous one, and they seem to vie with one another in the art of degrading their own natures. The stronger, more famous, and the more free an aristocracy has been, the more depraved will it then become; and however brilliant may have been

16   Chapter One

the luster of its virtues, I dare predict that they will always be surpassed by the splendor of its vices. [52]

At another point, he says,

In aristocratic societies the class that gives tone to opinion and has the guidance of affairs, being permanently and hereditarily placed above the multitude, naturally conceives a lofty idea of itself and man. It loves to invent for him noble pleasures, to carve out splendid objects for his ambition. Aristocracies often commit very tyrannical and inhuman actions, but they rarely entertain groveling thoughts; and they show a kind of haughty contempt of little pleasures, even while they indulge in them. [53]

Augustine argued that the tremendous licentiousness of the aristocrats was directly inspired by their pagan gods, whom the aristocrats hoped to mimic. Of a young profligate, he says, "He sees on the wall a fresco representing the fabled descent of Jupiter into the lap of Danae in the form of a golden shower, accepts this as authoritative precedent for his own licentiousness, and boasts that he is an imitator of God."[54] The divine honors adjudged to a goddess and the obscenities practiced in her honor were meant to puff up the high-souled man, Augustine wrote, and no vile theatrical entertainments could be penalized if the gods themselves had consecrated them. [55]

What both of these authors discerned in the aristocrat's experience of pleasure was more than simple hedonism. The aristocrat's voluptuous pleasures, his sumptuous banquets, his drinking day and night, his playing, his vomiting,[56] and his lewd stage productions were crimes that the holy powers of heaven delighted in, and the aristocrat's tremendous vanity was fueled by them. It was not mere pleasure that the aristocrat heightened when he did what he wished or whatever his lust suggested, but the most sublime feelings. It was not mere tactile stimuli that the aristocrat exacted from his objects of desire, but a feeling of power and dominance.

The contemporary expressive individualist may engage in more lewd and exotic behavior than Tocqueville's American, living in offbeat or unconventional ways, but it is not this aspect of the expressive individualist's pleasure experience that recalls the private life of the old aristocrat. Instead, what the aristocrat and the expressive individualist have in common is a tendency to nourish and sustain the idea of a higher self through pleasure. For the aristocrat, the higher self was the part of the self that was god-like, that conveyed greatness, that lifted one above the common man and groveling thoughts. The aristocrat's practice of magnificent crimes ranked him among the powers of heaven. For the expressive individualist, the higher self is also that which is deemed most noble, most honorable, and most superior. The difference is that it is not the highest as measured by the pagan gods of the aristocrat but by new things divine.

For some expressive individualists, the highest life is found in loving, feeling, passion, and emotion, and those mental phenomena attain the status of deities. They become the whole meaning of existence, the whole point of life. Records and tapes are listened to by such persons not merely for the sake of a good tune, not simply to laugh or smile, but to induce a wrenching emotional experience. Memories and passions swirl inside the head of the listener. The listener passes from sentimental to nostalgic to sad and is soon caught up in a kind of frenzy. But it is not a frenzy of pain, for the expressive individualist begs for his tears. The situation recalls the experience of Augustine before his conversion, when tears of misery brought him a perverse kind of joy. Weeping for a friend, he says, "So wretched was I that I held that life of wretchedness to be more dear to me than my friend himself."[57] In another chapter Augustine confesses his love for shows, how "I loved to feel sorrow, and I sought out opportunities for sorrow."[58] For the expressive individualist, passion and wrenching emotion provide tinder for his own fires. In the richness of his grief, he feels more noble; in the depth of his despair, he feels more "merciful."[59] Sorrow can be enjoyed, Augustine wrote, when it feeds one's own pride.

The aristocrat slew a thousand on the battlefield and then enslaved ten thousand more, making him more like the deity he aspired to be. The expressive individualist takes his or her soul to a different height, but one that he or she believes to be equally elevated. The aristocrat would not relish the death of any man. Some killings were low and contemptible. In the same way, the expressive individualist is not moved by any artistic performance and, like Augustine before his conversion, if the show cannot arouse grief or noble feelings of sympathy, one "leaves in disgust and with disapproval."[60] Both character types differ greatly from Tocqueville's American, whose tunes never soared so high, whose armies never killed so many in glorious battle, and whose pleasures would have been judged low and groveling.

Not all expressive individualist pleasures nourish a higher self that is conceived in tremendous passion and emotion, and certainly much new music, such as rap, explores the opposite dimension of human life. Nevertheless, the belief in a higher self can be found among these other expressive individualists.

Some expressive individualists buy houses of a certain vintage and stuff them with period pieces (e.g., old clocks, old frying pans, old chairs) because they desire to feel that they are a part of history, the carriers of a tradition. While living in such a house, an expressive individualist may self-consciously adopt the persona and values of someone from that era. This phenomenon might be observed, for example, among young professionals who have tired of urban life and moved to take over a country inn. Baking bread, milking cows, and waking to the crow of the rooster recall an age of rustic simplicity. In many of their gestures can be seen conscious and vigorous efforts by these people to relive and recreate an entirely different cultural experience, one that is clearly not their own. These people gaze upon what they love, and love what they can imitate. The objects within their field of view resonate within the part of their nature that desires to move closer to the ideal. Theirs is a vain ambition—to find the right inn sitting on just the right mountaintop, to "run the heights of the heavens and the lowest parts of the earth"[61] to seek the holy deities they want to emulate.

In this way, the experience of the expressive individualist is very different from that of Tocqueville's American. The latter demonstrated a much more shallow psychological connection with the products he purchased. True, Tocqueville's American, having just struck it rich, might have bought things to impress others and, in the quest for status, revealed a psychological connection with those products as well as a hope to prove himself higher. But if Tocqueville's American purchased the finest house or the best horse and carriage in town, he did so not because those objects "felt" right or because they reverberated in his soul or because they moved him closer to a particular understanding of the divine. It was not a complex image of the self that was nurtured in his purchases. "Higher" meant something completely different. Tocqueville's American merely wanted the notion of success to be attached to his person. He merely wanted his own identity to be attached on the surface to one simple idea—that he was not just any person, but a rich person.

The aristocrats observed by Augustine and Tocqueville saw in objects of purchase a testament to their own magnificence, a proof of their existence as superior beings. Mixed in with the tremendous pleasure derived from possessing certain objects was a feeling of triumph, and simple parties of celebration became bacchanals or glorious festivals fit for a king or god. Lavishly decorated items with no utilitarian purpose fulfilled essential status needs, the needs of a higher self.[62] In the graceful contour of a piece of furniture an aristocrat saw the noble feature etched on his countenance, and from each family jewel that adorned his body he felt the centuries of tradition, of the noble history of his ancestors, move through his body. It was not just to show that one was a rich person that the aristocrat purchased things. That was the simple and unidimensional attitude of Tocqueville's American. Rather, it was to show that one was imperial in every true sense of the word. The aristocrat, like the expressive individualist, formed a deep psychological connection with the objects he consumed, one that touched on his very identity as a person and brought him closer to the ideal.

The individualists Tocqueville observed clung to small and immediate objects, and they dwelled on the few things that could make them content, such that soon those objects "last shut out the rest of the world and sometimes intervened between itself [the soul] and heaven."[63] In the consumer culture of expressive individualism, products do not shut out the rest of the world but bring a person into greater contact with the world. Through art, music, and books, an expressive individualist merges his experience with those of other people. He or she feels what others are feeling and comes to understand them. By living in old houses and among antiques, the expressive individualist feels a connection with another world and another time. Such attitudes do not suggest a tendency to withdraw from the world or a desire to live in a hypnotized state of complacency and contentment. Rather, they indicate a conscious effort by the expressive individualist to place himself firmly in what he believes to be the current of life, thus making his life's experience higher, richer, and more worthwhile. This attitude has definite aristocratic undercurrents.

2

The Expressive Individualist, the Donatists, and the Honor of Work

How the New Standard of Honor for Those Holding High Office in America Recalls Certain Donatist Principles

In fourth-century Roman Africa, a schism occurred in the Catholic Church when a sect called the Donatists broke off from the main body.[1] The Donatists argued that they were the bastion of the most moral and the most pure, and their assertions of exclusive holiness often took a fanatical and violent bent. Their judgement of morality turned on whether one had been a *traditor* (a traitor), more specifically, on whether one had delivered up copies of the Christian sacred books to the persecuting authorities. The Donatists were extremely puritanical. They tried to implement visible standards of morality as a test of membership and demanded an empirical sanctity then and there in every member of the Church. In the particular principle that is relevant to this section of the analysis, the Donatists believed that the giver of sacraments must meet the test of holiness and that the cleansing of baptism proceeded from the merits of the minister and not simply from God's unseen grace. They insisted that the man representing the office, rather than the office itself, conferred sacramental grace. This is why the Donatists refused to recognize any baptisms performed by non-Donatist priests.

Augustine argued against this position, saying that there was a difference between the sacrament and the use or effect of the sacrament. The Donatist principle breaks down, he insisted, because it is impossible for humans to determine who is pure or impure.[2] Such final judgments are the preserve of God, not man. Since the sacrament is the gift of God and not the gift of man, its efficacy is not reduced if it is administered by an unworthy minister. Ministers may vary, but "the gift of God is constant and trustworthy."[3]

The Donatist principle attacked by Augustine has resurfaced in the American society of expressive individualism. Many expressive individualists believe as if the person holding office, rather than the office itself, is the crucial element in determining the legitimacy of the service rendered by that office. For example, within the narrow confines of American religion, numerous recent scandals have involved the leaders of certain sects (e.g., The Reverend Jim Bakker), and conventional wisdom presumes that all confidence in the integrity of these sects will evaporate. Even without transgressing the law, some religious figures clearly have become very rich indeed on the contributions of their followers, which would seem a sufficient reason to condemn them and their special brand of theology. Nevertheless, the sects do not disappear, much to the confusion of mainstream expressive individualist thought, and not because their followers are mere simpletons. These people believe that the man who fills the office of church leader is merely a man, marred by the same defects as other men who live in a fallen state. For this reason, they are not shocked and overwhelmed by discoveries of misconduct. The theology and the human form that give voice to that theology are kept separate in their minds, with only the former being holy and eternal. They, like Augustine, look at the church not as a society of the most moral but as a society of the redeemed, and they do not presume to judge.[4] They believe that a net once cast may be filled "with good fish and bad fish," but the fish are not to be separated until "the net is drawn to land" (in other words, by God himself).[5]

Some expressive individualists in America have been put off by religion because of the recent exposures. They laugh at the scandals and use them in evidence against all forms of organized religion. They consider most believers to be simple boobs. But this is only because, like the Donatists, they do not discriminate in their minds between the God-inspired beliefs that permeate an official position and the frail, defective human being who may hold that position.

Ironically, this is the reason that some expressive individualists who poke fun at the crimes of church leaders find it extremely difficult to discuss the moral defects in their own champions. For example, much attention has been focused recently on the sexual escapades of President Kennedy while in office, and it is very difficult for some of his inspired followers to admit the truth about the man. For some supporters, it was not the high office of the presidency, but the man himself—his person, his family, the idea of Camelot—that formed the crucial element of their worship. Like the Donatists, these people found purity and truth not in the minister's pronouncements, but in the minister himself.

Curiously, those who are perhaps more forgiving of these recent discoveries are the members of the church sects themselves. Many of them may not have idolized President Kennedy, and some are political conservatives, but in their minds they are able to separate the man from the office he held. For these people, the office of the presidency is not absolutely identified with Kennedy's human qualities; the official pronouncements of the Kennedy administration are not necessarily colored by the man's personal frailties and defects. In the same way, neither have President Nixon's crimes destroyed respect for the office of the presidency among religious conservatives, as it has for some expressive individualists. These sect members are quite comfortable with separating the office from the officeholder.

This expressive individualist fusion of the person and the office held by the person is evident in much of contemporary American politics, not only in the tremendous scrutiny now aimed at the private lives of politicians but in the entire theatrical production that American politics has become. Image-makers and public-relations experts put great effort into building a composite of the politician for mass consumption, replete with hobbies, favorite foods, musical tastes, and likes and dislikes, for they know that some expressive individualist voters will be moved on the basis of their feelings towards the politician's person rather than by his or her specific ideology. The likableness of the politician and the comfort level that a voter has with that politician (e.g., could he be family?) are often more important than the politician's program or beliefs. Like the Donatists, these voters scour a person's human side, inspecting it in great detail. This is because their respect for the office to which a person is elected and their whole attitude towards the concept of democratic governance hinge on their respect for the officeholder himself or herself.

This situation is very different from the experience of Tocqueville's America. Tocqueville admired in the Americans that "manly independence that respects the office more than the officer."[6] Just as the priests in Augustine's church derived their authority from the grace of God, so did the public officers in Tocqueville's America derive their authority not from their special set of excellences but simply from the intangible assent of the governed. Tocqueville's Americans perhaps admired some who filled official roles more than others, but they were generally able to look beyond the officeholder and discern something more august and unchanging, like the Constitution, the Bill of Rights, and republican principle. Their enthusiasm for political life and the idea of democratic governance did not wax and wane according to the "likability" of the person who happened to hold power.

Tocqueville noted that, unlike in Europe, public officers in America did not have official costumes and that this was the logical consequence of democratic principles.[7] Still, American democracy permitted an occasional ceremony, with public officers clothed in "silks and gold," but since these privileges were only transitory and belonged "to the place and not to the man," they did not compromise any democratic principles. In a way, the expressive individualist fusion of office and officeholder is far more disconcerting than the occasional magisterial pomp displayed in Tocqueville's America even though, in the latter, the officeholder is put on a pedestal while in the former, he stoops down low because he wants to know you, because he wants to be your friend. Implied in the new state of affairs is a shift from a perfect idea of government expected to be carried out by imperfect men and women to an imperfect government expected to be run by men and women presumed perfect.

How the New Idea of "Honorable" Work Recalls the Experience of the Aristocrat in the City of Man

There is an expressive individualist type in America that is distinctive and represents a modern adaptation of the old aristocratic outlook. The expressive individualists who belong in this category are eager to work, but not merely at a "job." To them, the idea of using work simply as a means of making money and obtaining gratification in private life is contemptible. They find in work the potential for much more. Work is a source of self-esteem, a series of achievements and advancements that extends through one's entire life or, for some, even an "ideal of activity and character" that is "morally insepara- ble" from one's life.[8] Rather than hope for a job, these expressive individual- ists aspire to a "career" or a "calling."

The mind-set of the expressive individualist who works in a career or a calling differs greatly from the mind-set of Tocqueville's American. It recalls the prejudices of the old aristocrat.

Tocqueville notes that because the democratic individualist lives in a country where there is no hereditary wealth and labor is a necessity, the notion of labor for honor is "always palpably united"[9] with the notion of labor for profit. Tocqueville writes,

> Even those who are principally actuated by the love of fame are necessarily made familiar with the thought that they are not exclusively actuated by that motive; and they discover that the desire of getting a living is mingled in their minds with the desire of making life illustrious.[10]

In contrast, the aristocrat despises labor done with a view towards profit.[11] According to Tocqueville, the aristocrat keeps the profit motive separate from the idea of honor. The desire for honor and the desire for profit "intermingle only in the depths of his soul; he carefully hides from every eye the point at which they join; he would gladly conceal it [the profit motive] from himself."[12]

The difference between Tocqueville's American and the aristocrat on this issue is very relevant to the idea of the career and the calling among expressive individualists. The career and the calling as they are conceived in contemporary America do not really appear in Tocqueville's observations of nineteenth-century America. Tocqueville suggests that early American individualists were very aggressive in their effort to acquire fortune, power, and reputation in their occupations, but this is also true of contemporary expressive individualists. The difference between Tocqueville's American and the expressive individualist lies elsewhere.

For Tocqueville's American, it was the remunerative consequence of work and not the intrinsic virtue of the task being performed that encouraged one to labor. While Max Weber's extensive analysis of the work ethic and the calling in the capitalist economies of nineteenth-century Protestant societies demonstrates a purpose to labor beyond profit, it was still, for Weber's Protestant capitalist, the act of work itself and not the nature of the task performed that reminded a worker of God's promise and stirred within him feelings of virtue.[13] For Tocqueville's American, such feelings could be stirred during the performance of any task, just as profit could be extracted from any task. Work was not sought according to its position in a rank-ordering of virtuous activity for, according to Tocqueville, there was generally no rank-order of honorable tasks in America.[14]

Tocqueville's American mixed a part of himself into the finished product of his labor, and he took a certain pride in ownership, but that is not the same as mixing the title of a job with one's personal identity. Tocqueville's American worked hard and achieved, which fed his pride, but the task he engaged in was not adorned with a particular virtue that fulfilled some vague and mighty hope. Work did not provide Tocqueville's American with meaning or a sense of purpose; the unique and special features of a task did not contribute to his feeling of being a unique and special self. Work simply made him rich. To link one's deepest attitudes about the self to the nature of one's work is a distinctly aristocratic practice. It is also a practice evident among some contemporary expressive individualists, particularly among those who view work as a calling.

According to Bellah, a calling has "meaning and value in itself, not just in the output or profit that results from it."[15] In the expressive individualist idea of a calling, the notion of honor and the notion of profit are uncoupled just as they were in the mind of the aristocrat. Like the aristocrat, the expressive individualist employed in a calling submerges the profit motive and affects not to think of income at all. This phenomenon is clearly evident in the attitude towards work expressed during some of the interviews conducted by Bellah. For example, Margaret Oldham, a psychotherapist, is concerned that psychology may not be the most fulfilling place for her, and she is "plagued by the idea that nothing I'm [Margaret] doing research-wise is ever going to have any relevance to anybody's life."[16] The profit motive, if it is present in Margaret, is hidden beneath an expressed desire to find honorable and meaningful work, which means work where she can "share her emotions" and "give to other people."[17]

The same aristocratic tendencies can be observed in the contempt shown by social workers, counselors, and therapists graduating from elite universities towards those who are about to enter the world of business and manufacturing. The "caring professions" are understood to represent higher or more noble callings because they are uncontaminated by the urge to make money. In the same way, it is commonly observed among individuals working in the caring professions that the importance of the mission will crowd out from their conversation the interest in making a profit. Sometimes it is only at the bottom of his or her consciousness that a caring professional will admit that the mission also satisfies the very important task of providing one with a living.

The aristocrat and some contemporary expressive individualists share an attitude towards work and the idea of labor for profit. This similarity between the two types is punctuated by differences in small details. The calling of the expressive individualist differs from the post of the aristocrat only in the actual task being performed.

Both the aristocrat and the expressive individualist work for honor and conceal the profit motive, but the two are guided by different conceptions of honor. The aristocrat was elevated by tasks that ennobled the self, that allowed one to display courage in battle and poise in public, and that allowed the self to be wrapped in "dignity and splendor." The aristocrat practiced virtues that were "combined with pride and the love of power."[18] The honor of the aristocrat was inseparable from the inherent virtue of the task being performed, and he therefore deemed only certain tasks honorable.

The expressive individualist is elevated by tasks that allow the self to share with others. He or she is elevated by tasks that permit a full display of one's benevolence, compassion, and sense of justice, virtues rooted in the ideals of fraternity and community. The identity of the expressive individualist is inseparable from the virtue of the task he or she performs and, as for the aristocrat, varying shades of virtue create for the expressive individualist a full spectrum of honorable and dishonorable work. For the expressive individualist engaged in a calling, a mere job would be demeaning.

The value structures of the aristocrat and the expressive individualist are different, but both are deeply affected by the nature of their work. This is because for both, an idea of virtue is mixed in with the description of the job. Both make careful distinctions between work that is ennobling and work that is humiliating, and both are degraded by certain tasks even if the job is legal and the profit is large.

The situation was very different for Tocqueville's American. In that figure, a principle of honor did not compete with the nature of one's work; Tocqueville's American did not expose himself to ridicule when he engaged in certain tasks. Tocqueville's American was never degraded because he worked, and because all honest callings were considered honorable and all men worked for money, all professions in Tocqueville's America had "an air of resemblance."[19] The fine distinctions made between jobs by the aristocrat and some contemporary expressive individualists were not made by Tocqueville's American.

3

Christianity, Public Opinion, and Republican Principle in the Imagination of Tocqueville's American

In this section, I will introduce three ideas or social phenomena that will be often referred to because of their tremendous impact on the imaginative experience of Tocqueville's American. These three concepts—Christianity, public opinion, and republican principle—help demonstrate how Tocqueville's American was a unique character type. They provide a series of coordinates to map that figure's interior sense, just as tables of income distribution and housing statistics provide coordinates to map the larger social world. They give structure and coherence to seemingly random psychic currents and, by transforming those currents into comprehensible and regularly occurring phenomena, they make Tocqueville's American more amenable to analysis. In this section, it will be shown how Christianity, public opinion, and republican principle fixed, or anchored, the mind of Tocqueville's American so that he would not be overwhelmed by the social disorder surrounding him.

The calm order that Tocqueville observed in the domestic life of the Americans was an effect radiating outward from an even more intense state of psychological control. Tocqueville observed of life in America, "Men are in constant motion; the mind of man appears almost unmoved."[1] Nineteenth-century American society was forever being shaped and reshaped by a torrential current of human endeavor, one that bore down on every man-made structure in the country. Every market, every technology, and every enterprise was susceptible to being swept away by that current. But amidst such chaos, the mind of the individualist was still. Tocqueville's American observed the unpredictability and commotion of democratic life from a fixed

29

point. Religion, public opinion, and republican principle were responsible for this seemingly paradoxical situation.

The first great force exerted on the mind of Tocqueville's American was religion. In his discussion of religion in America, Tocqueville states that religious worship is essential to the practice of democracy. He says that men cannot live without dogmatic belief and that the thoughts of men must be fixed by certain general truths.[2] The absence of any fixed beliefs causes men to become frightened at the democratic disorder surrounding them. Any disorder within the mind (in the world behind the eye) will lead to vigorous efforts by a person to order the society (the world before the eye) in which one lives. Tocqueville writes,

> When there is no longer any principle of authority in religion any more than in politics, men are speedily frightened at the aspect of this unbounded independence. The constant agitation of all surrounding things alarms and exhausts them. As everything is at sea in the sphere of the mind, they determine that at least the mechanism of society shall be firm and fixed; and as they cannot resume their ancient belief; they assume a master.[3]

Tocqueville argues that religion was essential to the preservation of freedom in America precisely because Christianity, in the specific form it took in America, instilled a certain order in the mind of the individualist.[4] It allowed people tremendous political and economic freedom while preventing them from becoming frightened by the disorder surrounding them. Christianity in America ordered the mind of the individual, but nothing outside of the individual. It focused its attention on the imagination of the citizen, not on the world external to the citizen, not on those realms of human activity (such as politics and business) that define the world before the eye. Tocqueville writes,

> In America religion is a distinct sphere, in which the priest is sovereign, but out of which he takes care never to go. Within its limits he is master of the mind; beyond them he leaves men to themselves and surrenders them to the independence and instability that belong to their nature and their age.[5]

Because religion in America concentrated its efforts on the imagination of man rather than on the society enveloping him, it required few external forms. Tocqueville says, "I have seen no country in which Christianity is clothed with fewer forms, figures, and observances than in the United States, or where it presents more distinct, simple, and general notions to the mind."[6] In Tocqueville's America, the physical structure of Christianity was almost invisible. Unlike in Europe, Christianity in America did not ally itself with a particular governmental faction or attach itself to a coalition of interests. Its presence in the external world was minimal. It exercised power by concentrating effort directly on a person's mind and will. Almost magically, it held the imagination of the individualist in thrall.

Tocqueville's American demonstrates a puzzling combination of rigid moral absolutism and aggressive individualism. But that combination is only puzzling when the purpose of Christianity in nineteenth-century America is misinterpreted. The purpose of Christianity in Tocqueville's America was to rigidly bind the imaginations of men and women, not to restructure the society in which they lived. Christianity did not assign great effort to realigning the structure of power and wealth in American society. When moving from religious issues to issues of politics and business in America, religious leaders quickly changed from omnipotent guides to simple followers. Tocqueville notes that when crossing from the realm of the human imagination to the external world, Christianity in America suddenly lost its great power, and the clergy would "readily adopt the general opinions of their country and their age."[7] When the ministers stepped outside of the sphere of the mind, they would become insignificant and would "allow themselves to be borne away without opposition in the current feeling and opinion by which everything around them is carried along."[8] The power of Christianity was directed at the mind of man. Beyond that realm, it lost its power of magic and could cast no spell.

Public opinion constitutes the second great invisible force exerted on the mind of Tocqueville's American, preparing the mold for what would become a unique configuration. Tocqueville comments on the tremendous power of public opinion in America, noting that its effect on limiting thought was greater than the police force of the mightiest tyrant. He writes,

> Monarchs had, so to speak, materialized oppression; the democratic republics of the present day have rendered it as entirely an affair of the mind as the will which it is intended to coerce. Under the absolute sway of one man the body was attacked in order to subdue the soul; but the soul escaped the blows which were directed against it and rose proudly superior. Such is not the course adopted by tyranny in democratic republics; there the body is left free and the soul is enslaved.[9]

Public opinion forced Tocqueville's American to behave in certain ways, but it accomplished this end by entering the human will rather than by physically obstructing human action. Like Christianity, public opinion lent a certain order to the imagination of Tocqueville's American and prevented it from moving beyond certain well-defined limits. The pressure of public opinion was so intense that for some cultural disciplines, such as literature and theater, it was almost strangulating.[10] At one point, Tocqueville declares that freedom of opinion is almost nonexistent in America. He writes, "I know of no country in which there is so little independence of mind and real freedom of discussion as in America."[11] In this particular passage, he is referring to the tyrannical power of public opinion, a power so complete that it could quell controversy and subdue a people with little effort.

Republican principle constitutes the third invisible force ordering the mind of Tocqueville's American. It exerted a power that, like Christianity and public opinion, invisibly passed into a person's will from where it would guide the smallest activities of life. For this reason, Tocqueville said of America, ". . . the Union is an ideal nation, which exists, so to speak, only in the mind."[12] Republican principle was so deeply impregnated in the mind of Tocqueville's individualist that it compelled even the wealthiest American to submit to the "authority of the pettiest magistrate."[13] Tocqueville describes how republican principle affected the smallest details of life in America when he writes, "The Americans transport the habits of public life into their manners in private; in their country the jury is introduced into the games of schoolboys, and parliamentary forms are observed in the order of a feast."[14]

How the power of republican principle could be concentrated on the mind of the individualist, providing a substitute for physical coercion, is also described in *The Federalist*. In *Federalist* No. 27 ("Ordinary Enforcement of Law Without Military Aids") Hamilton writes,

> The more the operations of the national authority are intermingled in the ordinary exercise of government, the more the citizens are accustomed to meet with it in the common occurrences of their political life, the more it is familiarized to their sight and to their feelings, the further it enters into those objects which touch the most sensible chords and put in motion the most active springs of the human heart, the greater will be the probability that it will conciliate the respect and attachment of the community. Man is very much a creature of habit . . . the authority of the Union, and the affections of the citizen towards it, will be strengthened, rather than weakened, by its extension to what are called matters of internal concern; and will have less occasion to recur to force, in proportion to the familiarity and comprehensiveness of its agency. The more it circulates through those channels and currents in which the passions of mankind naturally flow, the less will it require the aid of the violent and perilous expedients of compulsion.[15]

In Tocqueville's America, republican principle influenced business deals, friendships, and associations no less than it did the conduct of games and feasts and was so entrenched in the mental experience of the individualist that what was clearly a political paradigm soon became a natural phenomenon, almost an instinct of the species.

This concept is illustrated in other sections of *The Federalist*, particularly in *Federalist* No. 39. While the central government in America permitted local governments significant freedom and was thus called "federal," it also exerted tremendous force on the minds of individual citizens and therefore displayed certain "national" features. The central government exerted little administrative control on state and local governments, but the ideas promulgated in the Constitution penetrated deep into the mind of every citizen. The external world was free and disordered but the imagination of the citizen was fixed and ordered.

Tocqueville also comments on the hybrid aspects of the federal government, noting that while the government of the United States was centralized, its administrative apparatus was not. He writes,

> I have shown that in the United States there is no centralized administration and no hierarchy of public functionaries. Local authority has been carried farther than any European nation could endure without great inconvenience. . . But in the United States the centralization of the government is perfect; and it would be easy to prove that the national power is more concentrated there than it has ever been in the old nations of Europe.[16]

This statement basically sums up the point made about the influence of Christianity, public opinion, and republican principle on the mind of the early American. In the external world of Tocqueville's America—in the spheres of politics and public affairs, business and association, and social intercourse—tremendous freedom existed that caused that world to be marked by great disorder. But in the internal world of Tocqueville's American—in the world of the imagination—three forces combined to constrain and order the individualist's mental experience. Christianity, public opinion, and republican principle caused limits to be placed on the imagination of Tocqueville's American such that even if streams of human endeavor crossed each other randomly and chaotically in the external world, there existed within the mind of the American a narrow and ordered spectrum of thought.

How the Imagination of Tocqueville's American Refers More to an Augustinian than a Platonic Conception of the Soul

F. Scott Fitzgerald once described America as a country existing only in the "mind," which is exactly how Tocqueville described it a century earlier.

Old World countries have distinctive folk traditions, architectural styles, monuments, ceremonial dress, and cuisine, and those concrete structures in the external world are what stimulate the senses and trigger within the imagination the necessary idea of "country." In Tocqueville's America, modeled on the principles of democratic capitalism, there was little that continued or remained unchanging in the external world, and the idea of country came to exist only within the internal world of the mind. Its supports were not made of brick and mortar but of something less visible—of religious faith, the power of public opinion, and the idea of republican principle. Unlike the visible countries in the Old World, Tocqueville's America was truly an invisible country, for that which defined it had no physical substance. America transcended the world of force and matter to become almost pure idea.

This understanding of America will be explored later but at this point, it is important to establish the idea of America as an Augustinian rather than a Platonic concept.

The study of Platonic philosophy enabled Augustine to see things in a new way and move beyond the simple dualism of the Manicheans. Augustine embraced the Platonic idea of a world above the senses and beyond the material, one that is ideal and never-changing. The world in which man lives is mutable, argued the Platonists, and filled with passing spectacles. While it is beautiful, it is also superficial and ephemeral, and to stay in that world is to live in twilight. Yet another world, beyond the physical senses, does not change and is filled with truth and light, though utterly transcendent. That faculty of mind—the soul—that interprets physical stimuli is not part of the physical world but of this other world. The Platonists argued that it was the rational soul, the intellectual soul, that could aspire to know the light of this other world. By looking inwards and upwards, aided by understanding and reason, a man could loosen his bonds to sense and come to know this higher world.

Augustine came to appreciate that God, like the human souls He created, is not material or visible as the Manicheans had thought, but invisible and beyond matter. Augustine owed a tremendous intellectual debt to the Platonists, and in *The City of God* he refers to the Platonists as "justly esteemed as the noblest of the philosophers."[17] He says of the Platonists that their "gold and silver was dug out of God's providence" and that they "come nearest to the Christian faith."[18] But Augustine and the Platonists disagreed on certain fundamental points, one being whether it was through faith or reason that man could come to know the divine.

The Platonists, Plotinus in particular, argued that the part of us that reasons is easily distracted by the physical needs of the body, but by opening itself up to the light, the intellect could move man towards the eternal and the transcendent. Through reason, the Platonists argued, man ascended the great heights. Augustine argued just the opposite: that faith was the gateway to understanding. While Augustine had great respect for man's rational faculties, he believed that human reason was embedded in the human will, and it was faith, not reason, that moved the will.[19] Augustine believed that man could never know something completely unless it was coupled with his full consent or affection.[20] Such consent was derived from the will, a part of the human consciousness resting at a much greater depth than simple wisdom. The divine can be known through reason (as the Platonists knew it), but never completely acknowledged except through faith. This is because man's will, which impinges on his ability to reason, is fractured in its fallen state. Augustine believed that it was only through faith and by the grace of God that man's fractured will was healed. Without faith, the philosopher's reason could never catch more than a glimpse of the divine. One must first believe, Augustine insisted, in order to pass through the mists.

Augustine said that the Platonists emphasized reason over faith because they were too proud to admit that their power of reason was incompetent. He wrote, "the proud scorn to take God for their master"[21] and said the Platonists were too vain to admit that they must first believe in order to understand.[22] Of the philosophers of reason he says,

> Will you be able to lift up your heart unto God? Must it not first be healed, in order that thou mayest see? Do you not show your pride, when you say, First let me see, and then I will be healed?[23]

This discussion is extremely relevant to the notion of America as an idea. As a country that seemed to exist only in the mind, Tocqueville's America stands relative to the countries of the Old World as the invisible world stands before the visible world in Platonic philosophy. The countries of the Old World were defined by all that was physical and material—by the sights of gleaming palaces, by the smells of special meats and pastries, and by the sounds of age-old accents. Tocqueville's America was a country defined by the spiritual and the intangible—by a religious faith that had few external manifestations, by a public opinion that had no weight or mass yet could spread across an entire continent, and by a republican principle that was barely more than a geometrical axiom. A chaotic world surrounded the Americans, but the world of the American mind was oriented by certain fixed beliefs. Those beliefs were unchanging, as Tocqueville carefully noted. In Tocqueville's America, one could move from the farm to the city or from east to west, but in the invisible world that was America, such physical

movement was associated with no perturbation in the ideal of Christian faith
or in the commands of republican principle. Those ideals remained constant.
Compared to the visible world of Old World countries, where the tangible
markers of identity varied almost from county to county, the invisible world of
Tocqueville's America radiated a certain universality and Platonic simplicity.

Since Augustine accepted the Platonic notion of a transcendent, or
invisible, world, this conception of America is also consistent with Augustinian philosophy. What places the idea of America firmly in the Augustinian
camp is a recognition that the principles giving structure to the "invisible"
world of America—Christian belief, public opinion, and republican principle—were elements of faith, not reason. This is most obviously demonstrated
in the fact that Tocqueville's Americans were Christians, not pagan Platonists;
they were devout believers, not rationalist philosophers. But this understanding is just as apparent in the cases of public opinion and republican principle.
As Tocqueville describes them, these two phenomena were not actively
contemplated in the mind. They were not bits of logic springing from free
thought and discussion. On the contrary, public opinion and republican
principle almost limited free thought and discussion by insinuating themselves into the wills of Tocqueville's Americans below the level of consciousness. The informed and clever judgements of the American, whether at the
dinner table, in business, or in the games played by schoolchildren, rested
on the love of a mind that sincerely believed. It was an almost blind faith in
public opinion and republican principle that preceded the application of
democratic procedures to the political and commercial activities of American life.

Such faith humbled Tocqueville's American. Whether guided by Christian
ideals, the dictates of public opinion, or the rules of republican principle,
Tocqueville's American surrendered his will to a higher order. He saw the
world around him through a lens crafted by faith, and that faith prevented
him from always asserting himself, from always dominating, and from always
doing what his nature desired. His mind acknowledged, it had come to love,
certain democratic ideals of order, and in this spirit he waited his turn at the
bank, moved into line at the store, or acquiesced in the opinion of the
majority. Rather than always calculating its own self-interest, the rational
faculty in Tocqueville's American was made submissive to this particular
faith. Such passage from "knowledge to acknowledgement" recalls the Augustinian passage "away from the standpoint of autonomous reason, as yet
unhumbled by the Mediator, to a willing recognition of God in which reason
is operative but at length, being cleansed."[24]

Through faith, Tocqueville's Americans were made submissive to these
powers, but having once "stooped low," which the Platonists refused to do,

they used their "native vigor and "purified understanding"[25] to ascend the heights and create a democratic republic filled with thoughtful and educated citizens. Tocqueville's Americans, like the Platonists, had a great respect for reason and science. But unlike the Platonists, who always insisted on understanding before they believed, Tocqueville's Americans trusted and believed so that they could understand, and their commitment to Christian ideals, public opinion, and republican principle brought order to their business ventures, their scientific pursuits, and their explorations.[26] It is perhaps the case that for Tocqueville's American, unlike for the Platonists, the will was no longer free to be its own master. Yet a tremendous faith caused the American's energy and effort to be focused and made his restless disposition and excessive love of independence productive rather than dangerous. This is no longer the case in the society of expressive individualism.

4

Pelagianism in the Society of Expressive Individualism

At the beginning of the fourth century, Augustine was drawn into what is perhaps his most famous controversy. The British monk Pelagius presented a radically new understanding of man, one that received considerable attention and respect. Pelagius argued that man was free to pursue good and avoid evil independent of God's grace. He agreed with the traditional Christian position that man's will was created by God, but he insisted that the character of the will was independent of God. Pelagius argued that man could choose between good and evil, to be with God or against God, and that it was essential for man to be free to move in either direction. Without this freedom, the whole idea of human volition was emptied of significance. Moreover, if God, not man, was the author of all volition, then man's evil doings must be ascribed to God, which was unthinkable. Hence, to absolve God of any evil and to make human choosing and willing substantial activities, Pelagius proclaimed the character of the human will to be independent of God.

Pelagius also rejected the concept of original sin and the idea that sin was somehow transmitted to every individual at birth. Sin is not born with man, argued Pelagius, but is subsequently committed by man, not because of a defect in human nature but rather a defect in the human will.[1] He said infants were born in the same innocent state lived in by Adam before the fall and that "Adam's sin injured only himself, and not the human race."[2] This new view made (as Augustine noted) the purpose of infant baptisms unclear, as there was no longer presumed to be any sin needing to be cleansed at birth.[3]

The Pelagian movement appealed to a universal theme: the "need of the individual to define himself, and to feel free to create his own values in the midst of the conventional, second-rate life of society."[4] Its social program had a definite reformist bent, for if human nature was free and good, not defective, then man could transform society for the better. Completely free individuals responsible for themselves and their actions could build a more loving and joyful community.

Unlike the Manichean or Donatist movements, which could be located in expressive individualism only after they were translated into a modern sense, Pelagianism occupies a central position in expressive individualist America, almost unchanged in form. Pelagianism does not imagine God as an "immense shining body" nor does it preach intolerance, and thus it need not be cleansed of irrational or antidemocratic tendencies before being inserted into the movement of expressive individualism. This is why the ideas in Pelagianism—the belief in the individual, in the individual's great capacity for love and good, and in the need of the individual to define himself or herself—are not only compatible with American democracy but have found a home in that country's dominant religion. Mainstream American Christianity has absorbed expressive individualist ideals and, by doing so, provides almost an exact replica of the Pelagian heresy attacked by Augustine fifteen centuries ago.

How the Pelagian View That Man Has a Natural Capacity for Love Is Also Dominant in Christian Expressive Individualism and Other Areas of Agreement between the Two Movements

Pelagius discerned in man a natural capacity for love (a capacity for love "embedded in man's nature") and made a distinction between this capacity and the power of God.[5] The power of God was viewed by Pelagius as merely an assist device, one that guided man as he exercised his natural powers of love and charity. God's role was simply to aid or supplement the flow of love emanating from the human will. Pelagius writes in his *Defence of the Freedom of the Will*, ". . . But that we really do a good thing, or speak a good word, or think a good thought, proceeds from our own selves."[6] The Pelagians said that while man does sin, he does not sin automatically, for man has a special capacity to do good without God's grace. In this way, man is not inherently defective.

The same idea is quite prominent in Christian expressive individualist thought. Christian expressive individualists believe that man has a capacity for love separate from the power of God, one that can be used to achieve "wellness" and improve the lives of others. One Christian expressive individualist writes, "We are in fact free to love, free to be kind and generous and even great of soul. We can best communicate this message not by emphasizing our need to be rescued from negative possibilities, but rather by emphasizing *our potential for living in a loving and faithful way*"[7] (my italics). The Christian expressive individualist discerns in man a capacity for good separate from God, one that does not require absolute faith in God to be rendered operative.

Both the Pelagian effort to lessen the need for God's grace and the Pelagian assumption that man alone "can either perfect righteousness, or advance steadily towards it"[8] are evident in Christian expressive individualist thought. Greg Anderson, in *The 22 Laws of Wellness*, writes, "Religion tells us that the greatest thing to possess is faith. . . Sadly, the pursuit of faith has a checkered history that is long on wars and oppression, short on peace and personal compassion."[9] He continues, "It is the daily practice of the greatest of the non-negotiable laws of wellness, the Law of Unconditional Loving. Unconditional, nonjudgemental loving. This is our aim, life's single highest and most rewarding pursuit."[10] For Anderson, it is human love, not faith in God, that is most important.

For both the Pelagian and the Christian expressive individualist, the human soul is elevated by *our* practice of loving and not because God's secret, ineffable spirit has worked its will on our minds. Both believe man has the capacity to do every good thing by action, speech, and thought because God "has endowed us with this possibility," with God returning afterward only to "assist it."[11] God is merely a support in the process of an individual's own self-flourishing; He serves to heighten and intensify a person's own loving instincts. For both the Pelagian and the Christian expressive individualist, the merits of the self precede God's intervention and it is merely an awareness of God's law that helps one accomplish the good.

The Pelagians argued that man is not inherently defective or sinful ("we are able to sin and not to sin,"[12]) and that sin is not propagated through the species by the simple act of birth. Innocent babies are already in Christ, said the Pelagians, which appears to correlate with the empirical view that babies have not yet had time to sin. This Pelagian idea is readily apparent in Christian expressive individualism. It can be observed, for example, among some of the expressive individualists interviewed by Robert Bellah in *Habits of the Heart*. For one such person, Art Townsend, a "cheery mysticism eliminates any real possibility of sin, evil, or damnation,"[13] and problems are simply "welcomed as opportunities for growth."[14] The same idea is present in an interview conducted by James Fowler with a newly ordained Unitarian minister in his book *Stages of Faith*. The interview goes as follows:

Miss T: Sin! I don't use the word sin, *ever.*
Interviewer: Why?

Miss T: I think, on the whole, people are doing the best they can with what light they have. And I think more in terms of mistake than I do of deliberate sin.[15]

In another work of Christian expressive individualism, the whole concept of original sin is described as foolish and out of date. C. Randolph Ross, writing in *Common Sense Christianity*, says,

These implications of the traditional idea of "original sin" stand in opposition to the whole of Jesus' life and teaching. The God of Jesus Christ loved the world, sought out sinners, and forgave those who repented. Anyone who shares the Christian understanding of God can not help but find these ideas—humans as unworthy of God's love, babies as evil, and God not forgiving anyone until innocent blood has been shed—to be repugnant and blasphemous.[16]

To both the Pelagian and the Christian expressive individualist, the idea that we are born in sin, with sinfulness passed down from generation to generation, is ludicrous. ("Horsefeathers!" exclaims Ross). Both believe man is no more inhabited by sin than he is by righteousness, for if man did not have the ability to choose between right and wrong, there would not be the good in the world that there already is.[17]

The freedom attributed to the will of man by both Pelagianism and Christian expressive individualism causes the idea of the self to assume central importance. It is the freestanding, autonomous self in Pelagianism who decides whether or not to go to God, whether or not to be sinful, and whether or not to love. Similarly, in Christian expressive individualism, the self is awarded a high degree of "autonomy," so much so that it is elevated to a "cosmic principle."[18] It becomes "the source of all religious meaning."[19] In the case of Art Townsend, " 'there is nothing that happens to me [Art] that is not for the fulfillment of my higher self.' "[20] Townsend believes that he possesses by himself the necessary resources to live a full and loving life. A belief in God merely helps him to develop those resources and improve on the fine qualities he already shares, thereby enabling him to achieve an even higher state of being.

This belief in "autonomy" rests firmly on the Pelagian conviction that human nature has never been depraved or corrupted by sin, that it is not necessarily imperfect, and that the individual human spirit can stand well on its own. The relationship between man and God achieves a kind of equal balance in Pelagianism and Christian expressive individualism. In Pelagianism, God does not inspire man. Instead, Augustine observed, man happily conforms to certain divine edicts and receives the joy of faith as if it were a reward from heaven. The same "contractual" relationship between God and man exists in Christian expressive individualism. God and man are given almost equal status; they meet each other halfway. God opens the door for the believer in the spirit of reconciliation, "waiting for us to respond and walk through."[21] In Christian expressive individualism, it is our choice[22] whether to move towards God or reject Him, and man receives great gifts if he makes the right choice. The expressive individualist does not need to be saved from sin. Rather, he must decide on his own whether or not to commit to a life of faith. God makes an overture to man, but it is man who responds, with the first step being a move towards God and a willingness to live faithfully. God reaches out to the Christian expressive individualist, but it is the expressive individualist who remains firmly in control.

Since both Pelagianism and Christian expressive individualism view love as simply a matter of the will, tremendous possibilities for social reform arise. Immense good can be achieved, independent of God's grace, because man possesses a natural capacity for love. An educated mind with a modicum of self-control can choose good and reject evil, and both the Pelagian and the Christian expressive individualist emphasize how benevolence can be opposed to the excesses of competitive individualism through the conscious and deliberate activity of the loving person. Man has fallen, but not irreversibly, and with an effort of the will, paradise can be regained.[23] In this spirit, the Christian expressive individualist voluntarily places his or her social activism and denial of self-interest in opposition to the inequities of society and the problem of selfishness. Through education, the Christian expressive individualist believes a person can be made to realize the beauty and great value of a loving community.

The Conflicting Impulses within Pelagianism and Christian Expressive Individualism

The Christian expressive individualist is so radically autonomous and believes so strongly in the self as a cosmic principle that one wonders why religion is even necessary in the life of such a person. He or she chooses whether or not to go to God, as if religion were no different than any other consumer product. The expressive individualist weighs competing options and chooses God, with faith believed to originate in thoughtful calculation rather than in divine inspiration.

The idea of choice in faith implies that a person can be upright and "good" even before entering into a "contract" with God, and that a person can already have sublime feelings and an advanced conscience before choosing God. In this way, an appreciation of God's "value" precedes the "decision" to become religious. The high value placed by the expressive individualist on God causes him to choose God, and that awareness of value is recognized by Christian expressive individualism to denote a prereligious state of goodness. It is precisely such goodness in men and women that prompts them to go to God.

Augustine observed the same phenomenon among the Pelagians and asked probing questions. If a person already possesses within himself the capacity for good, separate from and preceding God, why does he pray to God?[24] The act of prayer, for example, implies a high degree of helplessness. It suggests someone does not yet know the good but is desperately trying to know it. If a person is believed to be capable of acting freely and deliberately, of achieving a higher self through self-education, why does he bother to mouth the traditional Christian appeal to God for rescue? If a person believes that man, through choice, makes man religious, and not God, what exactly is the purpose of God?

Augustine noted this contradiction in the Pelagian act of prayer, and the same contradiction can be discerned in the prayers of Christian expressive individualists. The Christian expressive individualist also locates the power of love and kindness within himself. Instead of praying that one will perform a loving act, that a mysterious and invisible spirit will work its power on a helpless and confused psyche, the Christian expressive individualist prays that he will exercise his own capacity for love in order to perform a loving act. Both the Pelagian and the Christian expressive individualist pray to God, but they are really trying, through prayer, to empower their own power. Augustine commented on how odd it was to watch the Pelagian plead to God, praying that he will act with the very power of love that he attributes to himself. Augustine writes, "For what is more foolish than to pray that you may do that which you have it in your power to do."[25]

The Pelagian idea of prayer can be located in numerous Christian expressive individualist texts. In one book, for example, the author writes,

> In praying . . . we cannot help but consider God's will for us. If we pray with the right attitude, if we bring "willingness" to listen for an answer, this will make us more sensitive to the pull of God so we in fact may get an "answer" by becoming aware of the direction in which we need to go to live towards God. And lastly, this whole process prepares us to face our problems and to deal with them in the most constructive way by properly grounding us and focusing us and even energizing us.[26]

The author is in a difficult situation, as was the Pelagian. He does not want to give up the institution of prayer, but if he is to preserve individual autonomy and the idea that man's will is completely free, he can only grudgingly impart real power to God. In the passage quoted above, the act of prayer suggests a humble appeal to a superior being. But on closer inspection, one can see how the expressive individualist remains firmly in control of the prayer experience. Prayer depends on *our* "willingness" to engage. Faith in God is preached, but it is faith in God at a distance, allowing a person to modulate the extent to which he or she is "pushed" or "pulled" by God. It is *we* who "consider" God's will. Prayer depends on *our* inclination at the moment, on *our* impulses, on *our* "right attitude." The expressive individualist, like the Pelagian, may believe in God, but his real hope is in man. It is man who leads himself to the well of inspiration.

This situation reveals an important paradox in Pelagianism and Christian expressive individualism. Both try to move a force within themselves (the power of love) with a force they already believe to be within themselves. Both attempt to stir feelings of love within themselves through the free and loving act of prayer. But prayer is an appeal rooted in powerlessness, an admission by the person that one can not stir feelings of love within the self, and it conflicts with the Pelagian and Christian expressive individualist position that one has a natural capacity for love.

This leads to a second contradiction in Pelagianism and Christian expressive individualism. Both movements believe that human "choice" and human "will" are the same, that a loving action need only be preceded by a pure thought. But as Augustine notes, simple calculations of love do not necessarily translate into action. It is in this spirit that Augustine warned Pelagius, "it is not because we do not will, or do not do, that we will and do nothing good, but because we are without His help."[27]

Not even the loving thought, let alone the loving action, is under human control, warned Augustine. Pelagius insisted that our ability "to think a good thought comes from God," but that "we actually think a good thought proceeds from ourselves."[28] Augustine noted that our minds are not so clearly under our control. All men desire to be happy and think happy thoughts, but they do not possess the control to do so. Man is more a prisoner of his own imagination than a freethinking spirit. It is the imagination that generates the phantoms that haunt him, the feelings that terrify and plague him, and the cravings that crowd out his contemplation of the good. Man can contemplate the good, but he cannot command the good to come into his mind.

In the same way, man can perform acts of love, but such acts do not mean that a capacity for love resides within man or exists under his control. The choice of performing a loving act and the will to do so are separate phenomena.

Augustine uses an analogy to convey this idea. Man has the power to smell, see, and hear, but he argues convincingly that those senses are less under the power of man than they represent "natural necessity."[29] A man can see, but if his eyes are forced to remain open and the lights kept on, he cannot not see. A man can hear, but if his ears are laid bare and sounds continue, he cannot not hear. A man can smell, but if his mouth is covered and he is forced to breath through his nose, he cannot not smell. It is the same with sinning, argues Augustine, for the "actual capability of sinning lies not so much in the power of man's will as in the necessity of man's nature."[30] Man can sin, but there is a certain "necessity" about this. It is not under his complete control to sin (or to love) at will, just as it is not under his control to hear and see at will. The act appears to suggest control, but by probing deeper one can discern a definite lack of control.

The sin in man does not refer to the part of a man's constitution that refuses to love at will, but rather in the "incapacity of the will to do what it wills."[31] Acts of love merely demonstrate how the defective and perverse will of man, which can "darken and weaken all those natural goods,"[32] must be healed through God's grace in order to be guided in love. A person can love, but that does not mean a human capacity for love exists separate from God. Quite the contrary, the will cannot love "freely," just as it cannot hear or see freely, and the sin in man is not that man fails to love, but that his nature is flawed such that he cannot do what he wills.[33] It is only through God's grace, said Augustine, that man can do good. This line of argument weakens the entire premise on which Pelagian and Christian expressive individualist belief is founded, for it demonstrates the impotence of the human will.

In Christian expressive individualism, it is argued that man, through choice, can become an even higher and more virtuous being. God exists not to justify the self, but only to make improvements on an already very independent self, and the free will of expressive individualists is what enables them to build loving communities.[34] This is why hypocrisy is considered to be one of the great evils in modern Christian practice.[35] If a person does not completely fulfill the divine commandments, it is presumed that a defect exists in the autonomous self that the self has failed to correct with his or her own power. In Christian expressive individualism, acts of love are the accomplishments of man, not God, and acts of self-interest are believed to be rooted in a failure to realize one's full potential, not in the failings and frailty of human existence.

As Augustine demonstrates, this is a dangerously naive and simplistic understanding of human volition and will. Human nature is much more imperfect than either the Pelagian or the Christian expressive individualist thinks. The human will suffers from a profound and permanent dislocation.

Mere self-control, education,"getting in touch with one's feelings," and rational discussion are inadequate solutions to the problem of sin. The fractured will of man prevents him from making "choice" synonymous with "will." In this way, the great visions of paradise, of achieving wellness apart from God, of growing through loving, of combating a natural capacity for self-interest with a natural capacity for love, of sharing our love with others, and of building "special loving communities"[36] are merely fantastic delusions of power. The capacity to love and do good does not belong to man. It is not a part of his nature. Love can sometimes be observed in human acts, but that is not a sufficient basis on which to claim love as a force at man's disposal or to begin prosecuting the design of the higher self.

This is why, Augustine argues, faith is most crucial. If whatever evil man performs comes from a defective will and whatever good he performs comes from a will healed by the grace of God, then faith in God is a prerequisite to doing good. The will must be healed; otherwise, it will simply remain trapped in perversity and impulse. In this light, the idea of a "contractual" relationship between God and man is absurd. Man cannot be an equal partner in a relationship with God because man depends on God to do good, to heal his pain, and to love his neighbors. It is not "we who by virtue of the freedom of our wills cooperate with God, but God who by virtue of the gift of grace *cooperates* with us."[37] It is faith, not a human capacity for love or a "willingness" to meet God halfway, that precedes all the good works of man.

It is interesting to observe Pelagianism and Christian expressive individualism try to have it both ways. Both movements pay respect to the idea of God and recognize the superiority of God as God, but they also try to discover a part of the human experience separate from God and still good, where God is no longer God. This phenomenon is evident not only in the attitude of Christian expressive individualists towards prayer, but in their attitude towards original sin, baptism, and grace. Both the Pelagian and the Christian expressive individualist believe that baptism is an important sacrament denoting the cleansing of sin. Yet it is unclear why the sacrament is necessary if humans are not born in sin. The paradox is similar to the one in which the Christian expressive individualist prays to God for the inspiration of love, all the while presuming the power of love to reside in himself or herself.

According to the Pelagian and the Christian expressive individualist, innocent babies not yet baptized do not burn in the fires of hell, but are in Christ. Augustine points out the contradiction,

> If he is already in Christ, why baptize him? If, however, as the Truth puts the case, he is baptized for the express purpose of being with Christ, it certainly

follows that he who is not baptized is not with Christ; and if he is not "with" Christ, he is "against" Christ. . . And how can he be "against" Christ, if not owing to sin?, for it cannot possibly be from his soul or his body, both of these being the creation of God. Now if it be owing to sin, what sin can be found at such an age, except the ancient and original sin?[38]

Some Pelagians and Christian expressive individualists argue that babies are judged by the good things they would have done had they lived and for this reason are saved although they die before baptism. But Augustine demolishes this idea in *Against Julian*, noting that if this were true, an adult could just as easily be judged by evils he might have committed had he lived a few years more.[39] The idea of condemning a good man on the basis of evils he might have committed had he lived is absurd. The judgment rendered on a person's existence is done so according to a person's actual life, not potential life.

The Pelagians and the Christian expressive individualists are forced into a corner, for unless they are willing to give up the institution of baptism and the idea that one needs to be with God, a moral distance they refuse to travel, the unavoidable conclusion is that infants are born with defective natures and are corrupted by sin. It is not a volitional sin that babies are guilty of, but a sin inherited from parents who themselves are tainted by the fall of Adam.

In sum, the difference between the Augustinian and Christian expressive individualist (or Pelagian) can be located in their radically divergent views of man and his world. The Christian expressive individualist and the Pelagian see in the world outbursts of joy and laughter and presume that man and the world are basically innocent and good. They view human sin as a "superficial" matter, one of choice. They say, "Wrong choice might add some 'rust' to the pure metal of human nature; but a choice, by definition, could be reversed."[40] Augustine finds something very different in the human experience—tortured wills, rage, a "pressing throng of desires," hatred, suffering, pain, pestilence, illness, and disfigurement—all of which we see if not in ourselves in others, and concludes that man has fallen far indeed. It is with this view of the world, colored by the fall, that Augustine finds no person to be innocent. All who enter this world are forced to carry the same burden, which is why infants must be baptized. The difference between Augustine and the Christian expressive individualist is that, for Augustine, his view of the world and the role of church institutions like prayer and baptism match up, while for the Christian expressive individualist they do not.

How the Tension between Christian Expressive Individualism and the Therapeutic Ethos Is Basically a Tension between Pelagianism and Manicheism

Expressive individualism has been described in this book as a coalition of ideas rooted in the experience of late antiquity. Those ideas are expressed at different levels of intensity in any given person, and thus different expressive individualist types exist according to which ideas have coalesced (e.g., the ambitious entrepreneur, the hippie, or the social worker have divergent attitudes and beliefs, yet all can be expressive individualists). Some expressive individualists appear more like the pagan aristocrat than the Donatist or more like the Pelagian than the Manichean. Yet the major philosophies exemplified by the pagan aristocrat, the Pelagian, the Donatist, and the Manichean can be located in the intellectual and spiritual atmosphere of the society of expressive individualism.

In this book, these philosophies are discussed in relation to Saint Augustine. But they also represent conflicting worldviews in their own right. In the particular case that will now be discussed, the conflict between Christian expressive individualism and the therapeutic ethos, two ideologies strongly represented in contemporary America, will be examined as a conflict between Pelagianism and Manicheism.

Christian expressive individualism (or Pelagianism) argues that man possesses a natural capacity for love and is capable of choosing a religion of love. Yet there is also a strong Manichean element in expressive individualist society that, as noted in Chapter 1, is associated with the therapeutic ethos. It posits that man has two natures and not a single will that is free to choose. For the therapist, the will and the "I" are not free because much that is evil, sinful, or painful is often unaffected by rational control mechanisms. Through treatment, the effort is made to contain feelings and anxieties comprising this other nature and impinging on the higher self. Both the Pelagian and the Manichean believe in a higher self independent of God, which is why Augustine condemned both as vain, but the Pelagian and the Manichean imagine the idea of a higher self differently. For the Pelagian (and the Christian expressive individualist), the higher self is identified with the freedom of the single will to choose and to love. It is rooted in the conviction that the human will is not inherently defective. The Manichean (or the therapist) argues that one is weakened by having two natures, and that evil is not simply a matter of "choice" but, rather, manifests itself in a war between two different wills. For the Manichean, the higher self does not emerge from mere self-control but only after great struggle.

According to Christian expressive individualism, man has a natural capacity for love which he can control and use as a basis for his actions. The therapeutic ethos arises from another tenet of expressive individualism, one that says it is difficult to disentangle love from other feelings, even the feeling of self-interest that Christian expressive individualism tries to combat. One character in Bellah's book learns through therapy that, "Being in love one day can mean, like, being selfish. I mean, doing something just for yourself, which I never thought you can and still love."[41] There is an element of impulsiveness in the human psyche addressed by the therapist and ignored by the Christian expressive individualist. The therapist helps the individual discover his or her feelings.[42] Those feelings are then evaluated through therapy in a way that suggests that love is no less unfathomable and mysterious in origin than other human feelings. For the therapist, love is not a natural capacity in man to be used at his discretion.

The Christian expressive individualist has bold plans for man, and the natural capacity for love is to be used to build "loving communities." But the therapeutic ethos in contemporary America presents an understanding of humanity that rocks the entire premise on which Christian expressive individualism stands. The therapeutic ethos says that love is an element of the human personality that is no different than any other feeling, moving in and out of the human psyche for inexplicable reasons and with unpredictable frequency. The Christian expressive individualist is challenged by the therapist's belief that the self is not in full control after all, that certain moods and feelings actually lie beyond the control of the self. Basically, in this debate, the Pelagian is being challenged by the Manichean.

Curiously, this is exactly how the Pelagians interpreted Augustine's challenge to their idea that man was not inherently sinful but rather free to choose. They called him a Manichean. The crucial point on which the Pelagians believed themselves to differ from their opponent rested on a line separating themselves from the Manicheans. To the Pelagians, the critical issue was whether man had a free will or a will rent asunder in strife. This is the same point that divides modern-day Pelagians—the Christian expressive individualists—from modern-day Manicheans—the therapists.

The consequence of the struggle between Christian expressive individualism and the therapeutic ethos (i.e., between Pelagianism and Manicheism) is very different from that of the struggle between Augustinian Christianity and Manicheism in late antiquity. The triumph of Augustinianism ended the presumptuous vanity of the Manicheans, who believed that men could be made higher and more divine through such practices as asceticism. The conflict between Christian expressive individualism and the therapeutic ethos is different because it is a conflict between two different versions of the higher self, with no opposing force to restrain the vanity of either. The result is actually an exacerbation of the very kind of human vanity that Christian expressive individualism tries to combat—namely, individual self-interest.

The therapist encourages individuals to tend to their self-interest and focus on their emotional needs and feelings. Therapeutically self-actualized individuals who find loving and caring to be complicated and confusing sentiments are, according to Robert Bellah, encouraged to resist self-sacrifice and retain a high degree of independence.[43] Self-interest, which Christian love in the society of expressive individualism is designed to oppose, can actually be encouraged by therapy when therapy tries to help individuals resolve the confusing elements of loving and caring relationships. The therapeutic ethos encourages people to resist obligations and prevent external circumstances from interfering with feelings that arise spontaneously within the self. In nurturing the self and feelings of love, "a kind of selfishness is essential to love"[44] from a therapeutic point of view.

The therapeutic defense of the self and one's feelings is called self-validation.[45] While feelings may ebb and flow within the self, whichever feelings come to dominate the self, and thus define the self, are supported by the therapist. Therapy supports rather than judges the individual.[46] It does not defend the idea of a higher self by positing within man a natural capacity for love, but rather by helping a person "handle"[47] uncontrollable feelings and declaring the final emotional mix to stand for a new, sovereign self. The new combination of feelings and impulses is defended in the name of "liberation," almost as if it signified an accomplishment of the self. This is how an uncontrollable phenomenon, the ever-changing mood of the psyche, is redefined as a manifestation of personal growth.[48] The individual undergoing therapy may not house a component of the divine (a natural capacity for love) but, in a slightly different way, can still emerge higher from his or her struggle.

The therapist, like the Christian expressive individualist, believes in the idea of a higher self, but by rejecting the proposition that love is under human control, the therapist grounds the higher self in whatever feelings do arise within the imagination. For the Christian expressive individualist, the individual is a higher being because he or she contains an element of the divine called love. For the therapeutically self-actualized individual, the individual is a higher being, capable of growth, because of the unique and ever-changing psychological composition of the self.

Thus, a tension exists between Christian expressive individualism and therapy, even though both grow out of the movement of expressive individualism. Christian expressive individualism, because it attributes to man a natural capacity for love, tries to oppose love to the problem of self-interest. But when the individual proves to be less in control than once thought, expressive individualism responds with a therapeutic model that merely exacerbates the problem that religion was meant to oppose. Therapy encourages self-interest instead of weakening it and makes a community based on loving and sharing more unlikely than ever.

How the Animating Spirit of Tocqueville's Christian Individualists Was Augustinian and How the Religious Experiences of the Expressive Individualist and the Aristocrat in the City of Man Come to Approximate One Another

The practice of Christianity described by Tocqueville in nineteenth-century America differs in important ways from much of contemporary American Christian practice. Christianity in Tocqueville's America was not rooted in the movement of expressive individualism. Its purpose was not to combat aggressive individualism or reform society. Its purpose was not to combat self-interest with human love. Rather, its purpose was to combat disorder. Tocqueville's Christian individualist was not a Pelagian. He or she was an Augustinian.

Robert Bellah interprets a passage in Tocqueville's work that analyzes the purpose of Christianity in nineteenth-century America. He finds in Tocqueville's understanding of Christianity a link between Christianity and the goals of contemporary expressive individualism. Religion, Bellah argues, is a mechanism that helps moderate the excesses of competitive individualism. He writes,

> Tocqueville saw religion as reinforcing self-control and maintaining moral standards but also as an expression of the benevolence and self-sacrifice that are antithetical to competitive individualism. He said that Christianity teaches "that we must do good to our fellows for love of God. That is a sublime utterance: man's mind filled with understanding of God's thought; he sees that order is God's plan, in freedom labors for this great design, ever sacrificing his private interests for this wondrous ordering of all that is, and expecting no other reward than the joy of contemplating it." Here Tocqueville expressed the hope that the destructiveness of utilitarian individualism could be countered with a generalized benevolence, rooted in sublime emotions "embedded in nature," that is, in expressive individualism.[49]

I believe Bellah seriously misinterprets Tocqueville's understanding of religion in nineteenth-century America and conceals the great change that has taken place within the practice of American Christianity. Bellah opposes Christianity to the problem of aggressive individualism. According to Bellah's interpretation of Tocqueville, Christianity encourages "caring" and "compassion" in a society organized according to the principle of self-interest. But this is the expressive individualist view of Christianity, not Tocqueville's view, for Tocqueville does not oppose Christianity to the problem of self-interest so much as he opposes it to the problem of disorder in democratic society. [50] For both Bellah and Tocqueville, Christianity is a religion of love, but for Bellah and the movement of expressive individualism, it is a love expressed by man for his fellow creatures. For Tocqueville, love is the "order that is the purpose of God." [51] In reference to Bellah's citation of Tocqueville, it was "order," not compassion, that constituted "God's plan" in Tocqueville's America.

Tocqueville says Christianity "teaches that men ought to benefit their fellow creatures for the love of God," [52] and while the Christian acts freely, he or she receives joy from contemplating the order of God. [53] Tocqueville finds in man's experience, including his most sublime feelings, the workings of a higher power. The benefit done to man's fellow creatures is done in the love of God, not as a testament to love that can be activated independent of God. The difference between the two kinds of love is crucial, and Augustine discusses this point in his book, *On Christian Doctrine.*

In the first chapter of *On Christian Doctrine,* Augustine tries to explain what it means to love one another "in God." [54] He describes spectators who have come together to watch a play, who are complete strangers to one another, and who become aroused by their admiration for one of the actors. In their applause, they find their own enthusiasm reproduced in others, and they "begin to love one another for the sake of him that they love." A bond is established as they applaud their favorite.

This is the same experience of love in Tocqueville's Christian. Love is not a resource natural to man, independent of some higher being. It is not a possession of the autonomous self, disclosed at will when the self feels inclined. On the contrary, love is that feeling that the Christian individualist expresses towards God and that radiates outward towards one's neighbors, but that owes its source to the inspiration of God and not to a calculation made by the self. Love is a "pleasure" [55] synonymous with the feeling that comes from knowing one has prosecuted the "great design" [56] of God. It was not man's power of love that gave Tocqueville's Christian individualist pleasure, but rather a glimpse of God's eternal order.

This understanding of love is not found in Christian expressive individualism. It is a distinctly Augustinian concept, one further explored in *The City of God.* In the work, the City of Man and the City of God are separated precisely according to the different human loves. Augustine writes, "These two cities were made by two loves: the earthly city by the love of self unto the contempt of God, and the heavenly city by the love of God unto the contempt of the self."[57] Those belonging to the City of Man are not united in any real sense, except that each manifests a tremendous love of self. The pagan aristocrat and the modern career-oriented expressive individualist, both excelling only to gain glory for themselves, clearly belong to the City of Man. But so also do the Pelagian and the Christian expressive individualist, for when they donate their love to others, they presume it is their love to give, that the capacity for love that allows them to care and to share at will is a part of their nature. They presume that this faculty makes them God-like, or at least independent of God, and when they love, they do not love "in God" so much as they love "in man." This can be observed while they perform their loving and caring duties, for when they do so, they, like the aristocrat, love the praise of man as much, if not more, than the praise of God.[58]

This love is very different from the love of those who belong to Augustine's City of God. Those who belong to the heavenly city are united by a love of God and of one another in God, and not by a love of one another separate from God. Love in this city is not manifested so much in active charity that ennobles the self, but in an inner peace derived from "the perfectly ordered and harmonious enjoyment of God, and of one another in God."[59] Human love does not rule the City of God, but rather the "peace of all things," which is "the tranquility of order."[60]

An important difference between the Christianity of Tocqueville's American and the Christianity of the expressive individualist rests precisely on these divergent attitudes towards religious love. Tocqueville's Christian did not champion the idea of a loving self independent of or prior to God. He or she did not separate divine power from a human capacity for love. In the Christianity of Tocqueville's American, man's merit does not precede God; man is nothing without God. The self is neither so autonomous nor superior that it can presume to choose religion as if it were merely an adjunct to an already fully developed self. This important difference between Tocqueville's American and the expressive individualist causes another link to be established between expressive individualism and the experience of aristocracy. This is not surprising, given that the loves of both the Pelagian and pagan aristocrat are, as Augustine noted, expressions of self-love.

Because the Christian expressive individualist locates the capacity for love in man, religious energy is focused directly on the problem of self-interest. The Christian expressive individualist believes that human love operating within and on the social order can be placed in opposition to selfishness. Through activism, it can help correct serious inequities in society. The Christian expressive individualist believes that the power of human love can build a more loving and caring community.

This idea leads to the creation of "caring" institutions within the American society of expressive individualism that aid, or are devoted to the study of, the weak, the disadvantaged, the lonely, and the miserable. These educational, therapeutic, and social service institutions, both secular and religious, stand in an intermediary position between God and man and are a testament to the divine power of love that is credited to man. They are recognized to be expressions of a God-like spirit within man, above the darkest side of human nature but below the purest expression of love that is articulated in the divine. Caring institutions represent what man, who is believed to be partly selfish and partly capable of initiating a divine and loving act, can accomplish in this world.

It is this practice that mimics the experience of aristocratic society. In reference to the religious beliefs of an aristocratic people, Tocqueville notes that such people "will always be prone to place intermediate powers between God and man."[61] The only difference between the Christian expressive individualist and the aristocrat is that while the Christian expressive individualist interposes caring institutions between God and man, the aristocrat interposes between God and man those institutions reflecting on the might and bravery of a man. Warrior rites, codes of honor, and schools of discipline exist in aristocratic society as a testament to the God-like position of superiority that a man can aspire to, not as a testament to a God-like capacity for love existing in man. These aristocratic institutions, like the caring professions in the society of expressive individualism, reflect a belief in a higher self, but one that is rooted in honor, not love, in the glorification of the most noble, not in charity for all.

Christianity in Tocqueville's America located the capacity for love in God, not in man and, as a result, the power of human love was not directly opposed to the problem of selfishness. Without a belief in the natural capacity for love, Tocqueville's American could not aspire to oppose love to self-interest. On the contrary, Tocqueville asserts that Christianity in nineteenth-century America actually allied itself with the principle of self-interest to produce a stable social order.[62] Instead of representing the antithesis of religion, individual self-interest complemented religion. Tocqueville notes how the American clergy would constantly emphasize those points where prosperity in this world and the commands of religion "are most nearly and closely connected."[63] Instead of attacking self-interest in the name of love, Christianity in Tocqueville's America was adapted to the principle of self-interest.

This position suggests that the American clergy of the nineteenth century firmly grounded religion in the principle of utility, but the conclusion is incorrect. The American clergy of the nineteenth century tried to show where religious ideals and the desire for material prosperity supported common action. Those efforts do not signify an attempt by the clergy to sacrifice religion to the principle of utility. Rather, they signify an attempt by the clergy to demonstrate how two separate and autonomous spheres of life, the spiritual and the material, could articulate codes of conduct that complemented rather than antagonized one another.

This arrangement is actually quite consistent with Augustine's understanding of the two cities in *The City of God*. The heavenly city and the earthly city need not necessarily oppose one another; it is possible for them to coexist on earth. The two cities have common ground, for temporal peace and prosperity are certainly blessings that provide the conditions under which individuals can work out their eternal destiny.

Tocqueville alludes to the difference between a religion made compatible with the principle of self-interest and a religion based on the principle of utility in his comparison of American and European Christianity. Of European Christianity, Tocqueville says, "men desert religious opinions from lukewarmness rather than from dislike; they are not rejected, but they fall away."[64] For such "disbelievers" in Europe, religion was "no longer considered to be true, but was still considered to be "useful"[65] and, on that basis, continued to influence the external world of "manners and legislation."[66] The Christian experience in Europe, in which religion adapted itself to the principle of utility and became involved in social and economic issues, differs greatly from Christianity in America, where religion exerted little power and influence in the external world, but held the mind of the individualist "under undisputed control."[67]

Tocqueville's Americans were fervent believers and not the lukewarm followers whom Tocqueville observed in Europe, and if self-interest and the principle of utility served as a basis for individual action in the external world, Christianity was allotted the realm of the mind. While Christianity and the principle of utility may have agreed on certain points, the relationship did not absorb Christianity into a debate over "policy," just as it did not allow the rules governing conduct in the material community of individualists to take hold within the spiritual community of individualists.

Unlike the Christian expressive individualist, Tocqueville's Christian did not presume that self-interest could be fought with the human power of love. Tocqueville's American simply accepted self-interest as an enduring facet of the human personality, one that was immune to the entreaties of love ("men can never be cured of the love of riches"[68]). Since a natural capacity for love in man was not imagined by Tocqueville's Christian, religion was not set against self-interest but instead was designed to funnel human energy, ambition, and drive into orderly and "honest" activities.[69]

For this reason, nineteenth-century American democracy, unlike the society of expressive individualism and aristocratic society, did not possess institutions standing intermediate between man and God. The public association and the civic organization, much discussed by Tocqueville, were not expressions of human love or the higher self, but rather of the principle of self-interest "rightly understood."[70] They were founded on a principle that the Christian expressive individualist combats and the old aristocrat scorns—individual self-interest. As an institution, the civic organization did not ennoble those individuals who were associated with it or proclaim their work to be half-divine.

The aristocrat mimicked the divine through institutions such as monarchy and hereditary estates, where power, lineage, and superior position sustained God-like creatures who commanded eternal reverence and respect. The expressive individualist mimics the divine through institutions such as the caring social service agencies of the state, which elevate governance above the sleazy world of politics through an association with the God-like power of human love. Tocqueville's American neither proclaimed the existence of a superior being (an impossibility in the new age of equality) nor did he proudly build edifices to human love. The charitable acts of the public association observed by Tocqueville were grounded in utility and self-interest, the simple rules of mortals in the larger world. They did not reflect a movement of the soul towards the divine.

5

Donatism in the Society of Expressive Individualism

In struggling with the Donatists, Augustine charged that their effort to erect a separate church, one more holy and more pure, was conceived not in devout faith but in pride. It was an incredible vanity and presumption of superiority, Augustine insisted, for the Donatists to pit altar against altar and claim for themselves the power to judge the souls of others. Their break with the Church reflected not a love of God but a love of themselves and an inflated view of man's capabilities.

Augustine said that the "sin of schism" committed by the Donatists revealed a flawed understanding of the church of God. It was true that one aspect of the church was visible. It expressed itself in the world of force and matter—in the form of buildings, robes, and scrolls—and could be seen, touched, and heard. But the visible church, Augustine argued, was only an impure reflection of the invisible church that transcended the physical world and signified God's love. Men are forced to live in the earthly city, of which the visible church is a part, and in the earthly city there exist a multitude of languages, customs, opinions, and tastes that tend to divide men and move them in the direction of disunity. But the invisible church lying beyond the senses is devoid of such fine distinctions between men. It comprises a single unity. The invisible church is the true church, and to focus attention on the visible at the expense of the invisible, to expend great effort on dividing men according to the details of earthly existence rather than pondering the unity of mankind, is to be carnal-minded and sinful.[1] Augustine preached that one should humbly direct his or her faith beyond the visible church and towards the invisible church of God where unity, not divisiveness, reigns.

The impulse to form a "splinter group" is hardly unique to Donatism. Schismatics can be observed in many other movements, both religious and secular. For example, the aristocrats described by both Augustine and Tocqueville possessed the same urge as the Donatists to look over people and judge them carefully, to include some in the brotherhood and not others, and to separate themselves from the main body of society. It was by doing so that aristocrats came spend their lives in "vast enclosures,"[2] cut off from others. This tendency towards disunity was observed by Tocqueville throughout the Old World, as both aristocrats and nonaristocrats would spend their entire lives among groups that emphasized the sameness of their members. Each caste had its own "opinions, feelings, rights, customs, and modes of living."[3] Caste members, wrote Tocqueville, "do not resemble the mass of their fellow citizens; they do not think or feel in the same manner, and they scarcely believe that they belong to the same race."[4] Like the Donatists, both aristocrats and nonaristocrats would sniff out the differences between people—differences based on action, thought, or simply one's physical person—and proceed to join them to their brotherhood or banish them.

The Augustinian Catholic Church was the major force in the Old World that preached the unity of mankind. That unity called on people to control their urge to use sense and reason to discriminate between their fellows. It was only by looking beyond all that was visible that one could form a link in God with those practicing different customs, wearing different dress, or speaking a different language. Unity could be achieved only through faith in the invisible and the intangible—in God's invisible church. It was Augustinian Christianity that taught men to humble themselves before the invisible, to have faith in the unseen, and to lift themselves out of carnal-mindedness and see that which united all mankind.

In Tocqueville's America, a similar Augustinian phenomenon was operative. The realm of public opinion was the invisible world living beyond the world of force or matter. Public opinion could be given physical expression in human voice or in newspaper print, but that expression was simply an impure reflection of the wholly intangible phenomenon that was public opinion. Like Augustine's invisible world, public opinion was devoid of substance in the world of earthly sense. It had no beginning and no end, and it came to live only in the minds of men and women. It had presence on earth, yet it was greater than the visible society on earth, and it transcended all of the small microcosms of humanity and perceived differences between men and women to create a new unity. From some unknown epicenter, the power of public opinion radiated outwards, and though it lacked physicality, it carried with it sufficient force to move through every barrier and every human body until it penetrated the mind of every individualist. It was to that invisible power that Tocqueville's Americans humbled themselves, thus achieving a certain unity of mankind that spanned an entire continent.

Public opinion was as immutable and unchallengeable in Tocqueville's America as the Invisible Kingdom of God was in Augustinian Christianity. No schism in the church, Augustine noted, truly does damage to, or divides, the invisible church, for the unity that is the church is indivisible. Schism simply puts the violators in the position of apostates.[5] It separates them from God and excludes them from eternal salvation. In the same way, no individualist in Tocqueville's America could truly divide the unity of public opinion. Once public opinion rendered a decision on an issue, no higher court of appeal existed to overturn it. It was, according to James Bryce, as if Rome had spoken.[6] The man who went up against the tide of public opinion and violated the unity that it preached merely caused himself to be branded an apostate. Tocqueville describes in great detail the consequences met by the American who tried to break away from public opinion, how that person was forced to wander in lonely spiritual death as if he were excommunicated.[7]

Because of this American faith in the rightness of the majority and the humble pose assumed by the Americans at the invisible feet of public opinion, no culture could exist outside the culture of public opinion in Tocqueville's America. No schismatic activity was possible. Subcultures and small enclaves resisting the opinion of the majority simply could not survive.

In the aristocratic society of the Old World, no such omnipotent force existed, and subcultures existed to a much greater extent than they did in democratic America. The idea of the invisible church was known in the Old World, and it had its adherents, but the idea of discriminating between men on the basis of their person, their behavior, and their action was commonly accepted. The idea of mankind's unity could not efface the hundreds of castes, sects, and subcultures that physically set men apart from one another. This is why subcultures could exist in aristocratic society even though the governing regime was authoritarian. Tocqueville writes,

> In any constitutional state in Europe every sort of religious and political theory may be freely preached and disseminated; for there is no country in Europe so subdued by any single authority as not to protect the man who raises his voice in the cause of truth from the consequences of his hardihood. If he is unfortunate enough to live under an absolute government, the people are often on his side; if he inhabits a free country, he can, if necessary, find shelter behind the throne. The aristocratic part of society supports him in some countries, and the democracy in others. But in a nation where democratic institutions exist, organized like those of the United States, there is but one authority [majority opinion], one element of strength and success, with nothing beyond it.[8]

In aristocratic society, without the all-powerful force of public opinion to bear down on the mind and will of each individual, "protest" could exist in small, isolated enclaves.

In contemporary America, a new social pattern has emerged, one that is very different from the experience of Tocqueville's America and that recalls the pattern of life observed in old aristocratic society. There now exists a vast array of subcultures and islands of difference, each filled with people who are quite similar to one another. Both Robert Bellah and Richard Sennett describe this phenomenon, noting the emergence of extremely homogeneous communities in the United States over the last two decades.[9] In Bellah's book, these communities are called "lifestyle enclaves" and include such groups as religious sects, psychic institutes, the gay culture, and the youth culture. Sennett focuses his attention on the suburban community, which also represents a kind of lifestyle enclave even though its membership is quite large. Many in the suburban community make a concerted effort to establish a certain distance between themselves and other subcultures.

This new pattern of life represents a clear departure from the experience of Tocqueville's American. When the power of public opinion was at its zenith, Tocqueville's Americans radiated a certain mental unity despite the fact that accents and local customs varied across the continent. The Americans from Maine to Georgia, from Pennsylvania to Kansas, were virtually alike.[10] Tocqueville reports that Americans separated by great physical distances in the nineteenth century were more like each other than were the people of Normandy and Brittany, regions in France separated by a simple brook.[11] It was not so much that differences were absent among the Americans, but that those differences were overcome by a unity in outlook and spirit. Public opinion exerted subtle pressure on the mind of the American, creating a narrow spectrum of political thought and field of human endeavor.

Both Tocqueville and James Bryce commented on the omnipresence of the "business mind"[12] that accentuated the monotony and uniformity of American life. Millions of people would "think the same thoughts"[13] and devote their lives to material gain, leaving little possibility for variety in "knowledge, tastes, and pursuits."[14] In virtually every city and region, the rhythm of life was the same, and Bryce found this aspect of American life extremely irritating. Of the cities, he wrote,

> In all else they are alike, both great and small. In all the same wide streets, crossing at right angles, ill-paved, but planted along the sidewalks with maple trees. . . In all the same shops, arranged on the same plan, the same Chinese laundries, with Li Kow visible through the window, the same ice cream stores, the same large hotels with seedy men hovering about in the cheerless entrance-hall, the same street cars passing to and fro with passengers clinging to the door step, the same locomotives ringing their great bells as they clank slowly down the streets . . . their monotony haunts one like a nightmare. Even the irksomeness of finding the streets named by numbers becomes insufferable.[15]

In contemporary America, the power of public opinion is weak, and the Donatist principle of using sense and rational faculties to discriminate among people has reasserted itself. The unity that was the invisible world of public opinion has collapsed, resulting in schism in the visible world. Each of the lifestyle enclaves found in expressive individualist society, including, for example, the gay culture, the gun aficionados, the dance enthusiasts, the rappers, the golfers, the bar scene, the Elvis Presley fan club, the Scientologists, the inner-city gang, and the classical music lovers, radiates a certain purity that was evident in both the Donatist sect and in the Old World enclosure of aristocrats. The new lifestyle enclaves "celebrate the narcissism of similarity,"[16] and this has come about by Americans using their critical senses in the service of special values to sort human beings out from one another.

Many Americans will spend their entire lives in just one or two of these enclaves, finding support, friendship, common experiences, and a source of memories. In doing so, they willfully separate themselves from others. In each enclave, a new member is looked over very carefully to discern how much he or she is "like them," how enthusiastic and dedicated one is, and whether his or her manners and actions are appropriate to the group. This tendency to use the senses and other critical faculties to separate people can be observed across the political spectrum. It can be observed among conservative country-clubbers who refuse to extend membership to minorities as well as among those minorities radicalized by the "multiculturalist" ideal, who demand their own special eating places and dormitories on college campuses or who support bans on interracial adoptions. What forms the binding tie is that, in each case, human beings are being carefully separated according to the distinctive markings found on their persons.

It is curious, for example, to go into a bar frequented by rebellious, anticonformist types and find everyone there dressed in black. This occurs not merely because black dress is the fashion but because it is a testament to mental purity. It conveys how sincerely one is disgusted with bourgeois life and all of its pretty colors and insipid delights, and it helps one to be accepted by other fringe types. Hence, even this "anticonformist" sect demands a certain visible conformity and, like the Donatists, the members of the group look the new person up and down because they presume to judge the integrity and sincerity of those aspiring to join.

The same phenomenon can be observed in the suburban enclave, where the behavior and tastes of new neighbors are checked over very carefully. The color of paint used on the house ("Is it too loud?") and the landscaping techniques of the new neighbors are carefully scrutinized by the residents. Mixed in with this careful and thorough examination is a certain degree of trepidation, which is described by Richard Sennett in his book *The Uses of Disorder*. Sennett describes the suburban enclave as a "community of fear," one that tries to establish a pattern of living that is safe, ordered, and known.[17] The fear that organizes the suburban community is the fear of the unknown, and is not unlike the fear experienced by maturing adolescents who purify in their minds an ideal of how life should be and then proceed to live life according to that imagined ideal.[18] All that is visible and tangible is used in the service of constructing an idealized plan for living. The effort hardly differs from that of the Donatist in late antiquity. In both cases, the visible world, or earthly life, is given a certain coherence and predictability by employing man's critical faculties to probe the outer shell and inner spirit of other men. The end result is a visible world divided between the like-minded and the strange.

The weakening of public opinion has allowed new lifestyles to come into being. Instead of being united by the law of public opinion, contemporary Americans are divided by different outlooks and conflicting sets of values. Even the universal drive to accumulate wealth has become, in many enclaves, unimportant relative to the unique goals and projects of a particular community. The passion for making money persists among expressive individualists but, at times, becomes secondary to the dominant passion that brings people together in a group (e.g., fishing, windsurfing, ballroom dancing, or ethnic heritage). Life in the society of expressive individualism is varied, not monotonous.

In criticizing the Donatists, Augustine wrote, "To use visible standards of morality as a test of membership is to transfer the merit and glory from Christ to the members of themselves, and to set forth the church as a society of the moral rather than a family of the redeemed."[19] The unity of the church was the unity of those who were humbled in faith, who did not believe their critical faculties to be sufficiently precise to separate the "wheat from the tares," the good from the bad. In the same way, the unity of public opinion in Tocqueville's America was a unity of those who deferred to the transcendent power of the majority and its adjudicative power and who only with great caution resisted that power and struck out on their own. In both cases, a love of self was sacrificed in an awareness of the merit and glory of something beyond the self. The individual urge to construct a reality based on one's own imagined ideal of life was drowned out by a faith in some higher power. In the case of Tocqueville's Americans, they did not judge so much as they let public opinion judge, and they did not use their critical faculties to sort human beings out from one another so much as they yielded those faculties to the encompassing power of numbers.

This is not the case for the Donatist and the expressive individualist (or for the aristocrat). Both the Donatist and the expressive individualist wholeheart-edly love themselves. With that love, they carve up the visible world lying before their senses, scruple about the differences between men, and build sects and enclaves that represent, if not the most moral in man, at least what is believed to stand for man's highest aspirations. As Augustine noted, it is the love of self that hovers over the impulse to build a group that is simply a reflection of the self, and this phenomenon is evident in America now just as it was in Roman Africa fifteen centuries ago. The new subcultures or lifestyle enclaves in America have erected barriers that public opinion can no longer penetrate, thus shielding the minds and wills of individuals from the supreme power that once demanded absolute conformity on certain issues.

How the Lifestyle Enclave Differs from the "Small Private Circles" Tocqueville Observed in Nineteenth-Century America

Robert Bellah argues that the new lifestyle enclave is a kind of community, one built on a philosophy of individualism and bringing together those who reflect and affirm each other's selfhood.[20] He finds a logical continuity between the "small private circle" of friends in Tocqueville's America and the lifestyle enclave of the contemporary expressive individualist.

But the new order of lifestyle enclaves and subcultures in America is very different from the order observed by Tocqueville among the early Americans. In Tocqueville's America, the social order was composed of family units and impersonal institutions like the public association. Tocqueville's Americans formed friendships with those who shared common personal and professional interests, and those common interests formed the basis of a "multitude of small private circles" in democratic America.[21] But those private circles originated in "the accidental similarity of opinions and tastes"[22] and were never more than just small gatherings. The situation is very different in the lifestyle enclave, where contemporary Americans are bound together in much more profound ways. The rules of some enclaves, like the sports enclave, the animal-lovers association, the ecology club, and the musical fan club, almost carry the force of custom, religious rite, or mystical belief. In the sports enclave, for example, certain athletes command awe and reverence and the articles they have touched are worshipped like icons in a church. The experience in the lifestyle enclave is more intense and recalls not the "private circles of friends" in Tocqueville's America but the castes, clans, and religious sects of antiquity.

Furthermore, the small private circles in Tocqueville's America did not so completely dominate home life that a breakdown in communication resulted between members of different private circles.[23] According to Tocqueville, much of the life of the early American individualist was spent working in public associations and civic organizations in which dissimilar people were "forced to be acquainted and to adapt themselves to one another."[24] Richard Sennett notes that even into the early part of the twentieth century, American communities revealed "a multiplicity of contact points,"[25] as individuals from different walks of life would often meet and talk during their nonworking hours. Such interaction, he notes, is clearly absent from the modern suburban community. In a social order composed of lifestyle enclaves, members often remain within the confines of their respective enclosures and do not mix with individuals from other groups.

Just as the lifestyle enclave is different in quality and intensity from the small private circle of friends in Tocqueville's America, so is it unrelated to the nineteenth-century American experience of public association. The public associations in Tocqueville's America were founded on the basis of self-interest and not to enhance "meaning" in private life. For Tocqueville's Americans, the basis for public contact was generally a material need that prompted individuals to act in concert. A particular public association might be only as enduring as the material interests of its members. Unlike the lifestyle enclave, it did not provide its members with a sense of purpose in life or satisfy some personal quest for deep emotional meaning.

In the public associations of Tocqueville's America, individuals from different backgrounds and with different recreational interests (in other words, "everyone"[26]) would come together to plan and execute civic projects, such as improving town roads, building public schools, electing delegates, strengthening the moral tone of the community, or forming temperance unions.[27] All citizens, both men and women, "took a hand in the regulation of society."[28] While they shared a common moral outlook and a common conception of government and politics, they differed in ways that all individuals differ—in business goals and leisure interests, in their interpretation of what was new and fashionable. It is precisely because tastes differed and because it was possible in the new democratic society for individuals to gratify their particular desires that Tocqueville's America was in a state of constant commotion, with each person dashing about trying to reach his or her goal. In this way, "community" in Tocqueville's America came to be based not on the private interests of a subset of the population but on participation in public life. Individuals with a myriad of private interests would come together, sharing only general attitudes towards morality and politics.

It is true that Tocqueville's Americans did share common religious values, and those values seem to parallel the shared private goals of the modern lifestyle enclave. But nineteenth-century American society was largely a Christian society and since, according to Tocqueville, Christian morality was everywhere the same,[29] Christian morality could not provide the basis for a lifestyle enclave any more than public opinion could. Because it was embraced by virtually everyone, Christian morality could not delineate a particular lifestyle or subgroup of individuals in nineteenth-century America. It could not serve as the basis of a closed community.

In the same way, neither could the American obsession with making money make the public "community" of Tocqueville's individualists homogeneous. The passion for riches made American society monotonous, not homogeneous.[30] The desire for money was, like Christian morality and majority opinion, expressed in virtually all of the Americans studied by Tocqueville. It made everyone seem the same and all human activity motivated by this singular intense passion look alike. For this reason, the obsession with making money could not provide a basis for a private enclave. It could not be used to make a distinction between Americans. It could not be used to divide Americans into groups.

The situation is very different in the lifestyle enclaves of contemporary America. Within a particular enclave, the expressive individualist does not expect to find merely a stranger who shares a few general notions of morality and a common understanding of democratic procedure. This is what the Tocqueville's American expected to find in the public communities of the nineteenth century. The expressive individualist expects to find someone with the same recreational interests, the same hobbies, the same sexual proclivities, the same educational background, the same political convictions, and/or the same musical and artistic tastes. The expressive individualist expects to find, in his or her small private enclave, a community of human duplicates.

For this reason, I disagree with Bellah's position that the move from the nineteenth-century American "small private circle of friends" to the new lifestyle enclave constitutes a logical progression within the movement of American individualism.[31] Bellah argues that the narcissistic culture of similarity demonstrated in the contemporary lifestyle enclave is rooted in a longstanding desire of American individualists to mix with those who share similar tastes, values, and goals. But while the individualist in Tocqueville's America may have felt detached from others,[32] he did not yearn for a life spent in the company of like-minded persons. He did not love himself so much that he expected all social intercourse to be conducted according to his interests, his tastes, and his values. This is not how the public associations and civic organizations of nineteenth-century America operated.

How the Political Order Created by a System of Lifestyle Enclaves Recalls the Experience of Old Aristocratic Society

Tocqueville feared that individuals in a democratic society might withdraw completely into private life and, by doing so, become easy prey for despotic rulers. He feared that the private "circle of interests"[33] would displace the public association and sap the individual of all initiative and power needed to resist a tyrant. It is true that the lifestyle enclave in contemporary America is also an association of those who have withdrawn. It is composed of people who no longer try to find common ground with strangers in public space. But as institutions, the private circle of interests and the lifestyle enclave are not related. The lifestyle enclave is a far more extensive association in terms of membership and activity and, contrary to Bellah's assertion, even more a political one than the small private circles into which Tocqueville feared the Americans might retreat. This is true even though the contemporary lifestyle enclave is still rooted in private life.

Tocqueville argues that the public association helped counteract the American tendency towards self-withdrawal. The public association was a mechanism designed to preserve energy and vitality in a democratic society, one that encouraged interaction between citizens outside of domestic life. Tocqueville did not foresee that such energy and vitality could be demonstrated in associations rooted in the leisure activities of private life. He did not realize that an extreme love of self was very compatible with an intense interest in the world of politics and public affairs. The lifestyle enclave is, in the Tocquevillian sense, neither a "public" association nor simply a small, private circle of friends. It is an association that is substantial, energetic, and active even though it remains private, and it brings to mind the castes of late antiquity in which Augustine lived.

The lifestyle enclave has now become an important feature in American politics. Certain lifestyle enclaves form essential elements of the liberal and conservative coalitions in American politics. The liberal coalition includes such enclaves as the gay culture, the environmentally concerned, the arts community, and some segments of the youth culture. The conservative coalition includes such enclaves as the suburbs, certain religious enclaves, and the gun enclave. It is important to note that modern conservatism ("Reaganism"), which encourages local control, is not a throwback to the political practices of Tocqueville's America, where administrative power was decentralized and citizens were encouraged to participate in community affairs.

Contemporary conservatives praise the decentralization of government but for a different reason than did earlier proponents of local control. The lifestyle enclaves in contemporary America do not contain Tocquevillian individualists who actively desire to involve themselves in community affairs. Rather, they contain expressive individualists who have withdrawn from public life into small groups of the like-minded and who are often cynical about those who aspire to public life.

When conservatism defends the suburbs from a national governmental agenda (e.g., from forced busing to achieve integration) or defends religious enclaves from a uniform secularism (e.g., by fighting for school prayer or to defend the tax-exempt status of religious-based universities), it is defending local homogeneous enclaves of like-minded individuals who have withdrawn into private life, not vigorous associations of public-minded individualists. It defends enclaves of individuals who want to be left alone. The liberal tendency towards administrative centralization of government constitutes a threat to both the community of Tocquevillian individualists and the lifestyle enclave of expressive individualists. The contemporary conservative defense of local control does not necessarily signal a rebirth of Tocqueville's America.

Some of the more politically active lifestyle enclaves show how the lifestyle enclave differs from both the early American "private circle of friends" and the old public association. Many gays, athletes, artists, wilderness enthusiasts, animal lovers, and environmentally concerned people spend their private lives in the company of individuals who share their respective subcultural beliefs and lifestyles. Yet such people have also become very politically active. They have not withdrawn from the political process like Tocqueville's imaginary citizen living under administrative despotism, but instead have formed political organizations that energize the members of their respective enclaves.

This political activity, however, signifies the politicization of private enclaves, not public action, for it is an extension of a specific practice or belief shared with friends in private life. While the members of lifestyle enclaves obey the rules of public discourse, their politics are rooted in their separateness as a private group, not in those aspects of life that are common to all. While the enclaves are political, they are not public; their political activity originates in a private community of similar individuals and not in a public community of strangers.

The politicization of private enclaves signals another return to Old World practice. In his work *The City*, Weber compares the modern city with the city of antiquity. He argues that the modern city encourages the growth of professional organizations and associations and the mixing together of people from different backgrounds at the expense of rigid caste and clan systems.[34] This pattern of social intercourse differs considerably from the pattern governing the city of antiquity. There, individuals were confined to specific caste institutions, guilds, and fraternities tightly regulated by custom and tradition (e.g., by magic, taboo, totemic cults, superstition, or the traditions of noble families). These castes absorbed the lives of their members and little communication existed between members of different groups. Such institutions formed the basic units of political activity within the ancient city.

In the modern city, notes Weber, individuals sever ties with traditional groups and become "citizens" capable of communal action and civic cooperation. Social mixing is encouraged, and if devotion to a private caste is weakened, interest in a "public" realm is instilled. The individual citizen replaces the clan or the caste as the new unit of political activity, and social intercourse between individuals previously unfamiliar with one another becomes possible in a newly created "public" realm.

The politicization of private enclaves in contemporary America (in both the conservative and liberal coalitions) recalls the experience in the city of antiquity. The lifestyle enclaves in contemporary America are like the ancient private castes. They are homogeneous in their membership, organized according to a specific rite or pattern of living, and composed of individuals who rarely interact with the members of other castes. Moreover, their members are linked to a larger political body through clan political activity and do not really interact with "citizens" in a public realm of strangers. The society of expressive individualism is not a collection of detached citizens, but rather a mosaic of enclaves and subcultures. In such a society, the lifestyle enclave becomes the new unit of political activity.

How the "Traditional" Community Is Not an Appropriate Baseline for Comparison with the American Lifestyle Enclave and How the Old American Community Transcended the Confines of the Material World

Augustine believed those who inhabited the City of God transcended the mutable substance of the earthly city. The earthly city, Augustine argued, is merely an alliance of temporal interests, and the order it fosters is makeshift. It is formed by a chance combination of men's wills, all moving in different directions to attain things that are helpful to them in this life.[35] Occasionally, a certain commonality of interests is realized, with the result being civic obedience and calm. But that calm is superficial and transitory, waiting only for the next great storm to strike (war, revolution, economic depression, or natural catastrophe), which is why Augustine said the earthly city is not a continuing city.

The heavenly city is the continuing city. It is in the heavenly city where perfect order is sustained and harmonious enjoyment achieved. When the heavenly city is forced to sojourn on earth, it has an interface with the disruption and commotion that rages in the earthly city, yet it remains a realm apart. In this way one can live in the earthly city but still inhabit the heavenly City of God. Through faith in God and the sacrifice of one's love of self, a person can be otherworldly even while residing in this world. The heavenly city is filled with human wills that are united in their love of God, not rent asunder by vain designs and ambitious pursuits, and it is in the moment of repose achieved through faith that one glimpses God's eternal and unchanging order of things. This is what Augustine meant when he spoke of "resting in God." The heavenly city is the only city that can offer any semblance of continuity or true order.

Augustine's distinction between the two cities is extremely relevant to the American experience. This is because his understanding of the two cities is mirrored in the animating spirit of Tocqueville's individualists. For Tocqueville's individualists, the earthly city, or the Visible World of society, was absolutely chaotic. At one point, Tocqueville compares the American communities of the nineteenth century to rootless armies in the field, with their inhabitants always seeming "to live from hand to mouth."[36] Towns would spring up overnight and then disappear as quickly as they were created. Fortune, not tradition, was the mortar that held American communities together, and the extraordinary mobility of the Americans, each one looking to get rich, caused communities to blend together by virtue of their newness rather than diverge because a special tradition held them fast. James Bryce writes, "The web of history woven day by day all over Europe is vast and of many colours: it is fateful to every European. But in America it is only the philosopher who can feel it will ultimately be fateful to Americans also."[37] Contrasting America at the turn of the century with Europe, Bryce notes that in Europe, "many old institutions have survived among the new ones; as in a city that grows but slowly, old buildings are not cleared away to make room for others more suited to modern commerce, but are allowed to stand, sometimes empty and unused."[38] In America, he observed, this "scarcely happens" as cities are continually rebuilt so as to give institutions a "new face."[39]

Tocqueville also notes the lack of respect paid to historical tradition in American communities, causing him to conclude that democratic society, unlike aristocratic society, has an instinctive distaste for that which is old.[40] The communities observed by Tocqueville in nineteenth-century America did not revere tradition. There was no rock of cohesion founded on special village custom or the glorious history of a township's past. The American towns were not continuing in any way, nor was there any presumption that they should be continuing. This is because Tocqueville's Americans focused their attention on the future, on the opportunities to gain wealth and success, and each person moved hither and thither to advance himself or herself. The American communities observed by Tocqueville were caught up in the same torrential and unstoppable current of change that bore down on every other institution in that society.

The American communities observed by Tocqueville were not traditional communities. They could not be. They had no tradition because basically they had no past. Were it not for the newspapers, according to Tocqueville, the chain of time in these towns would have been completely severed.[41] According to Tocqueville, the nineteenth-century American community was not founded on memories or historical tradition, but rather on self-interest ("cupidity"[42]). Community involvement and the public association were driven by the principle of self-interest rightly understood. This effort of Tocqueville's American to stitch together visible communities by relying on ever-changing self-interest is quite consistent with Augustine's understanding of what basically underlies the order of things in the earthly city of men.

But this chaotic and ever-changing visible world in Tocqueville's America coexisted with an amazing calmness and serenity that reigned in the invisible world of the American mind. That invisible world was fixed and ordered and yielded a certain inner peace and tranquility often described by Tocqueville in his work. The interface between the two worlds—between a material world that was chaotic and ever-changing and a spiritual world that was ordered and eternal—recalls the interface between the earthly city and the heavenly city in Augustinian theology. Tocqueville's American was worldly and had a great regard for peace on earth, but he was also otherworldly and would sacrifice his love of self for the love of things divine. It was not in building edifices to human love that he would surrender his love of self—those edifices were still part of the visible world and merely a testament to another man's love of self, thus hardly representing sufficient cause to lower one's own ambition. Rather, it was in a moment of repose, in church, while contemplating the eternal and the unchanging, while walking thoughtfully and respectfully towards the altar, and when bowing his head in prayer that Tocqueville's American surrendered his love of self to gain a glimpse of a higher order. It was in that special realm of faith, and in that realm only, that the American individualist found something enduring and continuous in life or felt a true unity with others. That realm of Christian faith corresponds to Augustine's unseen, invisible heavenly City of God, and the unity Tocqueville's American experienced was a unity in God, not in man.

The heavenly city in Tocqueville's America will be described in more detail in the second section of this book. But at this point, it is important to examine one understanding of community in modern expressive individualist thought and relate it to the experience of Tocqueville's America. This is because many expressive individualists yearn for community in the visible world, something that Tocqueville's Americans never did. They desire that some element of the earthly city be continuous and unchanging. It is in this spirit that they bemoan old buildings being torn down in the neighborhood or look with sorrow at the disappearance of a local factory. And these expressive individualists erroneously believe that such continuity existed in the communities of the American past.

In *Habits of the Heart*, Bellah introduces the term "community of memory" and compares it to the lifestyle enclave of the expressive individualist. He argues that "communities of memory" are formed by people who share certain practices and a common history and denote the traditional form of American community that existed before the rise of the lifestyle enclave.[43] "Communities of memory" have a history. They are "constituted by their past."[44] Bellah writes,

> The communities of memory that tie us to the past also turn us toward the future as communities of hope. They carry a context of meaning that can allow us to connect our aspirations for ourselves and those closest to us with the aspirations of a larger whole and see our own efforts as being, in part, contributions to a common good.[45]

The tight-knit religious and ethnic communities found in American cities at the turn of the century are offered as examples of a "community of memory."

I believe Bellah has seriously erred in opposing an ideal called the "community of memory" to the modern expressive individualist's lifestyle enclave and in suggesting that the "community of memory" forms the model of the early American community. The "community of memory" does not represent the traditional form of American community so much as it does a kind of community that once existed in the Old World.

In his work, *The Urban Villagers*, Herbert Gans studies one such "community of memory" in the West End of Boston.[46] His analysis of that ethnic neighborhood allows him to conclude that urban communities like the ethnic neighborhood are not really modern communities, but instead peasant, almost quasi-feudal, forms of social organization. Gans suggests that the existence of such communities in industrial America was an aberration in American urban history; they thrived for one or two generations after their members emigrated to America because certain feudal traditions and peasant customs could be perpetuated in the isolation of the ethnic neighborhood. Eventually, the members of these communities assimilated into the mainstream of American life, leading to the demise of those neighborhoods.

The communities of memory have a strong link with the experience of life in the Old World, much more so than with the townships of Tocqueville's America. And they are precisely the kinds of earthly communities that Augustine hoped people would transcend through faith in God. Augustine preached to the peasants of his time that all efforts to build something solid and everlasting in the visible world was futile. He reminded them that it is the destiny of fallen man to live in time and not calm eternity, to live among those who were vain and aggressive and not whole, and to live at the mercy of the elements and not in a state of bliss without death. In the visible world, time creeps along and, slowly but surely, everything moves along with it. If is not aging that brings death and destruction, then it is natural catastrophe and, if not that, then it is man-made violence. Augustine looked about him and saw a world of human calamity—of peasants losing their entire harvest in a single storm, of whole cities destroyed in war, of famine, disease, and pestilence bringing death to thousands[47]—and concluded that no arrangement in the visible world was durable enough to satisfy the aspect of human consciousness that yearns for peace, tranquility, and order. The visible world is actually a testament to the fact that man has fallen. The peace man desires, Augustine argued, can only be achieved through faith in God the unchanging.

It is this spirit of understanding that courses through the community of Tocqueville's American, making it very different from the Old World "community of memory" and the ethnic neighborhood of early twentieth-century America. The unity of people in Tocqueville's America was not grounded in that which was substantial or in the memory of things substantial—in village traditions, local anniversaries, time-honored ways, the history of families, or the solidity of the old church standing in the square. In the mind of Tocqueville's Americans, such phenomena were understood to be very weak reeds on which to rest a hope for unity. Moreover, they conflicted with the natural urge of men to invent new things and advance themselves. The material world stood before Tocqueville's American to be conquered, not to be cherished or held the same. It was in this spirit that Tocqueville's Americans found unity not in a "community of memory" but in the community of the faithful. It was in the invisible world of mind and spirit, not in the visible world of force and matter, that Tocqueville's Americans received the gift of contentment.

6

Platonism in the Society of Expressive Individualism

Chapter 3 discussed the central issue dividing Augustine from the Platonists. The Platonists believed that "reason" was the spark of the divine essence embodied by man that, if shielded from the perturbations and distractions of human existence, could help move one closer to God. The Platonists imagined an ideal of independence, of reason no longer weighed down by the needs of the body, lifting man above the natural order of which he was a part. They argued that man could apprehend the eternal and the immutable by using his rational faculties. Through reason, for example, man could gain an appreciation of his own selfhood and his own genesis.[1] Left unhindered, the conceptualizing imagination could yield the source of all being, all wisdom, and all perfection, thereby paving the way towards self-sufficiency.[2]

Augustine criticized the Platonist's faith in reason, arguing that the follies and fantasies conjured up by the human imagination were never "external" to the thinking man, as the Platonists insisted, but rather symptoms of man's imperfection. Biased images projected by the mind could never be separated from "truths" discovered in reason. An element of love, hope, dream, or passion is mixed in with every scientific pursuit, and the grander the question asked, the more such feelings perturb the result. Human reason is a seriously flawed mechanism, capable of discovering only partial truths.

Augustine argued, for example, that it was mere fancy to go from a rational appreciation that one does exist to the idea that man is the creator of his own existence.[3] Augustine was confident that he was alive and could prove this to himself in his imagination, but the idea of his own creation remained a mystery.[4] He was forced to recognize himself as "created" and that his consciousness of selfhood would be "forever dependent upon an inexhaustible and unconditioned source of Being, Wisdom, and Power in whose 'image' he was made."[5] There is no rational explanation possible for the mystery of creation, and no philosopher's reason can ever bridge the gap between the created and the Creator. This is why, Augustine argues, man is forever dependent on God and shares none of His divine essence. As certain facts relating to one's own creation and selfhood are neither demonstrable nor verifiable, they have to be accepted on faith.

This concept forms the basis of Augustine's famous dictum that one must believe before one understands (and that one must believe in order to understand). The person who refuses to believe or accept on faith certain core principles will ultimately become entangled in a web of thoughts projected by his or her own imagination. Those projections multiply feverishly as the person searches for answers to basic questions. This is how, for example, the young imagination "searching" for God sometimes conjures up images of fiendish deities, such as "god the colossus" or the "god with the red hair."[6] Augustine noted that the imagined projections of the Platonists were perhaps more refined and sophisticated than those haunting children, but by trying to rationally and scientifically apprehend God, the investigations of the Platonists represented no great advance. The Platonists also looked "outwards" with their critical faculties. Their conceptions of God, ranging from the formless representation of the infinite to the unseen Being surrounded by demons, were nothing more than flawed, imprecise projections of the human imagination. Those conceptions were just as much a part of the sensible world as the superstitious images of the uneducated. By following their sense of reason, the Platonists had transcended nothing.

In order to understand the meaning of God, Augustine said one must travel inwards, not outwards, and go far beyond the reasoning mechanism located within the brain. He advised those who wanted to apprehend God more clearly,

> don't go outside yourself, return into yourself. The dwelling-place of truth is in the inner man. And if you discover your own nature as subject to change, then go beyond that nature. But remember that, when you thus go beyond it, it is the reasoning soul which you go beyond. Press on, therefore, toward the source from which the light of reason itself is kindled.[7]

God is not apprehended through reason, but only in the flicker of light standing behind the rational faculty. There is in the mind "no knowledge of God except the knowledge of how it does not know Him."[8] It is by recessing further into the inner man, beyond the senses, through the distortions, past the memories, and over the subconscious dreams that one approaches the Divine origin of one's being. Such a journey, by definition, cannot be made in reason, but rather must go beyond reason. It must be performed with a single leap of faith.

It was by believing first, Augustine said, that man gained his freedom. Faith preempts the exhausting and futile search for meaning. It shields the individual from the temptation to latch on to the imagined projections of self-proclaimed swamis and gurus. By recessing into the mind and believing first, a man can have his entire experience illuminated for him, providing him with absolute standards of value, truth, and goodness with which to interpret his experience.[9] The person who believes no longer has to rely on the ever-changing tablets of values carved by the philosophers of the day.

Augustine's contrast between faith and reason is crucial to understanding much of expressive individualist thought. This is because expressive individualism, like Platonism, emphasizes the rational faculty of man at the expense of faith. It is not faith as a "religious" conviction that is weakened in expressive individualism, but a belief in certain essential principles prior to the use of reason. The change from Tocqueville's American to the contemporary expressive individualist is a change from an Augustinian to a Platonic conception of the self, and the change has led to a reinterpretation of republican principle.

Both Tocqueville's American and the contemporary expressive individualist believe in individual freedom, civil liberties, procedural rights, and democratic government. But for Tocqueville's American, republican principle was an article of faith preceding the onset of much smaller quests. Republican principle established a basis for order in which the individualist could work out his ambitions and plans. Faith in the "self-evident" truths of republicanism sank deep into the consciousness of Tocqueville's American, giving him an understanding of how he stood in relation to his fellow citizens. For the expressive individualist, republican principle means something very different. It does not precede the onset of smaller quests but marks the beginning of much larger quests. Republican principle does not give the expressive individualist a framework in which to order his business, build a public association, or serve on a jury. Instead, it grants him "options" and "choices" as he begins a search for the "meaning of it all."

Republican principle stood at the edge of the imagination of Tocqueville's American. As an article of faith, its primary purpose was to guide the rational faculties, whether in the larger world of business and politics or the smaller world of games and feasts. In contemporary America, republican principle is used in the service of active reason. Rather than guide the imagination, it tries to liberate it. The expressive individualist asks: Is it this lifestyle I should join or that? Is it this religion I should "choose" or that? Is it this theory that gives "meaning" to life or that? In each case, republican principle is simply perceived to be a legal device, one that permits Americans as many options as possible in their quest to look "outside" of themselves and find the meaning of who they are. Republican principle is no longer an article of faith located within the inner man from which the American individualist derives his knowledge, but a vehicle by which the person looks outward and tries to find answers to questions about "identity" and "meaning."

This change from an Augustinian to a Platonic conception of republican principle provides an explanation for why laws have proliferated in America over the last few decades. In *The Republic of Choice*, Lawrence Friedman notes an interesting paradox: while law in the United States has dramatically increased in scale and scope, the increase has been associated with a furthering of individual choice.[10] The law is more ubiquitous, but its rapid expansion has occurred simultaneously with a rise in radical individualism; the law supports the movement for greater individual rights. Friedman concludes from this observation that the law is "a kind of replacement, a substitute for traditional authority,"[11] but one that increases choice. Laws may have proliferated in America, but the law does not command so much as it liberates.

This legal transformation appears to support Tocqueville's observation that, in a democracy, politics gradually seep into the smallest activities of private life. Many laws in contemporary America (e.g., laws protecting abortion, homosexuality, or freedom of expression) suggest an intensification of that process; the rules of democracy have simply been extended to support new freedoms in private life. But the link with Tocqueville's America is really a very shallow one.

Republican principle in Tocqueville's America was practiced by individuals in private life in order to prepare them for public life. The rules of democratic order became second nature to Tocqueville's American, practicing them as he did at home, at work, and in school. Yet those rules were few in number because they represented only the outer boundaries of reason in the American imagination. They were not the subject of reason so much as they were the starting point of reason. To Tocqueville's American, the rules of republican principle described an unchanging order of things, and while their truth could not be verified, he accepted it on a leap of faith. The truth became "self-evident." Beyond these rules, the American mind could not advance without losing the order it loved dearly.

Republican principle in the society of expressive individualism means extending choice and enhancing autonomy in private life, not preparing individuals for a common public life. When inspired by this understanding of republican principle, the number of laws in a society must be very large. This is because each law has to clear away a specific obstacle from the path of a human imagination. Each law must facilitate the human effort to look "outward" for meaning. The law must prevent any code, any regulation, or any prejudice from getting in the way. It must be adapted to the needs of particular human beings, basically to help them realize any newfangled theory of meaning that might cross their minds.

For example, laws must be passed to remove any restrictions on dress for those who rely on dress to express themselves (e.g., a bill in the California legislature that would guarantee a woman's right to wear pantsuits to work). Laws must remove obstacles to the partially disabled who are working through issues of self-esteem. Laws must eliminate obstacles interfering with the gratification of desire for those who find meaning in pleasure. Laws must eliminate obstacles to divorce for those who want to preserve their options while married. If a large enough segment of the population wanted to find "god the colussus" or the "god with red hair," laws would have to be passed to facilitate this search, too. In each case, the law is anchored in republican principle and the idea of individual freedom. But in each case, the law is anchored in a Platonic conception of republican principle. The law merely supports a person's rational faculties, his creative impulses, and any theories of meaning that pop into mind. The law facilitates the effort to look outwards and move in whatever direction people believe they will find the divine.

The change from Tocqueville's America to the contemporary society of expressive individualism can be understood in a slightly different way. Augustine argued that unity was achieved through faith, by loving God. This is because when people sacrifice their love of self for the love of something higher than themselves, it becomes possible for them to develop an affection for one another. When Tocqueville's American looked "inward" and discovered the eternal and unchanging principle of republican order, his faith in republican principle bonded him to others. It was through the joint worship of republican principle that Tocqueville's Americans worked with each other, even if they happened to be total strangers. Each individualist willingly dissolved himself or herself into a higher order and could converse with others, act in concert with others, or perhaps even defer to others on the basis of that order. This is how republican principle prepared Tocqueville's Americans for public life.

The expressive individualist looks "outward" and the rules of republican principle are designed to serve his or her love of self. They are not designed to establish a unity but to preserve diversity and "autonomy." They defend the private wanderings of the human imagination, its rational and irrational projections, and the human effort to "search" for meaning. They are designed to give a person a better chance to understand what it is he or she wants to understand so that, in the end, he or she might come to believe in something

and gain "fulfillment." This is the Platonic conception of republican principle. It cannot bring unity for it is steeped in a love of one's own imagined
projections. It is this conception of republican principle that allows individuals in the society of expressive individualism to retreat into private life.

How the Transformation in Republican Principle Has Affected the Family in the Society of Expressive Individualism

The change in republican principle just described and the new role of
republican principle as a support for "autonomy" have caused another link
to be formed between the society of expressive individualism and aristocratic
society. This is because the new interpretation of republican principle has
seriously perturbed the state of the family in America.

In aristocratic society, formal political relationships within the family cause
domestic life to have a unique structure. Tocqueville observes of the parent
in an aristocratic family that "the parent not only has a natural right but
acquires a political right to command them [the children]; he is the author
and the support of his family, but he is also its constituted ruler."[12] In
aristocratic families, Tocqueville continues,

> the father is not only the civil head of the family, but the organ of its traditions,
> the expounder of its customs, the arbiter of its manners. He is listened to with
> deference, he is addressed with respect, and the love that is felt for him is always
> tempered with fear.[13]

The political relationships that govern the larger world are transported into
the aristocratic family, where they are reproduced on a smaller scale. Within
the aristocratic family is the same emphasis on inequality and respect for
tradition and rank that exists in the world beyond the family. As the "link"[14]
between past and present, the father's position in an aristocratic family is a
political one, for he carries the customs and traditions of the larger society
into the family and thus preserves them.

The family in Tocqueville's America did not possess such a clear link with
the political organization of the external world. It is important to note
carefully Tocqueville's conclusion regarding family life in America: that
family relationships in democratic America were not more democratic than
those of previous eras, but rather more natural.[15] While the structure of the
aristocratic family, like aristocratic society, was hierarchical and unequal, the
structure of the nineteenth-century democratic family, unlike democratic
society, was not equal. The parent in the American family was placed in a

dominant position, especially early on in the life of the child, and the limits of authority only gradually receded. Moreover, such limits did not recede in accordance with formal democratic theory but rather in an environment of "familiarity and affection,"[16] of closeness and warmth. The nineteenth-century American family was not rent asunder by democratic individualism but tightened by natural feelings. Parental authority was not rendered less absolute because of the democratic laws of the state. Rather, it was tempered by a new "familiar intimacy."[17]

In aristocratic society, the organization of the larger political world affects relationships between family members, causing such families to be "always correct, ceremonious, stiff, and cold."[18] But it is not the political rules governing democratic society that permeate the relationships between family members and make the democratic family warm and sweet. In Tocqueville's America, the rules of inequality governing the larger world of aristocratic society were replaced with new democratic procedures, causing social ties to weaken and citizens to be thrown apart.[19] Those democratic procedures, however, did not enter the family in Tocqueville's America, and family members, instead of being thrown apart, were brought closer together.[20] Republican principle did not serve as the basis for the natural closeness exhibited between family members in Tocqueville's America.

In the society of expressive individualism, the family is structured according to republican principle. Like the family in aristocratic society, the family in the society of expressive individualism is organized according to the political rules and customs that prevail in the larger society. The family of expressive individualists becomes a miniaturized version of the democratic society of expressive individualism. Both the family in Tocqueville's America and the family in the society of expressive individualism are more egalitarian than the aristocratic family, but the family in the society of expressive individualism is more equal because it is organized according to the political rules that govern relationships in the larger world. Family relationships are more equal but less natural, and they are split apart in order to preserve "autonomy," rather than joined together by mutual affection and familiarity.

The "politicization of the family" is a phenomenon that has been observed in families of expressive individualists, and it is also a feature of political movements that attempt to further the civil rights of children, (a cause that is perceived to be a logical extension of other civil rights movements).[21] Attempts are made by families of expressive individualists to form relationships on the basis of "fairness."[22] The struggle against patriarchy is a political struggle within the family, and it is theoretically buttressed by republican principle. It signifies an attempt to render the power structure within the family more equal but not necessarily more natural. By becoming organized according to democratic principles, the family in the society of expressive individualism tends to approximate the experience of the family in aristocratic society. In both families, every place is marked out beforehand.[23] The only difference between the two families is that the aristocratic family is governed by the principle of inequality, not equality.

The philosophy of expressive individualism becomes a basis for relationships between family members in the society of expressive individualism.[24] It is logical, then, that the promotion of self-actualized, autonomous expressive individualists within the family leads to problems similar to those that exist in the larger political community, including social fragmentation and difficulty resolving conflicts between autonomous individuals.[25] Family relationships in the society of expressive individualism may not be as cold and stern as they were in the aristocratic family, filled with "respectful and frigid observances,"[26] but they remain formal and present serious problems with communication and coordinating actions between family members.[27] The difference between the two families is that in the aristocratic family, formality and poor communication between members are rooted in the doctrine of political inequality. In the family of expressive individualists, formality and difficulty with communication are rooted in a political theory that emphasizes political equality and individual autonomy. Both doctrines render the family tie an artificial one.

By focusing on the autonomy of the self, the family unit in the society of expressive individualism is split apart by political forces rather than brought together by natural ones. Expressive individualism has contempt for those social units that are artificial, contrived, and based on mutual self-interest. It praises those units where attachments between members naturally and spontaneously arise. It is ironic, then, that the only natural social unit that Tocqueville observed in democratic America—the family—is transformed in the society of expressive individualism into an artificial one precisely because it emphasizes personal "growth" and individual "autonomy." In Tocqueville's America, republican principle shaped the minds of individuals in order to prepare them for public action. In the society of expressive individualism, republican principle does not shape the mind of the individualist so much as it becomes a political custom by which to organize private, family life. The politicization of family life seriously perturbs the natural feelings, the warmth and sweetness, that Tocqueville observed in the nineteenth-century American family.

How Expressive Individualism Recreates the Aristocratic Experience of Childhood

The new order adopted by the expressive individualist family causes another link to be formed between the society of expressive individualism and old aristocratic society. In aristocratic society, the stage of life known as "child-hood" did not really exist, particularly among upper-class families. Children were simply thought of as a "little adults." In nineteenth-century America (and Europe), the perception changed. Children were removed from the sphere of adult life and "childhood" came to be viewed as a "special and vulnerable" stage of life.[28] In contemporary America, the status of children has shifted back somewhat towards the aristocratic model. Children are once again looked upon as little adults, as advocates for children believe that children deserve the same rights, the same opportunity for redress in the courts, and the same respect for feelings and experiences that are routinely awarded to adults.[29] In contemporary America, the line separating children from adults is blurred just as it was in old aristocratic society.

Philippe Aries, in *Centuries of Childhood*, argues that prior to the eigh-teenth century, adults in European society largely viewed children as crea-tures similar to themselves.[30] Children, he notes, did not constitute a special group of beings imagined to be somehow "beneath" the class of adults and requiring special protection. For example, in aristocratic society, there was barely a line separating the games children played from those played by adults; that is, as Richard Sennett notes, "there were few childhood pleasures which adults considered beneath their own interest."[31] Sennett writes,

> Dolls dressed in elaborate costumes interested people of all ages. Toy soldiers similarly amused people of all ages. The reason for this sharing of games, dolls, and toys was precisely that sharp demarcations between stages of life did not then exist.[32]

The blurring of the division between children and adults in aristocratic society was evident in other activities. Musical recitals and communal sings in aristocratic society included both adults and children as participants.[33] The dress of children in aristocratic society, visible in the paintings of that era, was not markedly different from that of adults.[34] Children did not wear special costumes, but on the contrary, just smaller versions of adult clothing appropriate to rank and wealth. Even the theater in aristocratic society was not set apart from the world of children, as it would later be in nineteenth-century Europe. Children in aristocratic society were treated as "incipient adults"[35] and not placed in a group separate from the rest of humanity.

In the eighteenth and nineteenth centuries, in both America and Europe, a stage of life known as "childhood" came to be recognized. No longer were children viewed as little adults, but rather as being part of a special, vulnerable class of human beings.[36] Children were now consigned to a sphere set apart from the adult world. In the new era, for example, "certain kinds of play were reserved to children, certain kinds forbidden to them," and children were now considered too "naive" to be allowed to gamble or participate in games of chance.[37] Reading out loud, once considered a practice suitable for both children and adults, became "childish" and an amusement for young persons, with silent reading becoming the more "adult" form of entertainment. By the nineteenth century, children wore costumes that clearly distinguished them from adults and, as Sennett notes, the "dressing to station and elaborate aristocratic dress of children of late seventeenth century paintings . . . were regarded as absurd."[38] Theaters, cafes, and clubs also came to be viewed as adult places and were closed to children.

In this new era, the child came to be viewed as a vulnerable, fragile, and dependent creature requiring care and protection, and the change in status is consistent with Tocqueville's observations of family life in nineteenth-century America. Tocqueville does not specifically comment on the status of children in America but when he notes, for example, that parental authority in the early American family only gradually receded, he suggests that children in democratic America lived a fairly protected existence. It is interesting to note that while the new attitude towards children dominated nineteenth-century America and Europe, the old aristocratic view survived in some quarters of European society. The aristocratic principles of upbringing, including "non-nurturance, harsh discipline and parental absence,"[39] when placed in relief against the new emphasis on nurturing and loving, reveal how much the status of children had changed.

In contemporary America, the stage of life known as childhood becomes less prominent as the line once separating the world of adults from the world of children begins to fade.[40] The children's rights movement (as conceived, for example, by such organizations as the Children's Defense Fund) attempts to award children not the right to be loved and cared for, which was the major goal of children's rights advocates in the nineteenth century,[41] but the legal rights possessed by adults in the larger society. The right to be loved and cared for emphasizes the difference between children and adults. It emphasizes the child's vulnerable status and his or her need for a nurturing environment. On the other hand, the right to defend one's "autonomy," to exercise "choice" in living arrangements and lifestyles, and to sue one's parents in court obliterates the distinction between children and adults. That new right is based on the discovery that "unfair" encumbrances have been placed on younger persons as members of families. Those encumbrances require a legal stance as aggressive as that assumed by adults who suffer from handicaps, such as poverty and disability. The effort is made in contemporary America to factor out childhood from a person's situation, just as the effort is made to factor out poverty and disability from the life of an adult, so as to guarantee a person full equality of opportunity and freedom of "choice."

The expressive individualist's emphasis on feelings and self-esteem also causes the experiences of children and adults to merge. The recognition that children and adults both have the capacity to "feel" and experience intense emotions makes a child's pattern of life hardly different from that of an adult's and certainly no less deserving of respect. Furthermore, if life in contemporary America is understood to be a series of emotional dramas, with personal "growth" measured by the number and intensity of emotional scenarios one is involved in, then maturation does not require the guiding hand of parental authority so much as it does the opportunity to learn more about the self. In this way, the experience of the adolescent who suffers emotional trauma, and survives it, causes him or her to be judged more advanced, more "mature," than the suburban adult who runs a business but who has never experienced tremendous confusion, psychic pain, or great passion.

This attitude is reflected in many of the televisions shows produced in contemporary America. In shows such as *Beverly Hills, 90210*, children are granted adult-like status by virtue of the intense emotional situations they must deal with in their day-to-day lives. Their experiences are, as they were for children in old aristocratic society, the experiences of little adults. What is understood by expressive individualist adults to constitute living, or "life," is simply practiced by children on a smaller scale. The scenarios hardly differ. Love, anger, confusion, failure, and friendship are part of the expressive individualist's panoply of vital experiences and include both children and adults as active participants. In one television show called *Party of Five*, the parents are removed from the family altogether, and five children raise themselves by "growing" through the intense emotional experiences they share with peers and adults. The vulnerable stage of "childhood" that existed in nineteenth-century America disappears altogether and is replaced with a life's experience that is traumatic and confusing at times, but which is no less traumatic and confusing than it is for adults.

That a "youth culture" exists in the society of expressive individualism suggests that the break with nineteenth-century attitudes toward children is incomplete. The youth culture appears to establish a line separating child-hood from adult life. But the youth culture does not define a group that is separate and beneath the experience of adults, as childhood did in the nineteenth century, so much as it defines a group that is separate and adjacent to the experience of adults. The youth culture is just another lifestyle enclave in contemporary America. It does not denote a special class of citizens. If anything, the fact that many adults in contemporary America actually aspire to rejoin the youth culture (e.g., by mimicking the activities of young persons, listening to the music of adolescents, and attending the same clubs as teenagers), suggests that the youth culture ranks above certain segments of adult life, and that rather than representing the games and amusements of a more primitive class of humans, it signifies an advanced state of existence.

This blurring of the line separating children from adults in the society of expressive individualism is intensified by the activities of the caring professions. If expressive individualism transforms children into adults, the caring professions transform adults into children. The caring professions, such as psychology and social work, apply the same terms to the experiences of adults that nineteenth-century children's rights advocates applied to the experiences of children. "Caring" and "nurturing" are emphasized and, in some schools of psychotherapy, adults are encouraged to give free reign to the "inner child" lying within. It is a sign of personal growth in an adult if certain child-like elements of thought and behavior are liberated from the hard and imposing confines of the adult personality. Once again, the experiences of childhood and adulthood that were kept separate during the nineteenth century start to blend together in the society of expressive individualism, just as they did in old aristocratic society.

7

The Expressive Individualist
and Self-Esteem

Some expressive individualists in contemporary America are exquisitely sensitive to verbal attacks that come in the form of slurs, negative images, and cultural stereotypes, so much so that a new phenomenon appears to be at work in the movement of American individualism. Neither Tocqueville nor Bryce observed a tremendous sensitivity in the American individualist of the nineteenth century. While that person tended to be petty and craving towards the perquisites of public office and feared being taken for merely the plain citizen of a democracy when traveling through aristocratic Europe, a reflexive outburst to mild verbal assaults was conspicuously absent. The new sensitivity of the American is symptomatic of a much deeper psychological change, and rather than representing a variation on the insecurities of the early American (caused by living in a society without fixed positions), it signifies a new disposition in the American character. In this change, the new obsession with self-esteem in America closely parallels the obsession with honor found among aristocrats in the City of Man. Another connection can be made between aristocratic society and contemporary America.

Tocqueville briefly refers to the extreme sensitivity of the aristocrat in his description of that figure. The identity of the aristocrat was embedded in his notion of honor, so much so that even the most minor personal slight was construed by the aristocrat as an attack on his very being. The imaginary attack often prompted an aggressive response, such as challenging one to a duel. Both Tocqueville and Bryce observed that the nineteenth-century American individualist lacked this extreme sensitivity. The American individualist was somehow able to detach himself, or shield that which he identified with the very essence of his being, from the affronts one would occasionally meet with during social intercourse. A saying that has become an Americanism, "sticks and stones may break my bones but names will never hurt me," crystallizes in a few simple words the attitude of the American individualist observed by Tocqueville and Bryce.

The mind-set of the contemporary expressive individualist recalls that of the old aristocrat. Epithets and conventional idioms are viewed as personal affronts by many expressive individualists in much the same way that a "tap on the cheek"[1] enraged the old aristocrat. They perturb the mind and elicit an aggressive response in the form of demanding controls on free speech (e.g., "speech codes"), with duels having already been outlawed. For example, the phrase "going Dutch treat" is potentially threatening to the self-esteem of people of Dutch extraction, and the term "short" has been changed to "vertically challenged" in order not to cause psychic pain to expressive individualists so affected. For the aristocrat, the deep core of one's being exposed to the larger world of social transactions was called "honor." For the contemporary expressive individualist, the deep core of one's being exposed to the larger world of social transactions is called "self-esteem." In both cases, a certain vital portion of the self is laid bare, unlike in Tocqueville's American, in whom it was buried beneath thick, protective layers.

Richard Post's essay, "The Social Foundations of Defamation Law: Reputation and the Constitution," is extremely helpful in demonstrating this important similarity between the contemporary American and the old aristocrat.[2] Post analyzes the transformation in defamation law in the United States, arguing that the new concept of "reputation as dignity" closely parallels the aristocratic concept of "reputation as honor," with both differing from the nineteenth-century American concept of "reputation as property."

According to Post, the nineteenth-century American concept of "reputation as property" treated reputation as the product of one's efforts or labor.[3] Reputation was something earned and therefore extraneous to the self. It was peripheral to the notion of identity. To injure another's reputation in nineteenth-century America, one had to "destroy the results of an individual's labor."[4] The loss of reputation in such a society was, according to Post, " 'capable of pecuniary admeasurement' because the value of reputation is determined by the marketplace in exactly the same manner that the marketplace determines the cash value of any property loss."[5] Reputation in Tocqueville's America involved only that aspect of the self that pertained to economic activity, and the destructive effects of libel on a reputation so conceived were manifested not as a decrement in a person's comprehensive life value, but merely in the prospects of that person advancing materially in the marketplace.

In the nineteenth-century American concept of "reputation as property," reputation was in no way believed to reflect on the intrinsic value of the self.[6]

The personal identity of an individual was considered to be separate from his or her social identity. Because an individual's reputation was measured only according to his prospects in the marketplace, it varied according to market conditions.[7] When reputation is conceived as property, as it was in Tocqueville's America, it does not penetrate very deeply into that part of the self determining most fundamentally who one is as a person.

In the aristocratic idea of "reputation as honor," reputation is linked precisely to that part of the self associated with identity.[8] When linked to the notion of "honor," reputation causes much more of the self to be exposed to the larger world of social transactions.

Honor, unlike property, does not vary according to market conditions. It is a fixed statement of who one is, a testament to one's worth as a person. Unlike "credit-worthiness," the principle of honor envelopes the entire person. Honor is not simply an asset. It can not be earned through labor. Rather, it is virtually synonymous with identity.

Because "honor" in aristocratic society was linked to social position, the concept of "reputation as honor" caused reputation and personal identity to be influenced by one's social position in the community.[9] In aristocratic society, one's value as a person was affected by how the facade projecting into the larger world was received. This is why honor, or sense of self, was exposed to fluctuations in status in the Old World, and the defense of reputation became a defense of the self as a person, not simply as an entrepreneur.

Post concludes that the change in American libel law over the last few decades is significant, and that the new concept of "reputation as dignity" approximates, in important ways, the old aristocratic concept of "reputation as honor." Once again, a crucial aspect of the self has become exposed to the larger world of social transactions, and a person depends on others to give a complete picture of himself.[10] "Reputation as dignity," like "reputation as honor," presupposes that the essence of the self, not just the self's "credit-worthiness," hinges on the attitudes and opinions of others. Reputation so conceived is not just a "private good," as it was in nineteenth-century America, but "both a private and a public good," as it was in aristocratic society.[11] When reputation is joined to the notion of "dignity," the social and personal identities of a person begin to fuse, just as they did in old aristocratic society where reputation was joined to the notion of "honor."

Post, basing his conception of "dignity" on Erving Goffman's definition of that term, writes,

> In this way our sense of intrinsic self-worth, stored in the deepest recesses of our "private personality," is perpetually dependent on the ceremonial observance by

those around us of rules of deference and demeanor. The law of defamation can be conceived as a method by which society polices breaches of its rules of deference and demeanor, thereby protecting the dignity of its members.[12]

When defamation law protects "reputation as dignity," it protects not simply one's capacity to make money but also "the respect (and self-respect) that arises from full membership in society."[13] It presupposes that "individual identity is in some sense constituted by reputation,"[14] which is the same presupposition made by defamation law that protects "reputation as honor."

Post's discussion helps put in perspective the extreme sensitivity manifested by some contemporary expressive individualists, as well as their obsession with self-esteem. The expressive individualist's sensitivity towards personal slights indicates that a fusion of his or her social and personal identities has occurred, recalling the experience of the aristocrat in the City of Man. The new obsession with self-esteem mimics the old aristocratic obsession with honor, for the psyches of both are raw and exposed, with little external stimulus needed to elicit an angry or defensive response.

Aristocratic "honor" is elemental to a society based on inequality, while the expressive individualist's "dignity" is elemental to a society based on equality. Yet honor and dignity are two sides of the same crystal, and by distilling away the principle of equality from the society of expressive individualism, one finds a character type hardly differing from the old aristocrat. Both the expressive individualist and the aristocrat are very different from Tocqueville's American. The latter person, armed and protected in the mail of some special belief, was able to preserve intact his personal identity despite the occasional attack on his social identity.

8

The Expressive Individualist and the Spirit of *Ressentiment*

The effort in the first section of this book was to show how the movement of expressive individualism shares much in spirit with the anti-Augustinian sects of late antiquity. By absorbing the principles of Manicheism, Donatism, Pelagianism, Platonism, and aristocracy, the movement of expressive individualism represents less a step forward in the historical experience of man than a return to old ways of living and thinking. The tie between the expressive individualist and the aristocrat is especially interesting, as the relationship between the two has a recurring theme. The two character types not only share beliefs and prejudices, but consistently rotate around a single axis. What separates the expressive individualist from the aristocrat in the City of Man is not wealth or education but divergent attitudes toward the principle of equality. The structure of aristocratic society is based on inequality. The structure of the society of expressive individualism is based on equality. If the aristocrat looked at the institutions of expressive individualist society, he or she would see something odd yet familiar—an inverse image caused by projecting aristocratic institutions onto a democratic surface.

This phenomenon can be observed in the parallels already drawn between aristocratic society and the society of expressive individualism. Both the aristocrat and the expressive individualist create a spectrum of work ranging from the honorable to the dishonorable, but while the aristocrat honors occupations where one stands above others, the expressive individualist honors occupations where one relates to (and "feels" with) others. Both the aristocrat and the expressive individualist attempt to preserve a certain fixedness in the institutions of society, but while the aristocrat fixes society in inequality through a rigid class structure, the expressive individualist fixes society in equality by securing an ordered public sphere and work habitat.

Both the aristocrat and the expressive individualist insert divine-like institutions between God and man, but while the aristocrat ennobles the warrior who dominates and raises him on a lofty platform, the expressive individualist ennobles those who care for others equally and praises them for spending their lives among the wretched. Both the aristocrat and the expressive individualist introduce the political rules and traditions of the larger community into the family, but while the aristocratic family is organized according to the principle of inequality, the expressive individualist family is organized according to the principle of equality. Both the aristocrat and the expressive individualist reveal an extreme sensitivity towards personal slights, but while the aristocrat fiercely defends his reputation to preserve a high standing relative to others, the expressive individualist fiercely defends his self-esteem to preserve feelings of equal self-worth relative to others.

These similarities between aristocratic society and the society of expressive individualism, and the single difference on which they turn, can be understood within the context of a psychological phenomenon known as *ressentiment*. *Ressentiment* is a form of self-deception that is triggered by a combination of fear and impotence. When a person finds something threatening in the world but is impotent to do anything about it, he or she tends to invert reality and call that which is threatening "evil" and one's small and powerless position "good."[1] For example, Nietzsche argues that the "slave," who is both fearful and impotent in his pathetic condition, revalues values and makes poverty and weakness "virtues" when before they had been "vices" or signs of failure. The "slave" forms in his mind an image of the poor and weak as being "honorable" and "virtuous" and the rich as being "evil." The pain of the slave's existence is eased by constant referral to this image, which acts as a kind of narcotic. This inversion of reality sustains and reassures the slave, although in reality the values of the "master" condemn him.

Nietzsche grounded his understanding of *ressentiment* in the experience of modern democracy. He charged that the belief in equality as a "virtue" was a manifestation of the "slave" revolt in values. In *ressentiment*, the "master" and the "slave" change positions so that the "slave" becomes "virtuous" and the "master" becomes "evil." Nietzsche argued that greatness was built on inequality, but that envious and resentful "slaves" poisoned their own minds with the belief that equality, not achievement, was the greatest virtue and persuaded the "masters" to accept the new value structure by making them feel "guilty." The result was a democratic order that reminded Nietzsche of a domesticated herd of cows.[2] No person, he cried, can aspire to greatness anymore because such action is now considered to be "evil." To be average and unthreatening, to be with the herd, is now "good" and "virtuous."

Nietzsche's tie between the spirit of *ressentiment* and modern democratic practice helps explain in what way aristocratic society and the society of expressive individualism are related. The difference between the two societies turns on the issue of equality, which is precisely the issue dividing Nietzsche's aristocratic master from the *ressentiment* slave. The expressive individualist stands before the aristocrat as Nietzsche's slave stands before Nietzsche's master. The expressive individualist embraces the reality of aristocratic institutions, but simply twists their meaning and adapts them to the scaffolding of a democratic society. The society of expressive individualism is aristocratic society's inversion, or *ressentiment* opposite, differing primarily in that its institutions—its honor codes, its castes, its family structure, and its religious institutions—are organized according to the principle of equality, not inequality.

In both aristocratic society and the society of expressive individualism, the human imagination is sent far afield, but while the aristocrat dreams of building castles for himself, of ruling men, and of winning glory on distant battlefields, the expressive individualist dreams of building global communities for all, of caring for all, and of tending to the poorest and the weakest in distant lands. In both societies, a hierarchy of jobs is created, but while the aristocrat honors those positions that glorify the strongest, the gifted, and the superior, the expressive individualist honors those positions that emphasize the oppressed and direct "care" and "love" to the weakest members of the community. In both societies, people spend their lives in castes and subcultures, but while the aristocrat spends life in a caste that is formally ranked above others, the expressive individualist spends life in a caste that is recognized to be only adjacent to others. In both societies, great attention is paid to the spirit of man, but while in aristocracy a person's honor is cherished, highlighting the superior position to which only a few can aspire, in the society of expressive individualism "feeling" and "self-esteem" are cherished, since anyone can feel and have self-esteem, even a "slave."

In each case, the shell of the aristocratic institution remains intact, but the animating spirit has been warped so that the exact opposite of what was originally intended is now consecrated. Aristocratic institutions and attitudes in expressive individualist society do not ennoble the singular and the mightiest, but rather the weakest and most pathetic.

This point requires that an important modification be made in Tocqueville's understanding of democracy. Tocqueville also uses the principle of equality to make a distinction between societies, arguing that what distinguished nineteenth-century America from old aristocratic society was the principle of equality. But in Tocqueville's model, it is only where islands of inequality exist in America (for example, in manufacturing, where the employer commands the employee,[3] or in the legal profession, where lawyers form an elite within the general population[4]) that an intrusion of aristocratic forms is perceived. Tocqueville separates aristocratic society from democracy on the basis of equality and concludes that the distinguishing feature of aristocracy is inequality. At one point, he asserts, "Aristocratic institutions cannot exist without laying down the inequality of men as a fundamental principle."[5]

The society of expressive individualism shows how a democracy can reveal aristocratic tendencies, not because of the residual presence of inequality but independent of that presence. It is not in the corporations and law firms of contemporary America that one finds the attitudes and prejudices of an earlier age, but in those institutions that are most democratic, where "caring" and "sharing" are being performed and where "autonomy" and "self-esteem" are emphasized. In this new light, the similarities between aristocratic society and the society of expressive individualism require a change in the definition of aristocracy. The distinguishing feature of aristocracy is not inequality, but rather certain practices that have within them the potential to be adapted to democratic ideals. Those practices include a rank-ordering of jobs from honorable to dishonorable, a tendency towards fixedness in the general plan of society, the presence of castes and enclaves that serve as the primary social and political units of the country, a family structure mirroring the political organization of the community as a whole, the presence of ennobling institutions in civil society, and a tendency for people to merge their social and personal identities. "Aristocraticism," the name to be used to refer to these phenomena and the pattern of living they represent, need not be confined to those societies organized according to the principle of inequality. It can, as the society of expressive individualism demonstrates, form the basis of a society organized according to the principle of equality.

Because Tocqueville never saw a democratic society based on expressive individualism, he did not realize that aristocracy (or "aristocraticism") was not synonymous with inequality and that the gate by which aristocracy might reenter democratic society did not lie only where inequality persisted. Tocqueville did not realize that aristocracy could reenter democratic society in the name of equality. He did not foresee the possibility of a "servant's" aristocracy, of aristocratic society's *ressentiment* opposite. He did not foresee the society of expressive individualism.

How Tocqueville's America Was Based on the Principle of Equality but Not on the Spirit of *Ressentiment*

Tocqueville's America, like the American society of expressive individualism, was also governed by the principle of equality. But Tocqueville's America was not a *ressentiment* inversion of aristocracy. It did not rotate around the same axis that divides old aristocracy from contemporary America.

It is true that Tocqueville observed flashes of *ressentiment* morality in nineteenth-century America, including the obsession of some Americans with equality of condition. Some Americans were convinced that "justice" required absolute equality, even if it required everyone to be equally misera-ble.[6] Tocqueville occasionally observed an envious and resentful poor de-mand of the rich that they sacrifice their "pride."[7] He saw even the slightest privileges anger radical egalitarians.[8]

Moreover, the values embraced by Tocqueville's Americans can be found on Nietzsche's list of *ressentiment* values. Tocqueville's American honored "public spirit, benevolence, consideration, industriousness, moderation, modesty, indulgence, and pity,"[9] which Nietzsche argues are the *ressentiment* virtues of the "herd man" or the "slave." Other virtues embraced by Tocqueville's Americans, such as "usefulness"[10] and friendliness, also appear to be consistent with the spirit of *ressentiment*. An embrace of such values implies that Tocqueville's Americans were successfully domesticated and rendered harmless to other members of the "herd." It suggests that the Americans preferred equality and averageness to ambition and greatness.

Even Tocqueville himself seems guilty of *ressentiment*-inspired idealism when he states,

> We may naturally believe that it is not the singular prosperity of the few, but the greater well-being of all that is most pleasing in the sight of the Creator and Preserver of men. What appears to me to be man's decline is, to His eye, advancement; what afflicts me is acceptable to Him. A state of equality is perhaps less elevated, but it is more just: and its justness constitutes its greatness and its beauty.[11]

Tocqueville appears to have conceded the "slave's" position that equality is "virtuous" and "just," and that inequality, especially in the eye of the "slave's" God, is "evil" and "unjust." Such values are diametrically opposed to the values of Nietzsche's aristocrat.

Yet the link between the democratic society of Tocqueville's American and the spirit of *ressentiment* is weak for the same reason that the link between aristocratic society and the society of expressive individualism is strong. Just as Tocqueville incorrectly judged the distinguishing feature of aristocracy to be inequality, so did Nietzsche incorrectly judge the distinguishing feature of *ressentiment* culture to be equality. Just as it is possible to combine "aristocraticism" with equality (as in the society of expressive individualism), so is it possible to separate equality from *ressentiment* culture, to have a thriving democracy without *ressentiment*.

It is more than just a curious paradox that Nietzsche, the critic of modern democracy, argued that religiosity was essential to aristocracy, while Tocqueville, the defender of modern democracy, argued that religiosity was essential to democracy. The contradiction can be resolved by understanding that Nietzsche was not defending aristocracy in his work so much as he was defending nobility. He was writing not in support of a political form but rather in support of a positive, life-affirming, noble human spirit. He incorrectly linked that spirit with the political form called aristocracy, arguing that aristocracy was the natural reservoir of such vitality.

This is why Nietzsche's general observations concerning "what is noble" are occasionally linked to the habits of a specific class. When, for example, he discovers nobility in a class that has "profound reverence for age and tradition" and "faith and prejudice in favor of ancestors,"[12] Nietzsche is clearly referring to the political class of aristocrats that is also described by Tocqueville, as opposed to a more general aristocratic or noble type.

The Americans observed by Tocqueville expressed an instinctive dislike for that which was old and traditional and in this respect differed greatly from the European aristocrats observed by Nietzsche. But Tocqueville's Americans revealed the very same qualities that Nietzsche admired and found ennobling in the class of aristocrats, even though Tocqueville's Americans were democrats.

Nietzsche argues that religiosity, or myth,[13] is an essential part of the life experience of the noble human being.[14] Religiosity signifies an adherence to capricious law, and Nietzsche argues that "freedom, subtlety, boldness, dance, and masterly sureness . . . have developed only owing to the 'tyranny of such capricious laws'."[15] Adherence to capricious laws helps one to gain self-mastery, to become "severe" and "hard,"[16] and to secure value in oneself. Such laws demand a certain kind of faith that is often impenetrable to reason. It is only through such laws that the noble soul reveals a "fundamental certainty" about itself.[17]

Tocqueville's American manifested the same intense religiosity and adherence to capricious law as Nietzsche's aristocrat. While longstanding custom and historical tradition ruled the mind of Nietzsche's aristocrat, Christianity, public opinion, and republican principle ruled the mind of Tocqueville's American. Those three forces were no less embraced as immortal principles, resistant to dissection by rational utilitarian philosophy, than the obscure customs and privileges that dotted the landscape of the Old World. The aristocrat obeyed capricious laws and traditions that were revealed to him in the external world. Honor codes, dueling etiquette, caste privilege, military achievement, and the history of land ownership formed complete and detailed systems in the visible world and caused the world in which the aristocrat lived to be fixed and ordered. Tocqueville's American also put himself under the dominion of capricious laws, but Christian morality, majority opinion, and the doctrine of inalienable rights had few visible forms. The visible world in which Tocqueville's American lived was disordered, and the complete and detailed system of laws fixed and ordered only the mind. This is how Tocqueville's American survived amidst chaos with the same boldness, self-discipline, and masterly sureness as the Old World aristocrat who lived in his changeless world.

Life in Tocqueville's democratic America, then, is misleading. The tasks accomplished by its citizens were less grand than those performed in the past by aristocrats in the City of Man and therefore appear to be less noble. But the same nobility of spirit present in the aristocrat was also found in Tocqueville's American.

For example, both the aristocrat and Tocqueville's American reveal a high degree of egoism in their personalities, which Nietzsche says "belongs to the nature of the noble soul."[18] But because much of aristocratic society was fixed, with little in life that fluctuated, the "haughtiest nobility" (i.e., the aristocrats) displayed crass ambitious urges in fewer "portions of their existence."[19] In a democratic society, much of life is contested and no position is fixed. For this reason, the egoism of Tocqueville's American spilled over into displays of "restless and insatiable vanity" in many portions of life. Compared with the aristocrat, Tocqueville's American appears craving and jealous. But this is more a reflection on the difficult and competitive environment in which Tocqueville's American lived than on the nature of his soul.

The hardness and severeness of Nietzsche's noble soul are evident in Tocqueville's American as surely as they were in the European aristocrats observed by Nietzsche, even though the accomplishments of Tocqueville's American appear less grand. Both the aristocrat and Tocqueville's American "placed courage as the highest virtue,"[20] but while the aristocrat prized martial valor, Tocqueville's American prized that courage which

> emboldens men to brave the dangers of the ocean in order to arrive earlier in port, to support the privations of the wilderness without complaint, . . . and which renders them almost insensible to the loss of a fortune laboriously acquired and instantly prompts them to fresh exertions to make another.[21]

Both the aristocrat and Tocqueville's American would toil, but the aristocrat would build a magnificent structure honoring the past. Tocqueville's American would drain a swamp in the middle of nowhere with an ambitious eye towards the future. The aristocrat would create an empire; Tocqueville's

American would build a business. The aristocrat would lead an army across two countries. Tocqueville's American would drive cattle across three states. The aristocrat would bring his capricious laws and instincts to govern distant lands. Tocqueville's American would bring his "political laws, his religious doctrines, his theories of social economy, and his domestic occupations,"[22] firmly embedded in his mind and holding fast to his will, from the "depth of the backwoods" to the "business of the city."[23]

The aristocrat would brave the dangers of nature for honor and glory. Tocqueville's American would brave the dangers of nature for commerce and profit. Tocqueville writes,

> The European sailor navigates with prudence; he sets sail only when the weather is favorable; if an unforeseen accident befalls him, he puts into port; at night he furls a portion of his canvas; and when the whitening billows intimate the vicinity of land, he checks his course and takes an observation of the sun. The American neglects these precautions and braves these dangers. He weighs anchor before the tempest is over; by night and by day he spreads his sails to the wind; such damage as his vessel may have sustained from the storm, he repairs as he goes along; and when he at last approaches the end of his voyage, he darts onward to the shore as if he already descried a port. The Americans are often shipwrecked, but no trader crosses the seas so rapidly. And as they perform the same distance in a shorter time, they can perform it at a cheaper rate.[24]

The nobility of Tocqueville's American, following Nietzsche's understanding of that term, is perhaps best captured in Theodore Roosevelt's essay, "The Strenuous Life," where he writes in support of

> not the doctrine of ignoble ease, but the doctrine of the strenuous life, the life of toil and effort, of labor and strife; to preach that highest form of success which comes, not to the man who desires mere easy peace, but to the man who does not shrink from danger, from hardship, or from bitter toil, and who out of these wins the splendid ultimate triumph.[25]

Roosevelt continues,

> We do not admire the man of timid peace. We admire the man who embodies victorious effort; the man who never wrongs his neighbor, who is prompt to help a friend, but who has those virile qualities necessary to win in the stern strife of actual life.[26]

Roosevelt made these remarks in support of virtues such as helpfulness and good neighborliness, but while these are the "herd" virtues condemned by Nietzsche, Roosevelt's praise of them did not prevent him from giving individuals encouragement to push, to strive, to create, and to triumph. "Herd" virtues such as neighborliness and helpfulness provide essential human supports in a chaotic society of democratic individualists where rank and position are no longer fixed. They are not necessarily manifestations of *ressentiment*, and their embrace is not evidence that ambitious and aggressive people have been neutered, successfully "tamed," or rendered safe. They may simply attest to the difficult existence that is part of everyday life in a democratic society where, because of that existence, individual achievements are less significant and grand than they were during the age of aristocracy. When such virtues find their way into the mind, the human spirit is not necessarily prevented from being noble, positive, active, and free. Their high presence in society does not necessarily mean that a culture of *ressentiment* has been established.

The torrential current of change that overruns a democratic society prevents fixed codes, laws, and traditions from ever taking root. Such institutions served as beacons to the noble soul in aristocratic society. Yet this feature of democratic life does not prevent the internal world of the mind from being ruled by capricious laws. Nietzsche says of the noble soul that "it can move among equals with their equal privileges, showing the same sureness of modesty and delicate reverence that characterize its relations with itself."[27] He continues, saying that "refinement and self-limitation in its relations with its [the noble soul's] equals—every star is such an egoist—it honors itself in them and in the rights it cedes to them."[28] He wrote this on the assumption that the noble soul could only honor a small subgroup of individuals as equals and still preserve his or her nobility, that the noble soul could only exist in the aristocrat. He assumed that democracy, or the recognition of everyone as equals, would transform the noble soul into the *ressentiment* herd man. Nietzsche did not realize that equal privileges could be extended to all without extinguishing nobility in human beings. Tocqueville's American is a testament to the fact that nobility in democracy is possible, and that the noble soul and the principle of equality are not mutually exclusive.

The tendency of Tocqueville's American to oppose freedom to equality[29] is consistent with this conclusion, which leads to a rather interesting contrast between the noble spirit of Tocqueville's American and the *ressentiment* spirit of the expressive individualist. Tocqueville's American realized his great worth not through an equal position relative to others, but through his freedom to pursue a high aim. It was through freedom and not equality of condition that Tocqueville's American tested his mettle and gave full expression to that which was positive and noble in his soul. This freedom is very different from the freedom of the expressive individualist, which comes under the name of "autonomy." The freedom of the expressive individualist is not the freedom of those who strive so much as it is the freedom of those who desire to shield, to hunker down, to cut one's losses, and to protect. Freedom is desired by the autonomous self, often in the name of tolerance, to defend feelings and impulses spontaneously arising within the self. Freedom for the expressive individualist is not the vehicle by which a person aims for the most high. It is simply the vehicle by which all is leveled and all is respected.

Tocqueville's American and the Old World aristocrat adhered to capricious laws and felt a compulsion to obey them. The expressive individualist finds security in the "aimless wanderings" of the imagination, in just "feeling," and in the therapist's "letting go." Tocqueville's American and the aristocrat were egoists. The expressive individualist is also an egoist but a different kind, and he possesses a peculiar side to him that is an impulse to obliterate one's own ego in order to gain membership in a loving, harmonious "community." Tocqueville's American and the aristocrat possessed the needs of the noble soul—the need to strive and to create. The expressive individualist has a "need for what is noble," a desire to attain the "higher self," which, as Nietzsche notes, "is different from the needs of the noble soul itself and actually the eloquent and dangerous mark of its lack."[30]

Part Two

America and the City of God

9

The Creation of the Aristocrat in the City of God

In his *Confessions*, Augustine develops an original analysis of the meaning of time. Time does not exist except in the mind of a person. It is nothing more than the single moment of eternity distended within the human imagination. It is by recognizing "time" to be a kind of mental aberration that one can compress into the small space of the mind all that has passed or will come to pass in the physical world. In this chapter, the method Augustine uses to discover the difference between time and eternity will be adapted to the experience of America in order to show how Tocqueville's American was an aristocrat in the City of God.

In Book 10 of the *Confessions*, Augustine reflects on the joy and misery he has experienced during his life and finds them to reside in memory. He finds memory to be a vast cavern from which images move into consciousness and then out, not necessarily under the direction of mind.[1] Memories of events rush forward to the surface, asking, "Aren't we perhaps the ones?"[2] and then just as quickly are banished from consciousness by mind and forced back into the deep cavern that is memory. Memory is finally rendered distinct from mind when Augustine notes that it is possible for the mind to experience joy in remembering a past sorrow—the joy being present in mind, the sorrow being present in memory. He contemplates this phenomenon and muses, "Is it perhaps because memory does not belong to mind?"[3]

In Book 11 of the *Confessions*, Augustine builds on this understanding of mind and memory to make a distinction between time and eternity. Time appears measurable to humans, but it is only measured by the ruler that exists within memory. A long time to come can not really be judged any different than a short time to come because the event to come has not yet occurred and therefore cannot provide an endpoint for measure.[4] The "time" is merely conceived and distended within the image of memory. Just as future times cannot exist, neither can past times, for if future times have not yet come into being, past times have already passed. Past and future can only live as distensions of time that occur in memory. Even present time has no space, as the present can only be measured when it has raced from the future into the past.[5] In this way, Augustine concludes, all "time" is merely an artifact originating in the apparatus of memory. Time does not exist except as an imagined distension, and time, without the distortions created by memory and imagination, ultimately collapses into a single moment—eternity.

For Augustine, the moment of eternity is holy, arrived at when time has collapsed into itself. It radiates not enormous length or width, like the mathematical concept of infinity, but rather stillness and imperturbability. It exists not outside man but within him, and it lies within that aspect of man that is divorced from conscious thought. This is because conscious thought measures time, and time is nothing more than the moment of eternity distended (or distorted) by the human imagination. Eternity is discovered by mind through memory, but must remain unfathomable to mind, for to exist in the moment of eternity is to no longer think. It is to no longer be able to remember or to speculate, to imagine past or future. Such imaginative activities are, by definition, only done in "time." Thus, the moment of eternity can only be attained when the mind goes blank. The stillness of eternity and the activity of rational consciousness are mutually exclusive phenomena. All rational activity ceases when time is contracted into eternity and thus, apprehending eternity requires a leap of faith, not a leap of reason.

In drawing a distinction between time and eternity, Augustine makes some very interesting points.

First, from the perspective of eternity, past and future are not opposites. They are really the same phenomena, as both live only inside the human imagination. Past and future are projections of the mind that can function as powerful emotional stimulants. When they take the form of "memory" or "hope," they can trigger feelings of joy or misery or make one pause in deep contemplation. But in this way, past and future are simply equivalent forms of deception and, from the perspective of eternity, the psychological effect they exert is the same—they both cause the human mind to be distracted. Their existence rests on the tendency of the human imagination to construct layers and layers of time, and it is this tendency that removes a person ever further from the calm and imperturbable moment of eternity. The past and the future are both snares that throw a person into a state of flux. They sweep a person into the current of "time," which consumes much attention and energy. In this way, both the past and future are "distractions."

Second, that which exists or takes place in the physical world—the great clashes between men, the monuments stretching into the sky, the imposing palace of the king—can be understood as part of the deception that is the temporal experience of man. These structures or physical occurrences do not exist in the present except as images within the mind. They can exert a tremendous effect on the psyche (for example, they can command allegiance or reverence), but to do so they must exist in the form of memory. They must lie at the surface of the vast cavern of memory, crying out to mind, "we are definitely the ones," or "we are definitely the images that you want to ponder." This is because, as Augustine noted, the present "has no space." The presents exists only one millisecond later, when it has been stored in the human mind as an image of memory.

In this way, all structures living in the "present" are really nothing more than projections of the imagination. In order to exist for a person, they must take the form of memory. For the purpose of affecting the human psyche, the great power exerted by structures in the physical world lies not in their weight or matter but in the memory of their weight or matter, and it is that memory which brings about the desired psychological effect (e.g., allegiance or reverence). Mental pictures and real objects are, for the purpose of the human psyche, completely interchangeable. It is in this way that objects and events existing in the material universe can be transposed inward into the universe lying behind the portal of the eye. Blocks of substance can be changed into intangible spirit or idea because intangible spirit or idea can have the exact same psychological effect as blocks of substance.

It is by using these two Augustinian concepts that the following speculation will be made: *Tocqueville's American and the aristocrat in the* City of Man *are intimately related to each other because the entire physical world of the aristocrat was transposed into the mind of Tocqueville's American.* Aristocracy lived on through the democratic age, and it lived on because its entire physical structure was transmuted into spirit and poured into the mind of a single character type—Tocqueville's American. In this way, Tocqueville's American was an aristocratic figure. And in this way, Tocqueville's American was a special kind of aristocrat. He was not an aristocrat in the world of force and matter—in the City of Man. He was an aristocrat in the world of spirit or idea—in the City of God.

Shifting the External World of Aristocratic Society into the Internal World of the Mind

In *Sources of the Self*, Charles Taylor alludes to the kind of transposition I will describe. Taylor argues that the philosophy of Descartes initiated a process of internalization whereby a cosmic design in the external world was shifted into the internal world of the mind. Taylor writes,

> The ethic of rational control, finding its sources in a sense of dignity and self-esteem, transposes *inward* something of the spirit of the honour ethic. No longer are we winning fame in public space; we act to maintain our sense of worth in our own eyes.[6]

He continues,

> Strength, firmness, resolution, control, these are the crucial qualities, a subset of warrior-aristocratic virtues, but now internalized. They are not deployed in great deeds of military valour in public space, but rather in the inner domination of passion by thought.[7]

Taylor argues that a definite link exists between the rational, democratic individualist living in modern society and the feudal aristocrat preceding him. This book agrees with Taylor's idea but magnifies it tremendously. Building on Augustine's understanding of time and memory, it argues that the Old World aristocratic empire, not just an honor code, achieved its perfect reflection in the mind of Tocqueville's American.

The Old World aristocrat was strongly influenced by images of the physical world. The mind of the aristocrat was shaped by history as the past coated every church and every family name, serving as a constant reminder of the very origin of one's being. It was shaped by institutions of the local community, where small groups of people were fastened to a piece of land for generations, where lords forever ruled and servants forever obeyed. Operating within the confines of the community, the imagination of the aristocrat was bounded by detailed rules governing dress and dinner parties, courtship and sport, and by manners tightly regulating one's communication with others. The human imagination in aristocratic society was bombarded by so many images of the external world that its position became fixed in time and place. Those images of the physical world, of the concrete edifices of power and the unequal material relations between men, created a world for the aristocrat.

The imagination of Tocqueville's American was shaped by internal forces corresponding directly to those powers bearing down on the imagination of the aristocrat. A structure existed within the imagination of Tocqueville's American no less elaborate and comprehensive as the one enveloping the aristocrat in the world of force and matter. The difference between the experiences of the two is that the leading images in the mind of Tocqueville's American had no basis in the physical world. They were not reflections of physical substance but merely served the same psychological purpose as reflections of physical substance. Through the mind of the aristocrat raced images of tradition, local community, and elaborate custom—images of life in the physical world. Through the mind of Tocqueville's American raced images of an afterlife, public opinion, and republican principle—images that had no real basis in the physical world.

For Tocqueville's American, no history coated the walls of a church vestry, no ground was hallowed by the generations that had lived on it, no purple robes sustained an awe for royalty, and no leader stood so high on a pedestal. No images of the physical world could bring Tocqueville's American to his knees or make him bow in submission. But other images in the mind of Tocqueville's American, images not originating in perceptions of the physical world, could produce a related psychological effect. The belief in an afterlife, public opinion, and republican principle could make Tocqueville's American submit. They could make him respectful. In this way, the two sets of images are alike even though they have different origins, and this is how physical objects in the external world can be transmuted into spirit and crowded into the small space of a single mind.

The Transposition of Aristocratic Tradition (or "Time") into the Mind of Tocqueville's American

In the mind of Tocqueville's American, the stabilizing force of human time took on a new form. For the aristocrat, the illusion of time was sustained by physical markers in the external world, as every household relic, every gravestone, every family portrait, and every structure in the town square, each existing within the present, prodded the aristocrat to build in his imagination an idea of the past. The fleeting moment in which the aristocrat lived was dilated and distended as the physical evidence of the centuries preceding him bombarded his consciousness. The sheer quantity of sensory impulses in aristocratic society distracted him and caused his imagination to construct layers and layers of time, even though past time itself was without substance, neither present nor real. The aristocrat lived as others have, in short moments of life, but as he surveyed the physical evidence of all that had come before him, his imagination was telescoped into the past, and within that illusion he carried the yoke of centuries. Within that imagined distension of time, the aristocrat beheld life and ensconced his identity.

For Tocqueville's American, the illusion of time was formulated in a different way. According to Tocqueville, many of the early nineteenth-century American communities lacked an historical record and little effort was made to preserve remnants of the past. Unlike aristocratic society,

Tocqueville's America possessed few of the external stimuli that caused aristocrats to ponder history. But within the imagination of the American, the future in a single lifetime served the same purpose as the memory of a city's past.

Time was distended within the imagination of Tocqueville's American, but unlike for the aristocrat, it was projected far into the future, not back into the past. Real fixtures in the external world served as cues to the aristocrat, dilating his perception of time as he imagined the generations preceding him. Layers and layers of time were conceived in this way, creating within his mind a form of temporal space. For Tocqueville's American, intention, inclination, expectation, and anticipation, all forward projections of the mind, served as triggering agents that distracted him and caused the perception of time to dilate. Ambitions, hopes, and goals, not family crests and old churches, caused the American individualist to imagine layers and layers of time. Within this imagined distension of time, projected towards the future rather than into the past, a new form of temporal space was created, giving the American a psychological plane on which to locate himself. Fretting, hoping, impatience, and restlessness over that which might come to pass in an individual's future replaced longing, melancholy, and nostalgia for that which had already passed in the life of a larger aristocratic community.

The imagination of Tocqueville's American was telescoped far beyond the present. But within this new distension, Tocqueville's American saw prospective business success and grand plans of what might be, not the physical evidence of an ancestor's accomplishments or monuments to grand plans that once were. He pondered an afterworld that he believed would follow his death, not the remnants of an entire society preceding his birth. Tocqueville's American beheld in his imagination a new phantasm of time. That phantasm was composed of abstract goals and yet-unrealized triumphs that might come to pass in the future of a lone, ambitious individual, not the images of large estates and ancient articles that recalled a glorious tradition. A long memory of a society's past became, in Tocqueville's American, a long expectation of an individual's future.

Some aspects of American life observed by Tocqueville and James Bryce are consistent with this mental transformation. In his chapter discussing the distant objectives of human actions, Tocqueville writes,

> The instability of [democratic] society itself fosters the natural instability of man's desires. In the midst of these perpetual fluctuations of his lot, the present looms large upon his mind; it hides the future, which becomes indistinct, and men seek only to think about tomorrow.[8]

Tocqueville believed that such mental instability was inherent to democracy but could be eased when individual advancement was made to appear "the result of some effort, so that no greatness should be of too easy acquirement and that ambition should be obliged to fix its gaze long upon an object before it is gratified."[9] In this passage, Tocqueville is alluding to the stabilizing power of imagined time on the human personality. When time is distended within the mind of man, impulses are guided and length is given to the range of his desires.

Tocqueville believed that religion helped combat the potential for instability within the democratic mind, arguing,

> When men have accustomed themselves to foresee from afar what is likely to befall them in the world and to feed upon hopes, they can hardly confine their minds within the precise limits of life, and they are ready to break the boundary and cast their looks beyond.[10]

In this way, religion in Tocqueville's America served the same purpose as historical tradition in aristocratic society. The afterworld became the one final goal, the most distant yet the most grand, that swept the imagination of the American into distant time. The strong belief in an afterworld provided Tocqueville's American with a kind of protective cover under which he could gain a sense of permanence and calm, although the physical world in which he lived was chaotic and ever-changing.[11]

A similar phenomenon was observed by James Bryce during his travels through America. Bryce, the Englishman, says of the American individualists,

> This constant reaching forward to and grasping at the future does not so much express itself in words, for they are not a loquacious people, as in the air of ceaseless haste and stress which pervades the West. They remind you of the crowd which Vathek found in the hall Eblis, each darting hither and thither with swift steps and unquiet mien, driven to and fro by a fire in the heart. Time seems too short for what they have to do, and results always come to short of their desire. One feels as if caught and whirled along in a foaming stream, chafing against its banks, such is the passion of these men to accomplish in their own lifetimes what in the past it took centuries to effect. Sometimes in a moment of pause, for even the visitor finds himself infected by the all-pervading eagerness, one is inclined to ask them; "Gentlemen, why in heaven's name this haste? You have time enough. No enemy threatens you. No volcano will rise from beneath you. Ages and ages lie before you. . . . Why complete in a few decades what the other nations of the world took thousands of years over in the older continents?"[12]

Bryce offered these thoughts to the members of a state legislature in the American West, and some responded by admitting that "the political point of view—the fact that they were the founders of new commonwealths, and responsible to posterity for the foundations they laid, a point of view so trite and obvious to a European visitor that he pauses before expressing it—had not crossed their minds."[13]

Bryce and the American legislator had difficulty understanding each other because the temporal envelopes containing their respective imaginations were constructed differently. Bryce came from the Old World, and he lived within an imagined distension of time shaped by the history of a society preceding his birth and that would long survive his death. The American legislator lived within an imagined distension of time encompassing only the period of a single lifetime, spanning only a few short years. The walls in the imagination of the American legislator enclosed a much shorter period of "time" than they did in Bryce's imagination, even though that period of time, for both Bryce and the American legislator, was an illusion conjured up by the imagination. This is why Bryce saw generations of mankind before him and behind him when he spoke of human progress, while the American individualist saw only "ploughs and sawmills, ore-crushers and locomotives,"[14] the tools of success in a single lifetime.

This connection between Tocqueville's American and the Old World aristocrat is definitely grounded in Augustinian philosophy. From the perspective of eternity, past and future are equivalent and, for psychological purposes, denote equivalent mental experiences. Past and future are distractions or "distensions" founded on the human tendency to construct layers and layers of time within the imagination. The aristocrat who gazes "long" into the past and Tocqueville's American who gazes "long" into the future are engaging in perfectly symmetrical activities. This concept establishes the first support in the aristocratic system of Tocqueville's American.

The Transposition of the Aristocratic Community into the Mind of Tocqueville's American

In the mind of Tocqueville's American, the image of the aristocratic community was translated into new form. For the aristocrat, the boundary separating the county in which he lived from the world beyond had tremendous psychological significance. Inside that boundary, the aristocrat joined with others to form a "little platoon" of life.[15] He lived among certain individuals and customs and did so according to a rhythm of life that he was bound to by destiny.

The image of this world has a corresponding image in the mind of Tocqueville's American—public opinion. The order of public opinion was invisible and confined to the mind, but like the aristocratic community, it could fix the identity of a person, instill prejudice, and radiate the warmth of common humanity. Public opinion, like the aristocratic community, could separate that which was comforting and familiar from all that was foreign and strange. This was true even though public opinion lacked physicality.

In the physical world, Tocqueville's Americans lived like an "army in the field," always moving from region to region. Little opportunity existed for a township's ways to solidify and begin a tradition. Nevertheless, Tocqueville's Americans were susceptible to a power that fixed attitudes and beliefs. Operating on the imagination, public opinion guided the American and preserved within him a feeling of connectedness, just as local institutions sitting in a small corner of the physical world did for the aristocrat. To adhere to the opinion of the majority was to adopt the ways of the community. Only public opinion, unlike the local aristocratic community, had no physical space and so could be transported anywhere. Public opinion was a wholly mental phenomenon, not a collection of tangible institutions, and its effect on a person was independent of where he or she resided in the world.

This interpretation of public opinion is consistent with Tocqueville and Bryce's discovery that nineteenth-century Americans were extremely similar despite their being separated by long distances. Both Tocqueville and Bryce noted that Americans had a tendency to "think alike," that in America everything changes but nobody differs, as opposed to aristocratic society where nothing changes but everybody differs.[16] The constancy in the goals, values, and prejudices of the Americans reveals how in the New World it was no longer necessary to confine the "platoon of life" to the county, the village, or the hamlet. Through public opinion, the little platoon of life could stretch across an entire continent. In the Old World, real sights and sounds bombarded the senses and kept the feeling of community from waning. But through public opinion, the human mind could be stabilized without daily physical stimulus. No longer was repetitive contact with the same townsfolk, the same churches, or the same monuments needed to keep the memory of what bound people together from growing dim. Public opinion allowed the old aristocratic community to become dimensionless.

There is a definite connection between this idea and Augustinian philosophy. What influenced the behavior of the Old World aristocrat was not the substance of the local community but the mental image of that substance. The mental image persuaded the aristocrat to situate his thoughts and experiences by referring them to what happened within the purview of his senses. This image of the local community corresponds to the order of public opinion. Public opinion is not formed by a reflection of physical substance onto the surface of the mind but, rather, is pure idea. Unlike the aristocratic community, the origin of public opinion does not lie in the world of force or matter. Yet public opinion serves the same psychological purpose as the image of the aristocratic community. Public opinion persuaded Tocqueville's American to situate his thoughts and experiences by referring them to the cumulative power of the majority. Public opinion and the aristocratic community generate two different mental images, but from the perspective of Augustinian philosophy, they are very much alike. This concept establishes the second support in the aristocratic system of Tocqueville's American.

The Transposition of an Aristocratic System of Manners into the Mind of Tocqueville's American

In Tocqueville's America, the manners of the Old World aristocrat were expressed in new form. When the aristocrat socialized with other members of his class, all conduct was guided by a detailed system of rules. The proper dress, the proper greeting, the proper gesture in courtship, and the proper seating at the dinner table were elements of a complex code of conduct. In Tocqueville's America, simple democratic rules replaced these ornate forms. The new "manners" were no longer visible through clothing, a parade of gestures, or style of address, but found their expression in abstract republican principle.

The manners of the Old World aristocrat were detailed, complex, and innumerable because no fundamental theory united them. No one scheme could reduce to a single idea the countless styles of dress, medals, hand movements, curtsies, and bows in aristocratic society. It depended on how much a jewel shined, how far back a robe swept, how fine one's hands were, and how stiff one's posture was that awe was instilled, respect was stirred, or order was brought. Compared to aristocratic manners, the manners of Tocqueville's Americans had an air of simplicity about them when expressed in the physical world. There are only so many ways to shake hands, wait one's turn, or stand respectfully in line. But that outward simplicity is misleading, for it obscured a carefully organized system residing within the imagination of Tocqueville's American. Like a geometric axiom, republican principle can order objects in physical space even though the principle itself cannot actually be seen, touched, or heard. When democratic principles governed the games of schoolchildren and the order of a feast in America, a simple pattern of conduct was hiding a well-considered form, one that was not amenable to ostentation.

Frances Trollope, in her diatribe against the manners of the nineteenth-century Americans, was misled by the simplicity of American manners. Unlike Tocqueville, she assumed that well-mannered behavior required a visual and auditory display of cultivation and refinement, and because the manners of the Americans were so plain, she condemned them. Compared with European aristocratic society, the Americans seemed to her to lack manners altogether. In her book, she notes the vulgarity of the Americans at the dinner table, their lack of decorum at the theater, and the omnipresence of spittoons.[17]

Trollope erroneously graded manners in accordance with the patterns of conduct she witnessed in aristocratic ("civilized") society. She did not see that manners and rules of conduct guided the new American individualist no less than they did the European aristocrat, but as American manners were applications of simple, democratic notions, they did not lend themselves to glittering display. Tocqueville's American, no less than the European aristocrat, had an idea of what comprised the proper order of men and women in physical space. While a knight's garter, an imposing uniform, or a special accent did not cause the Americans to close ranks and cower, republican principle succeeded in guiding them into their proper positions. The American with his spittoon was no less guided by "manners" than the European aristocrat. Only the manners of the American, when expressed in the physical world, took a form that was unelaborate and barely visible.

The connection with Augustinian philosophy is evident again. The mental images of the aristocrat's manners, dress, and gestures correspond to the mental image of republican principle. Unlike the image of aristocratic manners, though, the image of republican principle has no basis in the physical world. In aristocratic society, it was by reflecting an image onto the surface of the mind that a powerful object caused one to cower and show respect. Republican principle can also make one assume a position of respect, but its mental image does not originate in the world of force and matter. Its mental image is not a reflection of something solid. It stands for a universal and timeless axiom, independent of the physical world. The connection with the aristocratic experience is that the image of republican principle can have the same psychological effect as images of real substance. This concept establishes the third support in the aristocratic system of Tocqueville's American.

Tocqueville's American as a Reservoir of the Aristocratic "Spirit"

While structure in the physical world is measured in speed, length, and weight, structure in the world of the imagination has no such units of measurement. Yet within the mind of Tocqueville's American, behind the portal of the eye, in a physical space measuring only a few cubic inches, can be found the entire supporting structures of a society that once existed in the physical world.

The entire tradition of aristocratic society—its social and political past, its church vestries, its hallowed ground, its generations of families, and its hereditary peerages—was transmuted. Its physical substance was expressed in a new, nonmaterial form, that of the hopes and ambitions of the American individualist, which caused the mind to be distended far beyond the present. The memory of things past became the expectation of things future.

The entire aristocratic community—its landmarks, its inns, its estates, its heartwarming smells, and its repetitive sounds—was transmuted. Its physical substance was expressed in a new, nonmaterial form, that of public opinion. Public opinion guided the American individualist regardless of his or her geographical location.

The entire system of aristocratic manners, custom, and fashion—the splendor of the dinner table, the diamonds and gold worn on the chests of nobles, the furniture aged properly by time, and the complex pattern of gestures and salutations observed at the theater and the club—was transmuted. Its physical substance was expressed in a new, nonmaterial form, that of abstract republican principle, which spawned a new order at sport, business, and dinner.

The physical world of the aristocrat was reproduced inside the mind of Tocqueville's American. It entered a new dimension where size, weight, color, and speed could all be reduced to the unmeasurable state of spirit or idea. It was in this way that more than just a flash of exemplary aristocratic behavior survived the democratic revolution. An entire aristocratic world was poured into the mind of a single character type—Tocqueville's American. Tocqueville's American, by housing within his mind an analog of the entire aristocratic world, does not constitute a rebellion against aristocracy so much as he does a continuation of aristocracy in a brand new form.

In the new age of equality, the physical structure of aristocratic society could not survive. In an atmosphere of constant change and shifting ranks, with each person moving hither and thither to satisfy his or her desires, reverence for tradition had to crumble, local communities had to lose their integrity, and the ornate system of rank, privilege, and interpersonal communication had to collapse. But although Tocqueville's democratic America was from the beginning devoid of such Old World ways, aristocracy continued to survive in that new country in a new form and in a new space. It survived not in the physical world of America but in the spiritual world of the American imagination.

For this reason, Tocqueville's American is a direct descendant of the aristocrat in the City of Man. He belongs not so much among a list of common democratic types as he does in a genealogy of aristocracy. At the same time, aristocracy in Tocqueville's America was not an empire of the physical world, of the earthly City of Man. It was an empire of the imagination, coming to life only in the celestial City of God. This point will be elaborated in the next chapter but it remains an essential one, for Tocqueville's American provides the "missing link" between the contemporary American expressive individualist and the aristocrat of the Old World. It is by way of Tocqueville's American that a country like the United States, which has no history of either aristocrats or peasants living on its soil (in the forms they are generally understood to take in history) can demonstrate an important connection with old aristocracy. Tocqueville's American is the carrier of the aristocratic tradition.

The Imperial Self of the Aristocrat in the City of Man

While the movement of expressive individualism reveals a strong association with the sectarian beliefs attacked by Augustine in late antiquity, it also has a link with the spirit of *ressentiment* described by the nineteenth-century philosopher Nietzsche. A problem arises because Nietzsche did not subdivide the spirit of *ressentiment* into different types. This is important because the *ressentiment* experience of American expressive individualism is very different from the *ressentiment* experience of European socialism. America and Europe both have democratic traditions, but the two continents have followed different paths of development, with the American path ending in a philosophy of radical individualism that recalls the experience of late antiquity. American individualism is charged by a unique set of ideas affecting the whole term of its existence, and the progression towards its special well of *ressentiment* must be accounted for. The differences between American and European ideas of individualism must be incorporated into any speculation on how America has changed.

The idea of "individualism" was actually first promulgated in Europe, expressed in the form of "individuality," but it differed significantly from what would later become the dominant American type. In Europe, the "individual" was merely considered to be a transitional phenomenon before a higher stage of social unity and harmony was attained.[18] In America, "individualism" came to represent the final stage of human progress. For this reason, it was condemned in Europe as an expression of ruthless, selfish, and egocentric behavior, one that only masqueraded as a new philosophy.[19]

Unlike European individuality, American individualism seemed to ascribe new value to old base motives. From the perspective of the nineteenth-century Saint-Simonians, who propagated an extremely influential form of socialism in Europe, the spirit of detachment expressed in the movement of American "individualism" was synonymous with rootlessness, social fragmentation, destructive rationalism, and anarchy. [20] The Saint-Simonians contrasted those social maladies with the healthy environment of "individuality," where the full development of human capacities would be combined with fraternity and equality.

Since individuality, with its romantic emphasis on human creativity and the unity of community, has become a prominent feature in the American society of expressive individualism, it is apparent that the stream of cultural development in America has been fed by more than one tributary. It includes inflow not only from traditional American individualism but from this other pool of belief. For this reason, the concept of individuality must be traced further back to find its well-source.

Tocqueville associated individualism with the feeling of detachment. But unlike individualism in America, which was present at the inception of that country, "individuality" in Europe was preceded by centuries of feudal society during which no spirit of detachment in any form was evident. In feudal society, the absence of this spirit of detachment resulted in certain characteristic patterns of human behavior. Such behavior existed in quasi-democratic form in peasant villages, and because peasant villages have persisted through the modern era, it is amenable to description. [21]

The basic social units of the peasant village were large peer groups and extended families. Within these groups, members were intensely affected by the thoughts and opinions of others. Individual self-esteem was dependent on one's standing within the group. It varied according to respect, power, and status and, since those qualities could only be expressed relative to others, a peasant's sense of self was deeply intertwined with the state of his or her social relations. Every action and every word spoken in the peasant peer group had important psychological ramifications, and a display of dominance by one was quickly countered by the effort of others to return the group to the level of equality, to soothe hurt feelings, and to prevent a rupture within the group. [22]

Equality was an essential principle of the peasant peer group. The peasant's attitude towards himself or herself was quite dependent on the order of rank prevailing in the external world. Inequality threatened self-esteem, so a conspicuous display of wealth was condemned, and competition between members was restrained. Within the peer group it was essential that everybody held roughly the same rank and made the same amount of money. Equality and fraternity in peasant peer groups were virtues designed not merely to support human companionship, but to discourage selfish and competitive behavior. Such behavior could disrupt the egalitarian milieu of the peer group and threaten other members with feelings of inadequacy and smallness. The psyche of the peasant was raw and sensitive and was quickly disposed to feelings of envy and jealousy.

The peer groups in peasant society were affectionate and comforting, but they were also closed, thereby guarding against insults that might come from the outside world in the form of worldly success or haughty behavior. By being reduced to the status of "stranger," the outsider was disarmed and could not threaten the important project of maintaining equality within the peer group. The stranger did not have to be factored into the innumerable calculations made by peer group members in determining relative status.

The peasant was so sensitive to the opinions of others and so threatened by external markers of success that an entire social structure was developed to reduce anxiety, protect self-esteem, and bolster feelings of self-worth. Such behavioral traits, however, were not confined to the peasant peer group. They were also evident in the aristocratic peer group. This point is generally not discussed in the social science literature, largely because peasant forms have lived on through the modern era while aristocratic forms have not. Even Nietzsche, who carefully analyzed both aristocratic and peasant culture and described the tendency towards hatred, envy, and jealousy among the peasantry, did not report such competitive behavior in the aristocratic culture. Nietzsche did not emphasize that the negative consequences of emulation, such as destructive envy and resentment, were just as prominent among aristocrats as peasants, and that while the aristocrat was noble and dignified, he or she also demonstrated an extreme sensitivity towards the opinions of others.

Flashes of competitiveness and sensitivity in aristocratic behavior are described by Tocqueville and Bryce. Tocqueville notes how an aristocrat would "regard a tap on the cheek as an unbearable insult and [would] be obliged to kill in single combat the person who struck him thus lightly."[23] Bryce also comments on the vicious cycle of envy and arrogance in the Old World that was conspicuously absent from America.[24]

The extreme sensitivity of aristocrats and their obsession with relative position can also be observed among the characters in fiction who are designed to represent them. Lord Chiltern, in Anthony Trollope's *Phineas Finn*, is a gentleman. At the same time, he is exquisitely sensitive to the most minor personal slights, which at one point forces him into a duel. The same character type can be found in John Buchan's *The Free Fishers*, where Sir Turnour, a wealthy sportsman, chases all over England to find a young man who has insulted him simply to demand a retraction. In H. Rider Haggard's *Allan Quartermain*, the character of Umslopogaas, the Zulu chief, is designed by Haggard to show how conventional aristocratic behavior can exist in a variety of cultures, independent of their state of technological advancement. The oscillation between intense love and intense rivalry within the aristocratic peer group is evident in the verbal exchange between Umslopogaas and Macumazahn, the English aristocrat. Macumazahn says to Umslopogaas, "Thine is a strange love. Thou wouldst split me to the chin if I stood in thy path tomorrow." Umslopogaas replies, "Thou speakest the truth, Macumazahn; that would I if it came in the way of duty, but I should love thee all the same when the blow had gone fairly home."[25]

The extreme sensitivity of the aristocrat and his obsession with relative rank inside the peer group appear to be longstanding features of aristocratic behavior, and certainly Augustine describes them in his criticism of pagan aristocrats. In *The City of God*, he finds fault with their competitive nature, with their never-ending pursuit of glory, and with their frequent battles and duels.

In another text, Josiah Ober describes the vigorous, often savage, competition between Athenian noblemen in Ancient Greece. He writes,

> This pattern of behavior is not surprising in light of the degree to which the aristocratic ethos emphasized competition. Since archaic times, Greek nobles had competed at everything from tossing wine dregs at targets when attending drinking parties to state politics. And they competed specifically with one another; in order for the victory to be sweet, it had to be over a proper aristocratic opponent.[26]

Kautsky, in his *The Politics of Aristocratic Empires*, reports a similar phenomenon among the aristocrats of Asia and feudal Europe. In his chapter titled "Position and Rank," he describes the intense competition for the highest position within the aristocratic peer group, with small differences in rank looming large in the minds of aristocrats. Of these conflicts he writes, "Although the stakes in intraaristocratic conflicts have now been listed separately as opportunities to gain wealth, power, and prestige, to serve and do one's duty, to maintain one's honor and gain glory, they are in practice and in the aristocrat's mind closely interrelated."[27]

Wayne Rebhorn, in his "The Crisis of the Aristocracy in *Julius Caesar*" notes how aristocrats of both Shakespeare's age and the Roman Silver Age articulated the notion of the *imperial self*, in which a competitive ethos of heroic self-assertion urged the individual towards personal self-aggrandizement.[28] It incited one "to extend the terrain of the self until it entirely dominate[d] the human landscape."[29] That notion produced intense rivalry within the patrician class. In the case of the Roman aristocrats, for example, heroism in the service of the patria gradually degenerated into competition within the patria, resulting in destructive, internecine combat.[30]

The urge to emulate and rival is a common element in aristocratic and peasant peer groups. In both, the person within the group "identifies" with other members, making possible a bond of brotherhood or even a love for close associates that could be quite intense. At the same time, the person "rivals" other members, which leads to destructive feelings of hatred and envy. For both the peasant and the aristocrat, a part of one's identity is shared with other people. It is affected by another person's position in the social order relative to the self. Rebhorn's comments on the aristocrat apply equally to the peasant. He writes,

> Propelling everyone forward in an endless quest for glory, the emulation at the heart of the imperial self essentially makes human relationships into a "zero-sum" game. That is, it makes characters act as though the status they could accrue were a fixed commodity in limited supply so that one man's rise must literally entail another's fall, or alternatively, each man sees the rise of another as an impairment of his personal status and importance, as a degradation or loss of rank even when such a loss has not actually occurred.[31]

The major difference between the aristocrat and the peasant is that within the aristocratic peer group, the aristocrat retains the urge to compete, "to excel all others," to "out-imitate" [his] fellows."[32] He retains a belief in the imperial self. The peasant, through an inversion of the value structure, has eliminated such competition by declaring it to be evil. Robert Redfield and John Kautsky's descriptions of peasant behavior are consistent with this view. Kautsky writes (at one point, quoting Redfield),

> He [Redfield] finds among peasants "a distaste for violence, a disfavor of prowess, in any form of conspicuous aggressiveness." To the aristocrat, risk taking and personal exploits, warlike (and also amorous) adventures are opportunities to prove his manliness and his worth, to maintain his honor and gain glory. Violence is a normal and, indeed, desirable aspect of life growing out of the aristocrat's position in his society.[33]

The peasant values "peace," "harmony," and "routine,"[34] and these values serve as impediments to any member within the peer group who might dare act like an imperial self. This is a crucial difference between the value structures of aristocratic and peasant peer groups.

These peer groups formed the basic social structure of the Old World, and they are very relevant to the issue of modern individualism. An analysis of peasant and aristocratic peer groups reveals two patterns of behavior that on one level oppose each other but, on a much deeper level, share a common basis. These two patterns of behavior and their common basis are not extinct but have actually survived to form the psychological basis of socialist society and the American society of expressive individualism.

The peer groups of the peasant and the aristocrat reveal two distinct patterns of behavior. From the peasant peer group comes the effort to preserve group cohesion at the expense of individual achievement. The peasant's effort to preserve harmony, fraternity, and equality within the peer group is a virtue made necessary by the fragile and sensitive ego of the peasant, including his tendency to measure self-worth in the collective judgment of others. It has been suggested that the spirit of European socialism, including its emphasis on the group at the expense of the individual and the goal of complete uniformity and equality in social status, is derived from this aspect of peasant behavior. Leszek Kolakowski, in his *Main Currents of Marxism*, notes that the emphasis on harmony and equality in society is a common feature of both feudalism and socialism.[35] Socialism, he notes, was inspired by the belief that antagonism, conflict, and social inequality were contrary to God's plan. Such a belief matches exactly the value structure of the peasant peer group, especially the peasant's commanding belief in the importance of peer group harmony and the equality of its members.[36]

Arieli describes a similar link between the socialist philosophy of Saint-Simon and feudal patterns of behavior. The socialism of Saint-Simon argued that the individual had no existence independent of society and that humanity was a collective entity progressing through time, achieving finality only when the spirit of service and the spirit of fraternity combined to form a new community.[37] According to this philosophy, the "individual" was understood to be just a "crisis phenomenon," waiting to be absorbed into a larger social unit.[38] Again, there exists an emphasis on the group at the expense of the individual, on harmony at the expense of competition and individual achievement. Both of these goals and the strong belief in equality correlate exactly with the goals of the small peasant peer group.

Socialist society emphasizes unity, harmony, fraternity, equality, and cooperation and essentially replicates peasant peer group behavior on a much larger scale. It smothers both "individualism" and "individuality." Socialism's virtues, which Nietzsche declared to be inspired by *ressentiment*, are tied to the insecurity and extreme sensitivity of the peasant, who flashed with anger at the slightest deviation from equality within the peer group and who demanded absolute uniformity in the name of the group. Since the aristocratic peer group was also guided, in part, by the goals of brotherhood, spiritual union, and community, it is not surprising that socialism would thrive in countries with these feudal antecedents. The obsession with equality is derived from its expression within the peasant peer group; the obsession with fraternity and community is derived from its expression in both the peasant peer group and the aristocratic peer group.

The link between the spirit of socialism and the spirit of feudalism has been commented on in other works, including Ralf Dahrendorf's *Society and Democracy in Germany,* Oswald Spengler's *Prussianism and Socialism,* Friedrich Hayek's *The Road to Serfdom,* and Barrington Moore's *Social Origins of Dictatorship and Democracy.* What emerges in each is a picture of an arrogant aristocrat facing a resentful peasant, with the peasant standing as the aristocrat's *ressentiment* opposite. A crucial difference between the peasant and the aristocrat turns on a simple transvaluation of values, for the peasant simply inverts the value structure of the aristocrat and declares superiority, achievement, and individual glory to be evil instead of good. With the collapse of feudal society and the triumph of democracy, the pattern of emulation and rivalry persists but in the democratic form of the peasant peer group. The aristocratic model disappears. Democracy comes to be joined to an obsession with equality of condition.

Socialism is the union of democracy and *ressentiment* that Nietzsche observed, one grounded in hatred, anger, jealousy, envy, and resentment and demanding the complete leveling of society so that everyone has the same. Expressive individualism is also a democratic form of *ressentiment* but one that differs from socialism because it draws its vital force from the aristocratic peer group, not the peasant. While both the aristocratic and peasant peer groups were steeped in emulation and rivalry, there was a specific behavioral feature that seems to have been unique to the aristocrat and that the expressive individualist shares. That special aristocratic feature is the belief in the "imperial self."

When democracy is filtered through the aristocratic model of behavior, the principle of equality is joined to a belief in individuality, not a belief in equality of condition. It latches on to that aspect of aristocracy glorifying the individual. Rather than smother a person's ambitions as the peasant peer group does, the aristocratic peer group invites the superior being to extend himself. Individuality is a democratic application of this aristocratic belief. It encourages the person to set free the great power and creative energy residing within him or her.

At the same time, the democratic notion of individuality perverts the original intent of the aristocratic imperial self. Rather than encourage one to struggle against others and conquer them, it focuses attention on the self and one's inner trials. Rather than make one status-conscious, it makes one withdraw into a privately created world. Rather than hold a person to the highest standards of achievement, it "individualizes" standards and makes them relative. As a result, a person influenced by "individuality" often expresses a feeling of detachment like the one described by Tocqueville in American "individualism." This is why the philosophy of "individuality" fits comfortably in the American tradition. But the two experiences in detachment are not related, as will be shown in the last chapter of this book. The spirit of detachment in Tocqueville's America was not founded on the belief system of introspective imperial selves but on something very different.[39]

If "individuality" is a *ressentiment* form of democratic philosophy, but one that is adapted from aristocratic peer group behavior, it is logical to ask why Tocqueville's America evolved in the direction of expressive individualism. Eastern Europe had a long tradition of peasant peer group behavior, and it is not surprising that the overthrow of the aristocratic order moved the region in the direction of socialism. Upon destruction of the aristocratic peer groups, the peasant credo—"equality of condition"—and not "individuality" became the new organizing tenet. But Tocqueville's America had neither peasants nor aristocrats on its soil, so why has the philosophy of "individuality" become so prominent?

The answer to this question was supplied in the first part of this chapter. Tocqueville correctly notes that peasant life and peasant behavioral forms were absent from democratic America. But he incorrectly concludes that aristocracy was also absent from democratic America. Aristocracy was present, though not in the conventional form it took in the Old World. Aristocracy came to live in the imaginations of men and women, not in physical reality. Each individualist in Tocqueville's America embodied the transposition of aristocratic society into abstract, dimensionless mental space. This is why American individualism has evolved towards expressive individualism rather than towards socialism, towards "individuality" rather than towards complete equality of condition. The heritage of the expressive individualist, by way of Tocqueville's American, is singularly aristocratic.

Tocqueville's American supplies the missing link between the aristocrat in the City of Man and the new American expressive individualist. But he himself does not participate in either tradition. As the aristocrat in the City of God, he stands as a kind of way station, resembling neither the figure who enters nor the one who leaves, but who nevertheless influences the course that is traveled.

10

Tocqueville's American as an Aristocrat in the City of God

How the Aristocrat in the City of Man and the Aristocrat in the City of God Have Different Ideas of Peace

Above all, Augustine wrote, men desire peace. Peace is the attainment of order, the easing of tension, and the quiescence of fury and conflict. It is a state of being that is attained when all the discordant elements in a system are harmoniously joined, and flux has given way to silence and calm.

But there are two kinds of peace, Augustine noted. There is peace in the earthly City of Man, grounded in political agreement and mutual economic interest. Such peace is observed between states when they give up their competition for territory or between men who have given up their quarrels. Earthly peace is very different from the peace enjoyed in the heavenly City of God. Heavenly peace is gained through faith, not political agreement, and it causes the inner man to be at rest, not society to reach a standstill. In heavenly peace, the spiritual body feels no want and all the elements of a person's will act in concert. [1]

The difference between earthly peace and heavenly peace is very relevant to the American experience, for it helps distinguish between two kinds of aristocrats. The aristocrat in the City of Man aspires to earthly peace. The aristocrat in the City of God (i.e., Tocqueville's American) aspires to heavenly peace.

The Old World aristocrat envisioned immutability in this life. He may have struggled in battle and eventually succeeded in making himself a king among kings, but when tempted by the image of peace, it was for an earthly peace that he yearned. The calm and repose that he imagined were products of orderly manners, refined tastes, and a close attachment to one's place of birth. It was a peace in which the material world did not fluctuate. It was a peace attained when war did not consume, when towns did not change, and when man did not advance. Tocqueville says of the aristocrats,

> they do not presume that they have arrived at the supreme good or at absolute truth, but they cherish an opinion that they have pretty nearly reached that degree of greatness and knowledge which our imperfect nature admits of; and as nothing moves about them, they are willing to fancy that everything is in its fit place. Then it is that the legislator affects to lay down eternal laws; that kings and nations will raise none but imperishable monuments; and that the present generation undertakes to spare generations to come the care of regulating their destinies.[2]

The aristocrat in the City of Man imagines an earthly peace. He imagines the different elements of society assuming their proper position and living in complete harmony with one another. To the aristocrat in the City of Man, peace is achieved when society is calm and still.

For the aristocrat in the City of God, peace does not mean earthly peace. It does not mean peace in "time" or in "society." It does not signify an absence of change in the physical world, nor does it rest on a temporary agreement between human powers. For the aristocrat in the City of God, "peace" means peace within the inner man. It means the peace that is yearned for in the moment of eternity.

Augustine develops this idea of heavenly peace while arguing against the Platonists. The Platonists insisted that the soul is eternal, with no beginning and no end. The soul, they said, is related to eternity like the footprint is to the foot—created, but still always existing.[3] Yet the Platonists also argued that the soul experiences happiness only when it is not tethered to the body. When it is attached to the body, it is wretched. Augustine counters by saying, "If, then, the soul has always existed, are we to say that its wretchedness has always existed?"[4] Since the Platonists could not agree to this possibility, Augustine concludes that the soul has not always been. The soul is not synonymous with eternity but must have had its beginning in "time."

Augustine says the soul of man is born in time and that it is during its moment on earth that happiness is always coupled with wretchedness. Life in the earthly city is a series of dialectical intimates; ultimate happiness, or peace, cannot exist on earth in any pure form. It is always associated with that which makes life wretched, which produces erosion, decay, war, and death. Earthly life is a story of opposites—of health waiting for sickness, of joy waiting for misery, of excitement waiting for boredom, and of peace waiting for war—and like the soul, Augustine argued, these opposites have their beginning in "time."

For this reason, earthly happiness is very different from the "happiness" that exists in the moment of eternity. The happiness in earthly peace is the happiness that comes from thinking that one will never lose what one loves. But in the earthly city, everybody eventually loses what he loves, which is why earthly happiness is very imperfect. In the moment of eternity, "happiness," or peace, is in no way associated with normal human elation. It is not the same feeling produced when the material position of the city seems secure, when a town resists the force of change, or when a truce is declared between combatants. The "happiness" in heavenly peace is not related to earthly happiness at all. Rather, it is "blissful" and "blessed," "tranquil" and "without mental perturbations."[5] It is a happiness that does not come from preserving what one loves, but from having no loves or attachments to earthly life at all. It is the "happiness" that comes from existing in a moment of stillness, as Adam and Eve did before the fall, before "the eyes of both of them were opened."[6] It is an inner peace in which the human will is whole, where drives, tensions, and lusts no longer rend it asunder. It is a peace not in which one is happy, but in which happiness and wretchedness are no longer possible.

The aristocrat in the heavenly City of God emphasizes heavenly peace, not earthly peace. It is not social tranquility that he yearns for, but rather tranquility of the mind. Unlike the aristocrat in the City of Man, the aristocrat in the City of God craves not order and calm in the physical world, but rest in the war "between the spirit and the flesh." The peace that the aristocrat in the City of God experiences is not simply a pause before the next material catastrophe, but a moment of inner calm and stillness.

This is the peace yearned for by Tocqueville's American. Unlike the Old World aristocrat, Tocqueville's American did not yearn for immutability in this life. The constancy in the physical world that the Old World aristocrat tried to preserve was, in the life and mind of Tocqueville's American, something inconceivable. In Tocqueville's America, earthly life was unpredictable and turbulent, with every artifact created by man ultimately crushed by the force of democratic change that rolled on like a juggernaut. On and on that juggernaut rolled, leaving nothing standing in its wake. Whole towns were built overnight and then deserted just as quickly by those who pursued ambition elsewhere. Each decade, a new discovery in business or science would change the face of human relationships, causing a person's combination of neighbors, friends, and business partners to shift and the place called home to move. The world of democratic capitalism was a world of commotion and chaos.

But this is how the aristocrat in the City of God lives in the earthly city. This is how an aristocrat who cares less for calm and earthly peace functions in the world of force and matter. For Tocqueville's American, life in the physical world was restless—another goal always dangled before him—and his disposition was marked by an extreme love of independence. Tocqueville's American did not yearn for immutability in the physical world but in the heavenly world of spirit. Unlike the Old World aristocrat, Tocqueville's American believed that it was only in the afterworld that one could find the unalterable, the enduring, and the eternal. Only heaven did not change or grow old. Tocqueville's individualist imagined calm, peace, and repose, but he imagined them only in a world transcending the physical world. He contemplated peace by detaching himself from the cares of this world, not by shielding, securing, and preserving all that he had formed an attachment to. It is within the inner man, during one of the few quiet moments of life, that Tocqueville's American caught a glimpse of the peace and calm of eternity and opposed it to his chaotic life in "time."

In Tocqueville's work, a few passages transmit this sense of calm and reflectiveness among the Americans. He says of the Americans,

> They therefore profess their religion without shame and without weakness; but even in their zeal there generally is something so indescribably tranquil, methodical, and deliberate that it would seem as if the head far more than the heart brought them to the foot of the altar.[7]

In this passage can be detected the state of peace yearned for by the aristocrat in the City of God. It is a state of peace that is tranquil, not "happy," beyond emotion and beyond heart, one that is gained through deep contemplation. It is by looking inward into one's soul that the aristocrat in the City of God catches a glimpse of the divine order and the unchanging.

How the Aristocrat in the City of Man and the Aristocrat in the City of God Are Animated by Different Spirits

By adapting Augustine's understanding of time and eternity to the American experience, it was shown how the physical world of the Old World aristocrat came to live in the imagination of Tocqueville's American. Christian belief, public opinion, and republican principle in Tocqueville's American correspond to images drawn from the aristocrat's physical world. This is why touches of kinship unite Tocqueville's American and the Old World aristocrat. While their respective imaginations, like elastic bands, are stretched in different directions, certain fundamental relationships unite them.

Of those corresponding relationships, the perception of "time" in Tocqueville's American most clearly distinguishes between the animating spirits of the aristocrat in the City of Man and the aristocrat in the City of God. For both aristocrats, the imagination is dilated and distended, one glancing backward, the other glancing forward, as "length" is given to their perceptions of time (even though neither the past nor the future exists in any real sense). Within their respective illusions of time, both the Old World aristocrat and Tocqueville's American discerned a foreground and a distant horizon separated by a wide expanse. But these "distensions" in time generate different combinations of feelings, intentions, and sensibilities and cause the animating spirits of the two aristocrats to differ.

For the aristocrat in the City of Man, the fields of imagined space stretching into the past are littered with generations of families and age-old estates. It is between the imagined foreground and imagined distant horizon that the aristocrat in the earthly city nestles his character, defines his position in the universe, and captures a moment of repose. For the aristocrat in the City of God, the fields of imagined space stretching into the future are littered with private ambitions, long-range business goals, and way stations towards personal wealth, with the Christian afterworld serving as the distant edge to that wide plain. Within that imagined space, the aristocrat in the City of God finds his bearings and projects a course through life. But in doing so, he does not review images of a human past so much as he telescopes his mind into the future. Rather than calmly reflecting over a history of the earth, he restlessly approaches what is still unknown, and advances towards the celestial city that he believes to lie in heaven.

In his essay "On the Uses and Disadvantages of History for Life," Nietzsche argues that healthy life requires the human imagination to be bounded by a horizon.[8] The imagination of the individual, he writes, must be enclosed within an atmosphere shielding man from the chaotic and meaningless universe. Only within such an enclosure, separated from cold nature, can a person thrive. Only when surrounded by comprehensible norms, beacons of experience, and time-honored customs can the individual will with vigor, declare with confidence, and give meaning to his or her conduct. Without this protective, life-giving atmosphere, the individual shrivels and becomes cynical, losing all ability to march forward, to fight for a cause, or to be seized by a passion. Nietzsche argues that an overdeveloped historical sense, a mind that erases the horizon by dwelling on all that history has produced outside of one's own culture, softens and enervates the mind and makes a person weak from "sleeplessness." The bounded horizon may be antiscientific, he argues, but is necessary for healthy life.

In a way, both the Old World aristocrat's perception of the past and the Tocquevillian American's perception of the future are examples of imagined states bounded by a horizon. Within their respective temporal envelopes, the Old World aristocrat and Tocqueville's American played out the drama of life with energy, vitality, and confidence. Both secured a veiling cloud to protect fundamental beliefs from "timeless" knowledge. Centered within their respective illusions of time were particular visions that supported a unique complement of attitudes and convictions. The illusions of "time" may have been little more than misty vapor, but to the imaginations of both, they were as hard and unyielding as iron rings.

For the aristocrat, all that came before him helped preserve him and though he could not divine change, the aristocrat looked back towards the past with love, loyalty, piety, and reverence and preserved the past for future generations. Nietzsche's discussion of the "antiquarian" conception of the past provides insight into the mental experience of the aristocrat. Of the aristocrat, he writes,

> The history of his city becomes for him the history of himself; he reads its walls, its towered gate, its rules and regulations, its holidays, like an illuminated diary of his youth and in all this he finds again himself, his force, his industry, his joy, his judgement, his folly and vices. Here we lived, he says to himself, for here we are living, and here we shall live, for we are tough and not to be ruined overnight. Thus with the aid of this "we" he looks beyond his own individual transitory existence and feels himself to be the spirit of his house, his race, and his city.[9]

For Tocqueville's American, the imagined temporal space did not instill a drive to preserve or immortalize, but rather to change, to create anew, and to undo all that had come before. The early American individualist ignored tradition, as Tocqueville notes, "in the continual movement that agitates a democratic community, the tie that unites one generation to another is relaxed or broken; every man there readily loses all trace of the ideas of his forefathers or takes no care about them."[10] Instead, the American individualist contemplated a lifetime of potential accomplishments and satisfied ambitions. What dominated his thoughts was not the past that came before him but the future that lay ahead. That future terminated in an afterworld that, by the peculiar features of the faith inspiring it, demanded perseverance more than reverence, resilience more than respect.

This point is essential to understanding the differences between the animating spirits of the two aristocrats. For the aristocrat in the heavenly city, the Christian afterworld serves the same purpose as unchanging tradition does for the aristocrat in the earthly city. But the Christian afterworld and unchanging tradition have different effects on the human personality. The

Christian afterworld stands in the imagined distant future and demands continence and perseverance. Tradition draws the mind into the imagined distant past and demands reverence and respect.

Tradition forced the Old World aristocrat to carry a burden of memories, to immortalize all that had come before him, and to preserve the past in an unchanging state. In this way, his industry was infused with meaning and purpose. The idolized past flowed through the smallest activities of the aristocrat's life. Both the grandest church and the smallest ancestral treasure reminded him how glorious life was and how future generations depended on his unfailing power to preserve.

In a curious parallel, the Christian afterworld forced Tocqueville's American to carry a burden of longing, expectation, and unfulfilled hope, and to strive for that which he might achieve in this world before finding rest in the next. In this way, his industry was infused with courage and staying power, and the daily activities of life were endowed with holy meaning and purpose. Never sure of one's salvation, never sure that one had received the gratuitous gift of God's election, and always aware that one could "fall away" and become incontinent anytime up to the moment of death, Tocqueville's American was compelled to persevere, not to preserve. But behind both the perseverance of Tocqueville's American and the Old World aristocrat's urge to preserve were the same intense devotion to duty, the same unyielding and unwavering will, the same belief that life was a test not be failed, and the same belief that great and noble purpose was insinuated in the smallest projects of life.

The imagined temporal space of the Old World aristocrat provided him with a bounded horizon, and within that space he idolized all that had come before him, preserved that honored tradition, and affirmed life through an act of conservation. Tocqueville's American was also provided with a bounded horizon, and within his envelope he glimpsed an afterworld that would follow his death, reflected on the meaning of that most distant layer of time, and affirmed life through steadfastness, steadiness of will, and sustained drive. Tocqueville says of the American individualist, "Thus, forever seeking, forever falling to rise again, often disappointed, but not discouraged, he tends unceasingly towards that unmeasured greatness so indistinctly visible at the end of the long track which humanity has yet to tread."[11] That experience was different from the experience of the Old World aristocrat. In the American experience, change was incessant, and self-interest was the moving power. But Tocqueville's American had instilled within him the same intensity of purpose, the same focused energy, and the same confidence in direction found in the aristocrat. By linking the destiny of a human lifetime with the decrees of Eternity, earthly activity remained charged with purpose.

Within the temporal envelopes of the Old World aristocrat and Tocqueville's American, in imaginations that were stretched into distant "time," conviction, drive, and purpose took root and became not just accepted conventions but firm and unyielding instincts. For the aristocrat living in the earthly city, those instincts were sustained through reverence, respect, and awe for that which had come before. For the aristocrat living in the heavenly city (i.e., Tocqueville's American), those instincts were sustained through perseverance, tirelessness, and constancy as one moved closer to the Glory that was to be. The Old World aristocrat looked into the past until his mind grew dim among the gathering mists of oblivion. Tocqueville's American looked forward with the same effect. For both figures, imagined time drew a fence around the person and, within their respective enclosures, the two types approached life with confidence, self-assuredness, vigor, and fire.

How the Christian Afterlife for the Aristocrat in the City of God is an Augustinian, not a Platonic, Concept

Nietzsche was the philosopher of aristocracy, but he did not see that the Christian belief in an afterworld could distend the human imagination and create a life-giving atmosphere similar to the aristocrat's reverence for tradition. He did not appreciate that nobility, vitality, and confidence could survive with the support of this special religious mechanism and that Christians could possess a dynamic, aristocratic outlook. In part, this is because of his vehement opposition to any belief in an afterworld, especially the Christian afterworld. He argued that the popular belief in an afterworld was an expression of nihilism and *ressentiment*, and that an afterworld, like all "ideal" worlds, was created not in the service of life but to deny life. Such a belief, he insisted, was not in any way compatible with the life-affirming, noble spirit of the aristocrat.

In such works as *The Anti-Christ, Twilight of the Idols, Beyond Good and Evil*, and *The Will to Power*, Nietzsche describes the Christian afterworld as especially grounded in fear and hatred, serving only those who fear nothingness after death or who resent the success of others in this world. The Christian afterworld, he argues, is a pain-easing fantasy, a kind of narcotic, which soothes the troubled mind by promising another life after death—a life in which the poor will triumph and the rich will suffer for their sins. He declares the fantasy of the afterworld, replete with promises of gratified pleasure—endless food and drink, comfort and relaxation—to be inspired by fear, resentment, and unfulfilled desire. Such a belief is destructive of life since real life, life on earth, is sacrificed in order to gain the promise of a future one.

Nietzsche believed that the Christian afterworld was modeled on the Platonic idea of a "real" world. A "real" world is unchanging and absolute and formed by shearing away man's flawed and earthly coil (the "apparent" world) from the spiritual ideals of justice and virtue. Nietzsche argued that "real" worlds are debilitating, and with some justification. The "real" world calls on one to deny or ignore earthly happiness for the sake of happiness in another world, and can provoke intense feelings of guilt, frustration, and cynicism when circumstances in the "apparent" world, such as poverty, sickness, and unhappiness, are constantly compared with the higher, more perfect state said to exist in a "real" world. Nietzsche correctly saw that certain interpretations of the Christian afterworld were built on a Platonic conception of the "real" world. One such example of *ressentiment* psychology is the Christian who immolates himself and pleads for death because the world is evil and the Kingdom of Heaven is good. The fantasy is designed to give the poor and luckless a reason to escape life.

But there is an important distinction to be made between a "real" world and an "afterworld" that is not made in Nietzsche's work. It is true that an afterworld, like a "real" world, is only imagined and does not physically exist. But as a fantasy, an afterworld need not be defined by the finest human qualities or the good untouched by the bad. It need not be a utopian state, so unlike life, serving only to calm the fearful, appease the angry, or satisfy the envious. The afterlife described in the cultures of the ancient Greeks, the American Indians, and the nineteenth-century African Zulus, societies based on the warrior-aristocratic tradition, demonstrate that a belief in an afterlife can coexist with a noble and dignified spirit.[12]

The African Zulu, for example, believed that honor and noble conduct were as important in the afterlife as they were in earthly life.[13] The afterlife did not signify an escape from the rule of the brave and the superior, but rather a continuation of that rule and therefore a continuation of struggle. The Zulu warrior expected to meet his family in the next life and, because he did not want to meet them covered with shame, he strived to conquer in this world, to act bravely and resolutely, and to win honor and fair fame. The belief in an afterlife did not give the Zulu warrior an excuse for weakness or consolation in failure, but rather compelled him to fight and win. While the Zulu afterlife may have been a fantasy, it was not a fantasy like the Platonic "real" world. It was not created by extracting all that was good in earthly life, confining it to a utopian state, and then declaring earthly existence to be evil and a sham. It did not invert the value structure of Zulu society, placing dishonor and failure at the top and honor and victory at the bottom, or stand for the very opposite of what Zulu society stood for. Rather than promising to numb the pain of life, to satisfy the longings of the weak and the vindictive, the Zulu afterlife urged one to relish life, to be ambitious, to plot to be great, and, in battle, to savor the glory in the blow.

The afterlife in Zulu culture is an expression of nihilism (according to Nietzsche's definition of the term), which Nietzsche specifically condemns. Nietzsche does say in certain passages that nihilism, or the creation of a fictitious belief system, can be an expression of powerfulness and vital spirit,[14] and perhaps he would have admired the Zulu's belief in an afterworld. But Nietzsche certainly did not believe the Christian afterworld to be created in active or positive nihilism. He was convinced that Christianity was simply Platonism for the masses and that the Christian afterworld was just a modification of the life-denying "real" world of the Platonists.

It is a curious lapse, then, that Nietzsche does not recognize the tremendous energy that Augustine devotes in *The City of God* to criticizing "those who think we should worship them [the gods] for the sake of the life which is to be after death."[15] Augustine also heaps scorn on the Platonic afterlife.

Augustine exposes the contradictions in the theories of the Platonist, Porphyry, who repeated Plato's contention that the body is a prison to be escaped from, but who also argued that the "world is an animal, and a very happy animal, which [Porphyry] wished to be also everlasting."[16] Augustine points out that if Porphyry's modification of Plato is true, if life can be loved for the happiness it gives, then a person cannot avoid losing happiness in Platonic thought since Platonic happiness is contingent upon the soul leaving the body.[17] If happiness could be found in life, Augustine argued, then Platonic happiness would have to be completely redefined. Plato would have to learn to love life.

Augustine exposes other contradictions in the Platonic theory of the afterlife. The Platonists argued that the human soul is constantly leaving and reentering human bodies. But if this were the case, Augustine noted, their promise of eternal happiness after death would be impossible. This is because the Platonists also insist that the body is a source of misery, and for the soul always to be returning to the body is to return the soul to a source of misery.[18] The reward of the afterlife in Platonic philosophy, according to the Platonist's own theories, must be a lie.

Augustine mocks the Platonists who worship the afterlife at the expense of life, repeating Virgil's claim that, following death, purified souls "with a blind propension yearn, To fleshly bodies to return."[19] Porphyry's subsequent effort to disentangle himself from all condemnation of life, by noting that perhaps the soul is not necessarily recirculated after death, simply moves Augustine to sarcasm. Augustine charged that in reversing himself, Porphyry corrected the illustrious master, Plato, because Porphyry preferred truth to Plato.[20]

Augustinian Christianity has within it the idea of an afterworld, but one that differs considerably from the afterworld of the Platonists. God's grace, Augustine writes, is designed not to help people "escape their suffering," but to bear those sufferings with a stout heart.[21] This idea of grace helps distinguish between the two afterworlds. The afterworld in Augustinian thought inspires people to persevere and, with God's grace, to move forward to the time when they will gain eternal rest. This idea is extensively discussed in Augustine's essay *On the Gift of Perseverance*. The Augustinian moves towards God's kingdom and glory and obeys not just for a time but to the end.[22] The afterworld represents a call to be strong, to struggle through the trials of life, and to show fortitude in the long journey through earthly "time." This spirit is the opposite of that inspired by the Platonic afterworld. The latter promises an escape from life and excuses those who choose not to move forward at all.

Augustine's understanding of the afterworld can be discerned within the mind-set of Tocqueville's American. For Tocqueville's American, the belief in an afterworld dilated the imagination and created a temporal envelope that sustained healthy instincts, positive attitudes, and the will to live and succeed. Its main psychological purpose was to form the most distant edge of an imagined temporal expanse, separating the present from the future and giving the mind the perception of depth. It helped Tocqueville's American plot a course into the imagined future, one requiring struggle and perseverance to finish. Rather than contract earthly time by presenting to the mind a close-up of what was to be, a vision molded by the wants and desires of the present, it distended earthly time, or the perception of earthly time, by presenting itself to the mind as merely a dot on the horizon, without content or detail. Rather than instill guilt and fear among the successful or ease feelings of hatred and envy among the luckless, it inspired all to move through life with force and vitality and to look upon as noble that which could be accomplished in a single lifetime.

Tocqueville's Christian was not Nietzsche's Christian. His urge was not to crawl and serve. He was not the believer who, with bent brows and humble mien, muttered pathetically to some unseen divinity, hoping to be rescued from all that was hopeless. The afterworld of Tocqueville's American was not just a phantasm of the poor and the weak, a sweet dream in which for a little while all fears might be forgotten. There was enough of a difference in the way nineteenth-century Americans and (Nietzsche's) Europeans imagined an afterworld for Tocqueville to comment on the phenomenon.

Tocqueville says,

In the Middle Ages the clergy spoke of nothing but a future state; they hardly
cared to prove that a sincere Christian may be a happy man here below. But the
American preachers are constantly referring to the earth, and it is only with
great difficulty that they can divert their attention from it . . . and it is often
difficult to ascertain from their discourses whether the principal object of religion
is to procure eternal felicity in the other world or prosperity in this.[23]

In Tocqueville's America, the afterlife was not a reflecting mirror that
loomed close by, showing the oppressed all that they desperately wanted to
see and obscuring all that was too painfully real, but a distant world that was
itself obscure. Tocqueville recognized that the belief in an afterworld could
be inspired by a variety of feelings. It could be a nihilistic fantasy steeped in
anger and resentment, directing all human energy away from this life and
towards a "real" (fantasy) life in eternity, as it was for some during the Middle
Ages. It could be forged in fear, as it was for the Christian who was good
because he feared the pain of hell, of whom Augustine joked was not afraid
of sinning, but simply afraid of burning. Or it could form part of a belief
system that concentrated man's attention on this life, that gave length to
earthly time, and that encouraged steadfastness in the pursuit of worldly
success. The spirits behind the two systems of belief are completely different.
And it is the latter (Augustinian) view that has the potential within it to
transform a simple believer into an aristocrat in the City of God. The
aristocrat in the City of God, with his special belief in an afterworld, has
more in common with the aristocrat in the City of Man who worships
tradition than he does with the embittered Christian Platonist who condemns
life for the sake of an afterlife.

Tocqueville believed the practice of religion to be essential to the health of
a democratic society because, from time to time, it encouraged individualists
to glance beyond the world of material gain that so dominated their lives.
Religion, he believed, elevated a person's thoughts and lured the mind away
from everyday concerns. It lifted opinions and tastes to a higher level,
permitting a discrimination of value and a sense of proportion different from
what was taught in the common world of gossip and novelty. It is with this
idea that he praised the religious worship of the American. Such worship was
not conceived during a rush of petty passion, but rather only when "the
American at times steals an hour from himself . . . laying aside for a while
the petty passions which agitate his life."[24] The idea of an afterlife in
American Christianity was not forged in extreme emotion, in fear and anger,
but rather surfaced in the mind when fear and anger were pushed aside.
Religion in Tocqueville's America was not steeped in passionate feeling but,
in a way, was opposed to passion,[25] and hence constituted an expression of

spirit that is the very opposite of *ressentiment*. For this reason Tocqueville saw something positive in American Christianity and stated, in defense of religion and the belief in an afterworld, that it would be better for people to believe "that the soul of man will pass into the carcass of a hog" than to believe "that the soul of man is nothing at all."[26]

The Christian Afterworld and the Feeling of Detachment in Tocqueville's American

One person who came to America during the nineteenth century and failed to understand the country's new spirit of Christian worship was the novelist Anthony Trollope. Trollope studied America through the prism of European custom and found American Christianity to be seriously flawed. In *North America*, Trollope describes the "rowdy" manner in which the Americans recited their prayers, stripping religion of "that reverence which is, if not its essence, at any rate its chief protection."[27] He says, "There is, I think, an unexpressed determination on the part of the [American] people to abandon all reverence, and to regard religion from an altogether worldly point of view."[28] Later in the same work, Trollope lends support to the idea of a "national religion" as a way to counter the new American form. "National religion," Trollope believed, could lift religion out of the everyday world of petty disputes, competitive urges, and vulgar display that dominated American religious life.[29] Of American Christianity, he writes, "one hardly knows where the affairs of this world end, or where those of the next begin," and it is never quite clear whether the American preachers are "doing stage-work or church-work."[30] Even Bible chapters, he exclaimed, were the subjects of political debate and comedy, and it was "a common thing for a clergyman to change his profession and follow any other pursuit," as if religious work were no different than any other kind of employment.[31]

Trollope came to these conclusions because he surveyed American Christianity from an Old World perspective. In the Old World, religion was incorporated into a larger culture of tradition, with churches, old families, historical monuments, and time-honored customs sustained through common expressions of reverence. From the perspective of traditional, or reverential, Christianity, nineteenth-century American Christianity appears insipid, uninspiring, disrespectful, and vulgar.

Christianity in America was not incorporated into a culture of tradition because no culture of tradition existed on the continent. There was little that was continuing or changeless in America. But through a completely different mechanism, through perseverance rather than reverence, American Christianity was able to sustain in its followers an unconditional faith, a great hope, and a stern certainty in what was right. By preaching steadfastness and perseverance, Christianity in America was able to convey a sense of high purpose, and while its believers may have been "rowdier" and more disorderly than those who worshipped in reverence, the same resoluteness of belief found among Christians of the Old World was also evident among American Christians. Nineteenth-century American Christianity accomplished what traditional (or reverential) Old World Christianity had accomplished for centuries, but in an entirely new way, one that was strange and confusing to Trollope.

Trollope recommended strict rules of conduct in religious matters and urged respect and reverence for religious institutions. But in making these recommendations, Trollope was not really separating religion from the basest impulses of persons so much as he was integrating religion into a society founded on emulation and rivalry. By elevating the status of religion and calling for a "national religion," he was merely strengthening the tie between religion and a general culture that prized status. What disturbed Trollope most about American Christianity was not that it gave itself over to worldly things, but that within a hierarchy of worldly things, religion was not preeminent. It did not command sufficient reverence. Trollope's effort to accord religion higher status is really an effort to incorporate religion into a pyramid of status, one that in the Old World descended from the greatest lords and ladies to the lowest toilers and servants. Such action represents the very opposite of shielding religion from the world of opinion and prejudice. By not being incorporated into a pyramid of status, American Christianity was, in a way, far more otherworldly than the Old World form, even though its believers were "rowdier" and less respectful.

The obsession with relative status was a prominent feature of Old World culture, evident among both peasants and aristocrats. That obsession is rooted in the spirit of reverence, which is the same spirit animating the order of Roman aristocrats in late antiquity and which Augustine condemned. There is an important connection between aristocracy and the reverential form of Christianity supported by Trollope, and it is not surprising that an aristocratic culture tries to integrate religion into a pyramid of status.

After the collapse of Rome, aristocracy continued to flourish throughout the Old World and did so in a very interesting way. While it presented a view of the world that differed considerably from the Christian view, it absorbed many of Christianity's institutions. The Old World was filled with aristocrats who were nominally Christian, but the animating spirit of the Christian aristocrat was not the Augustinian spirit of perseverance. It remained the aristocratic spirit of reverence for a human past.

This idea is suggested in the work of numerous philosophers. Nietzsche argues that in the species of history most connected with aristocracy, it is a respect for the past and a strong belief in tradition that commands the mind, not revealed religion. Tocqueville notes that in aristocratic society, heroic and glorious human achievements are inserted along the chain that links the common man to the divine, and that the worship of religion in aristocratic society is often obscured by a more fervent worship of a human past. Of the French aristocracy on the eve of the Revolution, Tocqueville says it was ready at any moment to "return to its ancient gods: valor, glory, and . . . magnanimity."[32] Max Weber makes a similar observation, writing,

> a warrior's style of life has no affinity with the idea of a kindhearted Divine providence nor with the idea of an otherworldly God who makes systematic ethical demands. Concepts like "sin," "salvation," or religious humility" are not only remote from the feeling of dignity which is characteristic of all politically dominant strata . . . but they [are] also seen as a direct insult to that dignity.[33]

The Old World aristocrat may have been a Christian, but he still believed that earthly life was spent in a part of the world that God did not create. With a tremendous pride, it was a reverence for tradition, for a glorious human past, that inspired and motivated the aristocrat, not perseverance in God.

Reverence is rooted in fear, and it was through fear that aristocracy in the City of Man modified Christian worship. Reverence requires a person to look outside of himself or herself and fear someone or something, with that fear subsequently being translated into reverence.[34] Layers and layers of reverence are created as each person who fears that which is unknown, incomprehensible, or believed to be terrible is forced into a lower position when the fear is converted into reverence. Hence, the peasant reveres the noble, the noble reveres the king, the king reveres the wizard, and all revere monuments from the past, whose origins are often unknown but that have survived a length of time that is terrifying to the human imagination.[35]

The reverential form of Christianity is an aristocratic adaptation that dominated the Old World for centuries. It is the same form of Christianity that Trollope was most familiar with, and it is logically found in those societies guided more by a respect for tradition than perseverance towards some distant end. This is because a system of tradition is based on a reverence for the past, which is based on fear of the mysterious, the inexplicable, and the more powerful, and that fear can be directed towards a monument from the past, a conquering tyrant, or the priest of a higher religion. When Trollope argues that reverence is the "essence" of religion, he is espousing a species of faith that is based on fear and terror, that tries to make its followers awestruck, and that is part of the more general pattern of fear and reverence prevailing in aristocratic society.

The spirit of reverence leads to intense status-consciousness among its adherents. This is not simply because it categorizes people according to relative importance, but because it categorizes them on the basis of fear. Reverence leads to a fusion of imaginations. The one who is revered commands the entire soul of the one who reveres, as the higher recognizes the all-consuming fear in the lower. At the same time, fear envelopes the entire personality of the lower, for the fear must be of sufficient magnitude to reduce him or her to a state of awe. In this way, a bond formed in reverence is an extremely intimate one. It is not just a facet of one's self that is involved when bonding with others in reverence, but one's entire identity. The tie in reverence is a tie between one who has conquered and another who has surrendered. Hence, the gradations of status that follow when reverence is practiced on a massive scale do not merely divide people according to relative success or skill, but according to relative worth as a person. When one is surpassed in a hierarchy of status based on reverence, one is scorned, and if those who are scorned are not in awe of the higher, they are embittered by their fall and resent the arrogance of those who believe they have conquered.

If the animating spirit of the aristocrat in the City of Man is the spirit of reverence, the animating spirit of the aristocrat in the City of God is the spirit of perseverance. The spirit of perseverance was the spirit of Tocqueville's American, and rather than incite tremendous status-consciousness, it engendered the opposite feeling of detachment.

In Tocqueville's America, the reverential form of Christianity was not dominant. Perseverance towards the future, not respect for a human past, emboldened Tocqueville's American and charged that person with a sense of holy duty. But perseverance, unlike reverence, does not have within it the potential to establish intimate connections between people. The spirit of reverence can be applied to both religious worship and human relations because it is based on fear. Fear tightly couples people's imaginations, causing some to look up in awe and reverence and others to look down with scorn and contempt. Perseverance can be directed towards an earthly enterprise like a business goal, but, unlike reverence, it can not be directed towards others.[36] Only reverence can produce a reconfiguration of the ties that bind people. Perseverance is a completely internal experience and has no counterpart in reverence's fear and terror. It provides no conduit for those living in the present to commingle their imaginations and identities.

In the Old World, fear and reverence caused the mixing of imaginations to be so complete that the identity of one person could almost be absorbed into that of another. Tocqueville comments on the personality of the "confidential servant" in aristocratic Europe, noting that "the master readily obtains prompt, complete, respectful, and easy obedience from his servants, because they *revere* [my italics] in him not only their master, but the class of masters."[37] He continues, "In his predicament the servant ultimately detaches his notion of interest from his own person; he deserts himself as it were, or rather *transports* [again my italics] himself into the character of his master and thus he assumes an imaginary personality."[38]

The close ties between master and servant in aristocratic Europe were nurtured in an environment of fear and reverence. Fear and reverence caused the imaginations of the two figures to mix together, and while it made one person awesome and the other person "mean,"[39] it caused the two to build a deep and lasting bond. Tocqueville says of the master and servant in the Old World, "They are connected by common reminiscences, and however different they may be, they grow alike."[40]

Such a union is not possible among people animated by the spirit of perseverance because there is no socially relevant ingredient in perseverance to support the mixing of imaginations. Perseverance as a system of belief leaves people detached. Without reverence and respect, or fear and terror, with which to forge intimate linkages between them, individuals do not expose their feelings of self-worth to the thoughts and opinions of others. Status competition requires human minds to be connected in series, for in the quest for status, it is relative position that is most important and not one's absolute level of success. A high degree of intimacy is required between people for status-consciousness to arise, and this was not present in Tocqueville's America. Compared to the master and servant in aristocratic Europe, the people in Tocqueville's America were more equal and therefore "naturally almost alike," but they never achieved the same degree of closeness found between persons in the Old World and, therefore, they "always remain[ed] strangers to one another."[41]

Because the aristocrat in the City of God is animated by the spirit of perseverance rather than the spirit of reverence, extreme status-consciousness is replaced by a feeling of detachment. Like the aristocrat in the City of Man, the aristocrat in the City of God has piety and conviction, but he does not combine those feelings with the urge to emulate and rival. Status-consciousness requires a sharing of identity, for it is the sharing of identity that encourages the belief that one man's rise constitutes another man's fall. Sharing of identity is possible in reverence, but not in perseverance. In perseverance, a holy fervor directs the eyes of the worshipper away from the dominion of another's imagination and towards the dominion of a world after death. It provides no outlet or contact point at which a person might mix his or her imagination with the imagination of another. It yields no point of entry like that found in fear and terror, where the imaginations and identities of two persons cross into each other and become interlocked.

In postwar America, the decline in a belief in an afterworld has been followed by a decline in the spirit of perseverance and, with it, a decline in the feeling of detachment. While the spirit of perseverance can be observed among individualists in contemporary America—for example, in the planning of careers or the conduct of a business—that perseverance is not real perseverance, just as nostalgia for the past is not real reverence for the past. The perseverance of Tocqueville's American was part of a holy mission that encompassed an entire lifetime. It was not practiced simply a few years at a time. As Augustine wrote, the mind-set of the person who bears the yoke of eternity on his shoulders is different from the mind-set of the person who bears the yoke of his own immediate desire and who perseveres only to gratify that desire. Both persevere, but it is not the same kind of perseverance, even while the two are persevering.[42] The early American feeling of detachment, grounded in real perseverance, had to change as the meaning of perseverance changed. The result in postwar America has been a mixing together of human imaginations not seen since the Old World. The result has been a society based no longer on the spirit of perseverance, but on the spirit of fellow-feeling.

11

The Fall of the Aristocrat in the City of God and the Rise of the "Organization Man"

In the change in American culture, a transitional figure stands between Tocqueville's American and the contemporary expressive individualist. That figure, henceforth to be referred to as the "organization man" after William Whyte's characterization of the new type,[1] subscribed to values and aspired to goals that were distinctive in the movement of American individualism. The organization man of 1950s America, with his special character and unique rhythm of life, represents the earliest evidence that aristocracy in the City of God had come to an end. It is with the rise of the organization man that an empire of the imagination was overturned.

The End of Real Perseverance and the Feeling of Detachment

The feeling of detachment in Tocqueville's American was a consequence of the spirit of perseverance, and that spirit originated in a particular form of Christian worship. In Tocqueville's America, a strong belief in an afterworld distended the imagination of the individualist just as reverence for the past distended the imagination of the Old World aristocrat. Because of the special features of the American system of belief, Tocqueville's American combined nobility, confidence, and self-assuredness with a feeling of detachment, while the Old World aristocrat combined nobility, confidence, and self-assuredness with extreme status-consciousness.

When the mental commitment underlying early American Christian worship disappeared, when, more specifically, an afterworld no longer served as the most distant edge in an illusion of time, the spirit of perseverance began to weaken and the feeling of detachment began to fade. An unusual variant of human motivation died back into the common stock, and a new species was born. That new species, based on fellow-feeling, replaced the spirit of perseverance and established a new spirit of human motivation. As the spirit of perseverance is the animating spirit of the aristocrat in the City of God, its decline must signal a decline in aristocracy.

While a weakening of the belief in an afterworld initiated the decline of Tocqueville's America, the reason for its passage is unclear. The change is as fundamentally mysterious as that which caused feudal traditions revered for centuries to suddenly lose their capacity to instill awe and degenerate into novelties fit only for a museum or a library. In both cases, the exact force initiating change and overcoming the tremendous power of inertia within the human personality remains hidden. In both cases, the human beings concerned appear to be little more than the puppets of destiny.

Tocqueville says that change presents the greatest threat to tradition, for when something changes, it loses its awesomeness and ability to command respect. That simple explanation for the collapse of aristocratic tradition may be the most accurate one, though it cannot account for the collapse of the early American system of belief. While change threatens tradition, it does not threaten a strong belief in the kind of afterworld imagined by Tocqueville's Christian individualist, and this is most clearly evident in the fact that change in democratic America coexisted with fervent religious belief. When aristocracy lives in the City of God, it does not require the earthly city to be at a standstill. Instead, notes Tocqueville, the early American system of belief had a different competitor. It was an obsession with the present, with the "thousand petty selfish passions of the hour,"[2] with all the glitter that temptation spreads before lusting eyes, that posed the greatest threat to a religious belief that dilated a person's imagination by telescoping it into the future.

As the individual casts his glance beyond the present and focuses his attention on the edge of time, a lengthy path is perceived by the mind such that the rhythm of life becomes one of slow and steady advancement.[3] When that person no longer gazes on a distant horizon, but rather on the satisfaction of an immediate passion, the present looms larger than the past, and the imagined horizon encompasses a shorter period of time. That new period of time, from the Augustinian perspective of eternity, is really no "shorter" than the period encompassing an entire lifetime; both images of time are merely projections of the imagination and do not exist in physical space. But when the "length" of time within an imagined projection of time is "shortened," when the endpoint of that projection becomes the satisfaction of an immediate desire, the entire perception of time becomes linked to the instability of human desire, and perpetual fluctuation, rather than slow and steady advancement, becomes the new imagined experience of life.

Tocqueville saw the democratic tendency to focus on the irresistible wants of the present to be in conflict with a religion that emphasizes distant objectives and lengthens the perception of time. A fundamental tension exists between a distant afterlife and the material present in a democratic society, like the tension between tradition and change existing in aristocratic society. That tension may explain why the imagined temporal experience of Tocqueville's American began to contract, why the range between the immediate present and the object of desire living in the future began to "shorten," and why, for the individualist, the afterworld receded beyond the conscious edge of distant time, and some earthly objective took its place.

The decline of the spirit of perseverance has led to the reestablishment of bridges between human imaginations similar to those that existed in aristocratic society. The spirit of perseverance focused the mind of Tocqueville's American on a point in distant time and maintained that focus for an entire lifetime. Unlike reverence, the spirit of perseverance contains no secondary power within it to shape human relationships in the present. It closes off the imagination from the imaginations of others. It shuts individuals up within themselves, rendering them incapable of bonding with others through deep expressions of intimacy or slavish devotion. Tocqueville's American was wedded to a belief in eternity, and that belief separated each person from the next.

The decline of perseverance signaled a return of the American to the City of Man—to the fears, loves, hatreds, and competitive struggles of the earthly world. But instead of being based on the inegalitarian principle of reverence, the new connections between people in postwar America came to be based on the egalitarian principle of "fellow-feeling." The spirit of fellow-feeling establishes the link between the Old World and post-Tocquevillian America. It represents the principle of equality applied to a much older system of belief, one that encouraged the commingling of human imaginations.

The Collapse of Detachment and the Reestablishment of Status-Consciousness

The descriptions of postwar American life found in the sociology literature of the 1950s are so well known as to be almost banal, but by placing them alongside my earlier descriptions of behavior in the aristocratic and peasant peer groups of the Old World, they take on a new meaning. There is a startling resemblance between the society of the organization man and past aristocratic society. The small groups in which the organization man lived were not like the "small private circles"[4] of Tocqueville's America so much as they were like the peer groups of the Old World.

The organization man, like the Old World citizen, was extremely sensitive to issues of status, and he nestled his identity and perception of self-worth in the opinions of others. The organization man desired active approval, not just passive tolerance, for it was only within the "imaginary approval group" that he could define and evaluate himself.[5] He received direction and guidance not from an internal set of beliefs but from the external signals of peer group opinion. It was in this way that the organization man was "other-directed."[6]

Whyte notes that the organization man was a member of a group from the moment he left college.[7] At home, he was a member of a "court clique," a kind of subgroup within the suburban development. At work, he was a member of a "team." Whether he was attending church, involving himself in a neighborhood association, or playing during leisure hours, the organization man was joined to others in a vast "web of friendship."[8] In virtually every moment of his life, the organization man was firmly nestled inside some peer group.

The organization man pooled his imagination with the imaginations of others in the peer group, causing him to be guided and steadied from without. It was through "belonging,"[9] through the positive feedback of others, that the organization man improved the quality of his inner experience; the most fundamental aspects of his psychological being were dependent on others. His relative status within the peer group might stretch high or low, but the pressure for adjustment that would return him to the center of rest originated not in his own consciousness but in the imaginations of those surrounding him.

The experience in which identity is shared with others is very much like the experience of the peer group in the Old World. Whyte says of the peer group in postwar America that the "group is a tyrant; so also is it a friend, and *it is both at once*" (his italics).[10] The group demanded that a person yield a portion of his feelings to a larger body. In return, the person derived confidence and moments of good feeling from the positive thoughts of other peer group members. While the organization man cowered before the judgment of the group, he desperately craved membership in the group, for it was only through group membership that he recognized the power in his own spirit and the vital force of his own existence. Tocqueville's Americans clustered into small groups because of an "accidental similarity of opinions and tastes."[11] Organization men clustered into small groups because the meaning of life itself was a phenomenon experienced only relative to others.

In many ways, the peer group of the organization man functioned more like the peasant peer group of traditional society than the aristocratic peer group. The psyche of the organization man, like the feudal peasant, was raw and sensitive, and rather than honor the singular, the distinctive, and the victorious, the organization man inverted the aristocratic value structure and proclaimed harmony, community, equality, and sameness to be virtues. Like the feudal peasant, the organization man viewed competition and the potential for unequal outcomes as a threat to his own status.

Like the feudal peasant, the organization man experienced a decline in status when another person rose higher, and, with tremendous envy, he kept a careful watch on the material possessions of others. Small differences between people loomed large in the minds of organization men. Whyte says of the organization men,

> People have a sharp eye for interior amenities also, and the acquisition of an automatic dryer, or an unusually elaborate television set, or any other divergence from the norm is always cause for notice. Those who lack such amenities, conversely, are also noted. In one suburb, to cite a rather extreme example, a wife was so ashamed of the emptiness of her living room that she smeared the picture window with Bon Ami; not until a dinette set arrived did she wash it off.[12]

Mills describes a related phenomenon called "status panic," where a successful claim to prestige by one person meant another's recognition of that claim and a decline in relative status.[13] Relative status was such an important component of the organization man's feeling of self-worth that vacations became a way, if only for a short time, of buying the feeling of higher status.[14] Mills says of the vacation experience of the organization man,

> The expensive resort, where one is not known, the swank hotel, even if for three days and nights, the cruise first class—for a week. Much vacation apparatus is geared to these status cycles; the staffs as well as clientele play-act the whole set-up as if mutually consenting to be part of the successful illusion. . . . They provide a temporary satisfaction of the person's prized image of self, thus permitting him to cling to a false consciousness of his status-position.[15]

To counter the fear of lower status, harmony and sameness became important virtues in the peer group of organization men. No one in the peer group was permitted to dominate anyone else. Feverish attempts were made to keep everyone within the peer group on the same level, to "cut everyone down to size who stands up or stands out in any direction."[16] Riesman notes the change in the value structure in America, writing that "overt vanity is treated as one of the worst offenses, as perhaps dishonesty would have been earlier."[17]

The new value system permeated economic practices such as consumption. Weber's nineteenth-century Protestant capitalist limited his consumption because of strong ascetic beliefs, because he believed that a state of religious grace separated its possessor from the material world.[18] The organization man, on the other hand, was "kept within his consumption limits not by goal-directed but by other-directed guidance."[19] It was not the doctrine of worldly asceticism but the "fear of others' envy" that kept him from splurging, just as he was prevented from consuming too little "by fear of his own envy of others."[20]

The organization man of postwar America was taught to conform, to maintain harmony within the group, and to eliminate challenges to another person's feeling of self-worth by practicing the doctrine of sameness. In business, the organization man emphasized the importance of the team or the group. Well-roundedness and the ability to get along were considered essential qualities for success; unorthodox method, drive, imagination, and individualism, once held to be indispensable qualities for the successful entrepreneur, were now considered to be impediments to individual perform-ance.[21] When entering business, the organization man was subjected to a battery of psychological tests that were designed to assess whether he con-formed to a certain group type.[22] The person who was ambitious, who wanted to excel, or who would try to advance quickly was rejected.[23] The corporation in postwar America, like the peasant peer group in feudal society, demanded that people conform to a certain definition of what was average and normal. Any pattern of behavior deviating from the norm, any hint that one was unique or special or somehow higher, was threatening to the stability of the group because it threatened the inner confidence of peer group members.

The ideals of the organization man are quite similar to the ideals of Saint-Simonian socialism, which, as noted earlier, represent a continuation of the spirit of the peasant peer group into the modern age. Like the Saint-Simonian and the feudal peasant, the organization man praised harmony and group effort for their own sake; they were held to be moral ideals.[24] At work, group morale and the degree of harmony between organization men became, in some ways, more important than the efficiency of economic production.[25] At home, it was the group, not the individual, that determined when a luxury became necessary; the individual who vaunted worldly goods was offensive to the community and quickly ostracized.[26] The group was to the organization man what it was to the Saint-Simonian and the feudal peasant—the measure of all things.[27] By worshipping the group and proclaiming harmony within the group to be the highest virtue, the organization man tried to arrest or combat the impulse of individuals to stand out or excel.

The court cliques in the organization man's suburban development functioned very much like extended families, and the degree of intimacy expressed between clique members was, according to Whyte, a new feature in American community life.[28] In a way, the experience of the organization man in the court cliques was more like that of the immigrant in Boston's West End, studied by Herbert Gans, than of Tocqueville's American. What Gans observed in the immigrant peasant could also be observed in the organization man. Whyte says that the organization man might shrink or swell in status, but would always remain tethered to the clique.[29] Gans observed similar behavior in immigrant America, noting that peer group members would "act as if they were held together by ties of rubber, which they alternately stretch and relax, but rarely break."[30] The peer group of the organization man possessed the same egalitarian ideals, the same strict controls on deviant behavior, the same distinction between "us" (the court clique) and the outside world, and the same obsession with relative status as the peer group in immigrant America.

As a collection of numerous small peer groups, the entire structure of the society of the organization man resembles the structure of the Old World. The peer groups or court cliques were like the enclaves of feudal society. They were enclosures, defined by specific customs, rules of conduct, and levels of affluence and education, outside of which the inhabitants never ventured. Like the peer groups in aristocratic society, the peer groups in the society of the organization man created a vast array of different status positions, with horizontal layers measuring prestige and vertical strata measuring "differentness" (e.g., ethnicity).[31] The peer groups were like the cells of a honeycomb; inside they were calm, ordered, and stable,[32] and by staying within the confines of a cell, the organization man could mingle his imagination with others and be "other-directed" without subjecting himself to the high status claims of the highest and most successful. The grandest persons simply occupied another peer group, another "cell" within the honeycomb, and by identifying such people as "strangers," the organization man did not have to mingle his imagination with theirs. Thus, he was spared a serious threat to his confidence and feeling of self-worth. By creating an enormous number of status categories, by creating a giant honeycomb with many different cells, the person in the society of the organization man could mix his imagination with others and form a deep and intimate bond with them, all while shielding the deepest elements of his psyche from the power of another.[33]

Curiously, another personality type that existed in the Old World, but that

Tocqueville declared he never saw in democratic America—the *lackey*—also resurfaced in the society of the organization man. Tocqueville notes that in aristocratic society, there is a unique class a confidential servants that vanishes when a society becomes more democratic. Commenting on this type of servant, Tocqueville writes,

> He complacently invests himself with the wealth of those who command him; he shares their fame, exalts himself by their rank, and feeds his mind with borrowed greatness, to which he attaches more importance than those who fully and really possess it. . . . The servants of a great man are commonly most punctilious as to the marks of respect due to him, and they attach more importance to his slightest privileges than he does himself.[34]

The spirit of the *lackey*, of the employee who dissolves his or her identity into the identity of the employer, reappeared during the era of the organization man. Both Whyte and Packard note the conceit of the clerks and salespersons who proudly declared that they worked "for *Time*" or "for IBM." By merging their identities with the identity of the corporation, these employees hoped that by associating with a larger power, a certain reflected glory might be theirs.

Like the person living in the *ancien regime* who, with perverse pride, bragged about his dependence on the arbitrary will of the king,[35] the employee of the large corporation in the society of the organization man countered feelings of insignificance by dissolving himself into the corporation, and he felt a rush of personal glory by way of the might and power of the business entity that employed him. Like the king's subjects in feudal society, some of the organization men took pride in their own personal subjection, and this phenomenon persists in the society of expressive individualism.

This author, for example, has met hundreds of young professionals (e.g., doctors, lawyers, teachers) who work an enormous number of hours, often under grueling conditions, and do so with a perverse pleasure and pride that follows tremendous sacrifice. Because the institutions that they work for are so prestigious, they find honor in their debasement, glory in their submission, and gain a worthiness and kind of luster in their dependence on these powerful organizations. In the minds of these people, senseless and exhausting toil carries an air of grandeur, and thus they not only brag about the harsh conditions of their work, but fiercely defend the organization that they work for and construe any attack on the organization as an attack on themselves. Although it is to a large business and not a solitary master that some organization men and some contemporary expressive individualists have deferred, the spirit of the *lackey*, the "puerile vanity and paltry ostenta-tion,"[36] can nevertheless be discerned in the new state of servility.[37]

In sum, it is ironic that the era of the organization man, when judged from the vantage point of contemporary expressive individualism, is considered to represent the last "conservative" era in American cultural history before the rise of expressive individualism in the 1960s. The society of the organization man does not represent the last gasp of Tocqueville's America so much as it represents a rebirth of the Old World experience that actually preceded Tocqueville's America. With the rise of the organization man, a dramatic shift took place in America, and his society represents more the first moment of a revolution than the last moment of an *ancien regime*. In this way, it is not only expressive individualists who have erred in calling the society of the organization man "conservative," but also the traditional American conservatives who decry the movement of expressive individualism and long for the America of the 1950s. By embracing the values of the Old World, the society of the organization man represents in some ways the exact opposite of the spirit of Tocqueville's America, which traditional conservatives claim to defend.

Why the Society of the Organization Man Was Not a Form of Administrative Despotism

Tocqueville argued that the American democratic spirit was energetic and vital, grounded in ambition, confidence, responsibility, and a love of free-dom. But he believed that built into the democratic spirit was a tendency towards administrative despotism. Under administrative despotism, freedom and individual responsibility are exchanged for the promise of security and a guaranteed allowance of simple pleasures. That feeble spirit, which Tocque-ville prophesied, appears to be qualitatively similar to the spirit animating the American society of the organization man, especially given the latter's emphasis on harmony, stability, and security. But the connection between the two societies is really superficial, and Tocqueville's prediction concerning the path of change that American democracy would most likely follow is not accurate. The society of the organization man is not an expression of administrative despotism or a new variant of democratic existence. Rather, it signals a return of the interior sense of the American to the earthly City of Man.

Tocqueville notes that life under administrative despotism is similar to life under old forms of tyranny. But it is only in the authoritarian features of administrative despotism that Tocqueville discerns a similarity between the society that he prophesies and those societies that have come before. Even then the comparison is strained, as Tocqueville notes that authority in the society of administrative despotism is "more extensive," yet "more mild," and that compared to its practice in old, nondemocratic regimes, authority under administrative despotism "degrades men without tormenting them."[38] Tocqueville did not imagine a more important connection to exist between an aged and enervated democracy and the Old World. He envisioned administrative despotism as being nothing more than a mutation of a once-vibrant democratic form, without any serious psychological links to the Old World preceding the democratic age. He writes that the society of administrative despotism "is unlike anything that ever before existed in the world; our contemporaries will find no prototype of it in their memories."[39]

But the society of the organization man is very similar in spirit to a society that existed once before in the world. With its goals of "regularity," "budgetism," "harmony,"and "stability,"[40] and its antidemocratic tendency to view authority with less trepidation than change,[41] it has a prototype. The yearning for earthly peace, security, and contentment, the tendency of people to live in the mouths of admirers, the great concern for what another person thinks—each of these behavioral traits recalls the City of Man that Augustine described fifteen centuries ago. The society of the organization man does not represent a new form of human existence called administrative despotism so much as it represents just another mortal community built on the old theme of self-love.

Tocqueville says of individuals living under administrative despotism,

> Each of them, living apart, is as a stranger to the fate of all the rest; his children and his private friends constitute to him the whole of mankind. As for the rest of his fellow citizens, he is close to them, but he does not see them; he touches them, but he does not feel them; he exists only in himself and for himself alone; and if his kindred still remain to him, he may be said at any rate to have lost his country.[42]

But the spirit of atomism that Tocqueville described is almost the exact opposite of the spirit animating the society of the organization man—the spirit of fellow-feeling. In postwar America, "other-directed" persons fused their imaginations with the imaginations of others inside a tight-knit peer group, causing them to lose a certain independence of mind. A new intimacy was achieved in American society. Through a complex system of "radar," an organization man not only "touched" his fellow citizens but felt them intensely, for it was precisely the feelings and attitudes of other members within the peer group that gave the organization man a source of direction.[43]

The organization man was not atomized but in a way, as Riesman notes, even more "socialized" than the individualist type preceding him.

The American individualist had returned to the earthly city. He looked "outward" to find the meaning of who he was and in doing so came full circle, returning to the experience of a world preceding America. In his *Confessions*, Augustine describes how easily one can be pulled from the heavenly city of God back to the earthly city of man. In a chapter titled "Alypius and the Gladiators," Augustine's friend, Alypius, attends a gladiatorial show in Rome, but insists he will not be moved by it. He says, "Even if you drag my body into this place, can you fasten my mind and my eyes on such shows? I will be absent, though present, and thus I will overcome both you and them."[44] But during the show, Alypius is overcome by curiosity, and the roars of the crowd "entered him through his ears and opened up his eyes." Very quickly he becomes a full participant in the event, fixing all his senses on the fighters in the arena, becoming "drunk on blood and pleasure."

In this story, Augustine gives a full account of human weakness, the natural human tendency to shift attention away from that which is calm and immutable (i.e., God and eternity) and towards all that is shifting and clanking and roaring and glittering. It captures the meaning of the change from Tocqueville's America to the postwar society of the organization man. From the perspective of the earthly city, aristocracy in the heavenly city is without brightness, noise, or excitement. It lacks the pleasure one gains from being admired or praised, or from experiencing great passion or emotion. This is because aristocracy in the heavenly city is not built on the love of self but on the love of God. It is not built on a love of the moving and the shifting but on a love of calm order.

The rise of the organization man signals a return to the earthly city—to all the beautiful consumer goods that suggest status and "making it," to all the praise that comes from being "respected," to all the personal power that comes from having money, and to all the fears that one has neither respect, power, or money. Like Alypius, the eyes and ears of the organization man were opened, and he fixed his attention on all that occurred in his immediate surroundings. It was not order that he loved, as Tocqueville's American did, but all the moving and shifting.

Yet a difference remains between the earthly city of the Old World aristocrat and the earthly city of the organization man. The earthly city of the Old World aristocrat was animated by the spirit of reverence. The earthly city of the organization man was not. This is because there was no serious tradition in America to revere. In America, there was no great history of the human past. With the decline of the religious spirit of perseverance, it became no longer possible for the vastness of imagined time to enclose the infinite space of the human imagination, to give the mind borders. For the first time in human history, the supreme good no longer rested at either end of time. It is for this reason that the American individualist distended his imagination into the imagination of another. The organization man gained a knowledge of who he was not by peering into an imagined distant past or into an imagined distant future, but into the imagination of another person. It was there that he believed he would find the supreme good. The rise of the organization man signals a return to the earthly city, but to an earthly city animated by a new spirit. The spirit of the age is not reverence for the past or perseverance towards the future, but rather fellow-feeling within the present.

By blending his imagination with the imaginations of others, by bonding with others in a new intimacy, the organization man sought warmth and contentment to counter his longing, wholeness to counter his feeling of incompleteness, and stability to ease his anxieties and fears. It was not by reflecting on all that had come before him or by pondering eternity that the organization man established his bearings and made life comprehensible. Rather, it was by "meeting people," by "belonging,"[45] and by mixing his imagination with the imaginations of others that such essential psychological functions were performed. It was in this way that the organization man became "fulfilled."[46] The purpose of the peer group in the society of the organization man was not simply to bring together those who shared common interests, as was the purpose of the "private circle of friends" in Tocqueville's America. Rather, the peer group was a temple of souls in which each person established identity, found meaning, and discovered a reason for life's struggle.

One gets a sense of the momentous change ushered in by the organization man in the works of Riesman and Whyte. In *The Lonely Crowd*, Riesman alludes to a change in the imagined temporal experience of the American. Of the inner-directed person (i.e., Tocqueville's American) he says that "in general the ambition of the inner-directed person is directed to a long-range goal," that a "psychological gyroscope"[47] implanted within that person urges him forward and causes him to struggle "against both the intractability of the material and the limitations of his own powers."[48] What the inner-directed person most feared was that "he 'might not be able to make it,' "[49] that he might not be able to persevere or stay the course as he "pursued the stars."[50] Comparing that figure with the new, other-directed person who sought "the respect and, more than the respect, the affection, of an amorphous and shifting, though contemporary, jury of peers,"[51] one gets a sense of how significant the change was. The mind of the old American was telescoped into an imagined distant future while the mind of the other-directed person was telescoped into the imaginations of those who surrounded him in the present.

This same phenomenon can also be discerned in Whyte's comparison of the Protestant ethic of Tocqueville's American with the Social ethic of the organization man.[52] To Whyte, the Protestant ethic meant the "pursuit of individual salvation through hard work, thrift, and competitive struggle,"[53] and he contrasts that system of belief with the closer spiritual union that the Social ethic commands between people.[54] The Protestant ethic focused the attention of the individual on the idea of eternity such that in daily living he was "fortified by the assurance that he was pursuing his obligation to God."[55] The Social ethic directed the attention of the individual outward towards the imaginations of others, and "belonging" became the ultimate need of the individual.[56] The Social ethic was not grounded in a strong belief in an afterworld, but rather in the spiritual union of humanity in this world. It was no longer towards a goal in the imagined distant future that the American individualist struggled, but rather for the friendship and approval of those who lived in the present.[57]

Whyte notes that in the church of the organization man, with its "passive, live-and-let-live attitude," the old sectarianism was absent. The new church merely desired to be socially useful and that everyone "get along."[58] Whyte ponders whether the church of the organization man was really a church or just a social center since it did not attend seriously to doctrinal matters, which he felt to be an important church duty.[59]

In a way, Whyte's position as commentator on the church in the society of the organization man is similar to Anthony Trollope's position as commentator on the church in Tocqueville's America a century earlier. Trollope examined the church in Tocqueville's America from the perspective of an aristocratic society that was dominated by the spirit of reverence. In criticizing American religion, noting, for example, that one could barely tell the difference between "church work" and "stage work," Trollope did not see that a strong religious impulse permeated the new American system of Christianity and that serious and compulsive behavior could be expressed in a spirit of perseverance as well as in the old spirit of reverence he was used to.

Similarly, Whyte examines the church in the society of the organization man from the perspective of Tocqueville's America, which was dominated by the spirit of perseverance (i.e., the "Protestant ethic"). In criticizing the church of the organization man, asking whether it was really a church or just a social center, Whyte did not see that a strong religious impulse permeated the new system of Christian worship, nor that serious and compulsive behavior could be expressed in a spirit of fellow-feeling just as it was in the old spirit of perseverance he was used to. Both Trollope and Whyte reveal a tendency to analyze and judge the religious experience of a new society from the perspective of the society preceding it.

The Spirit of Fellow-Feeling

"Fellow-feeling" constitutes the spirit of a new age, an age that began with the society of the organization man and continues through into the present. Fellow-feeling is a variation on the love of self and for this reason resembles the spirit of reverence that animated the Old World. Like reverence, fellow-feeling finds the supreme good in that which can be touched by hand, seen by eye, projected by mind, and received by heart. It causes one to dwell on the corporeal, to be absorbed in small calculations of relative status, and to carefully navigate past the shoals of envy and arrogance, insult and flattery, and ambition and group-think so as to emerge proud and self-satisfied but still well thought of. People who are animated by the spirit of reverence and the spirit of fellow-feeling are charged with the same burden. At the same time, fellow-feeling represents a distinct form of human motivation, and it provides the basis for a new cultural form. For this reason, it is important to understand exactly what is meant by the term "fellow-feeling." In his work, *The Nature of Sympathy*, Max Scheler carefully analyzes this psychological phenomenon, and his definition will be used in this comparative study.

Scheler argues that fellow-feeling is a psychological state in which a deep and intimate tie has been established between two persons such that one person "participates" in the feelings of the other. Scheler writes,

> *All* fellow-feeling involves *intentional reference* of the feeling of joy or sorrow to the other person's experience. . . Fellow-feeling proper, actual "participation," presents itself in the very phenomenon as a *re-action* to the state and value of the other's feelings (his italics).[60]

In fellow-feeling, the imaginations of two persons are connected such that the experience of one exerts an effect on and produces a conformational change in the experience of the other.

William Whyte's organization man and David Riesman's "other-directed" person relied on the feelings of others to bolster their confidence and "adjust" themselves. Those people were, more fundamentally, animated by the spirit of fellow-feeling. Just as Scheler's actor "reacts" to the state of another person's feelings, rejoicing in another's joy or commiserating in another's sorrow, so did Riesman's "other-directed" person and Whyte's organization man "react" to the feelings and attitudes of peer group members. By building a bridge to another person's nature, by establishing a system of radar that would allow one to detect and interpret the psychological experiences of others, the postwar American sought to better define and evaluate his own internal experience. Another person's likes and dislikes, and the intensity of those respective feelings, were sensed by the organization man, who would then "adjust" himself, including his own likes and dislikes (e.g., his tastes and ambitions), in order to preserve harmony within the group.

It is in this way that fellow-feeling is similar to the old spirit of reverence. Both establish a basis for competitive struggle. Like an expression of reverence, an expression of fellow-feeling requires the presence of two people, not just one. It signifies a kind of communion of imaginations, where imaginations once separate and distinct are blended together. In both fellow-feeling and reverence, the internal experience of one person is influenced by (and actually comes to depend upon) the internal experience of another.[61] The subject becomes ensnared by what another thinks, by what another accomplishes, and by what another says.

The difference between reverence and fellow-feeling is that while reverence is based on fear and terror, fellow-feeling is not. When two individuals in aristocratic society were bonded together in reverence, they were bonded together in inequality. The mixing of their imaginations was grounded in fear such that one feared and the other was feared, making them unequal. Rather than "participating" equally in another person's imagination, the person who revered was dominated through that connection and, in the extreme case of the *lackey*, dissolved his entire imagination, his entire sense of self, into the imagination of another.

Because, in reverence, one whole being becomes bonded to another, a peculiar form of intimacy develops between the two persons. Few compartments within the personality of the one who reveres remain unexposed, by virtue of the terror consuming him, to the person who is revered. The person who is revered commands almost the entire being of the person who reveres. A peculiar and unequal union exists between two persons united by reverence, a union that in the Old World created a stronger and more intimate bond than that formed by self-interest in Tocqueville's America. In Tocqueville's America, the individualist shielded his or her imagination from those who occupied a superior position, and any bond of inequality was very weak, established only through the impersonal mechanism of contract.

In fellow-feeling, one "participates" in another person's imagination through a "knowledge" of another person's feelings,[62] not in fear. A bond is formed in a more voluntary and conscious manner than when it is created in reverence. In fellow-feeling, the imaginations of two beings are merged together on a more equal footing; the imagination of one does not overwhelm the imagination of the other. Nevertheless, in fellow-feeling, a relationship of intimacy is established between two people that did not exist previously. In that relationship one does not cower, as in reverence, so much as one "adjusts." By sensing and experiencing the feelings of another person, the subject's own feelings are affected, and a new pattern of behavior emerges. By repeating the experience of fellow-feeling over and over again, the subject becomes "socialized."

The experience of fellow-feeling was the experience of the organization man. Living in his court cliques and working in the Organization, his efforts to "get along" with others,[63] to "adjust,"[64] to be sensitive to others (even if the final purpose was to manipulate them),[65] to "feel" what his children were feeling and discern what they "felt" about him,[66] represent an effort on the part of the organization man to establish intimate connections with the imaginations of others. The organization man wholeheartedly loved himself, and it boosted his pride to serve as a gateway to both personal success and popular acceptance. His imagination was affected and guided from without, and while the state of union he entered into was more voluntary, or more "equal," than the state of union created in reverence, it nevertheless meant that in the society of the organization man, as in old aristocratic society, a door connecting the souls of individuals was suddenly thrust ajar.

The Spirit of Fellow-Feeling in the Workplace of the Organization Man

The difference between the organization man and Tocqueville's American on the point of "fellow-feeling" is quite subtle, for Tocqueville's American also had empathic qualities and could gain insight into another person's imagination. But in the case of Tocqueville's American, such knowledge did not necessarily lead to a conformational change within the imagination of the person who was sensing. That person did not necessarily "feel" with the other person or adjust his behavior in response to those new feelings.

Scheler notes the importance of such minute distinctions in the study of fellow-feeling, arguing, for example, that sympathy is not the same as fellow-feeling. Sympathy, in a way, implies a certain distance or detachment from the person who is the object of sympathy, and it is not the same as "feeling" what the other person is feeling. The experience of fellow-feeling, in which human souls are bonded together through a reciprocal participation in feeling, is the animating spirit of the organization man and not that of Tocqueville's American.

In his section on fellow-feeling, Scheler examines "brutality" and "cruelty," arguing that in a perverse way cruelty is more closely related to the experience of fellow-feeling than simple brutality. Cruelty is fellow-feeling's exact opposite; it requires one person to be quite sensitive to the pain of others.[67] Scheler writes,

> The cruel man owes his awareness of the pain or sorrow he causes entirely to a capacity for visualizing feeling! His joy lies in "torturing" and in the agony of his victim. As he feels, vicariously, the increasing pain or suffering of his victim, so his own primary pleasure and enjoyment at the other's pain also increases. Cruelty consists not at all in the cruel man's being simply "insensitive" to other peoples' suffering. . . . In contrast to cruelty, "brutality" is merely a disregard for other peoples' experience, despite the apprehension of it in feeling.[68]

Scheler's distinction between "cruelty" and "brutality," his observation that "cruelty, unlike "brutality," requires one to be both sensitive to and influenced by the feelings of another, (making cruelty a kind of perverse variant of fellow-feeling) can help distinguish between the animating spirits of the workplace in Tocqueville's America and postwar America. The harsh conditions imposed by capitalism in nineteenth-century America are well documented, as is the violence displayed by rapacious settlers on the frontier. It is often said that the American capitalist class in the nineteenth century was brutal and cruel, but in light of Scheler's analysis, it is important to discriminate between accusations. As Scheler notes, "brutality" and "cruelty" stand for completely different psychological experiences.

The experience of the workplace in nineteenth-century America was often brutal and insensitive, but not necessarily cruel. This subtle but extremely important point can be discerned in Tocqueville's general analysis of factory work in early America. Tocqueville writes,

> The territorial aristocracy of former ages [feudal society] was either bound by law, or thought itself bound by usage, to come to the relief of its serving-men and to relieve their distresses. But the manufacturing aristocracy of our age [democratic America] first impoverishes and debases the men who serve it and then abandons them to be supported by the charity of the public. . . . Between the workman and the master there are frequent relations, but no real association.[69]

The capitalists that Tocqueville observed demonstrated a degree of brutality, but not really cruelty, for they had an almost complete disregard for the experiences of their workmen. They did not take pleasure in the misery of their workmen so much as they simply ignored it. They were insensitive to the feelings of their employees; those feelings did not affect their inner experience or change their conduct. The employer and employee lacked any real "association," for no bridge existed between their imaginations along which feelings might be communicated. Early American capitalism was insensitive and brutal, but not necessarily cruel, which is why Tocqueville noted that "the manufacturing aristocracy which is growing up under our eyes is one of the harshest that ever existed in the world; but at the same time it is one of the most confined and least dangerous."[70] It was confined because, in that relationship, no connection existed between human imaginations, one that might have given rise to the soul of a *lackey* or the soul of a torturer, even though the new conditions were harsh. The detachment of Tocqueville's Americans contained the new economic relationship and made it less "dangerous."

This same phenomenon can be observed in Whyte's discussion of the workplace in prewar America, before the rise of the organization man. Whyte notices the same insensitivity, the same detachment, and the same harshness (and potential brutality) that Tocqueville observed. He links the experience of old America to the Protestant ethic, and he contrasts it with the new business atmosphere informed by the Social ethic of the organization man. Whyte recounts his experience as a young man in the Vick School of Applied Merchandising, noting how different it was in comparison with the training program offered by General Electric in the postwar society of the organization man.

In the Vick School, the major emphasis was "work and competition," not "managing others' work and co-operation."[71] The code of the school, Whyte says, was that "business was survival of the fittest."[72] He writes, "There was no talk about the social responsibilities of business or the broad view that I can remember, and I'm quite sure the phrase *human relations* never came up at all."[73] Noting the harsh and insensitive atmosphere at the school and contrasting it with the new effort of business in the society of the organization man to encourage positive feelings, loyalty, and morale, Whyte says, "The Vick School was frankly based on the principle of elimination. It wouldn't make any difference how wonderful all of us might turn out to be. . . . the rules of the game dictated that only six or seven of us would be asked to stay with Vick."[74]

As in Tocqueville's description of the workplace in early America, one gets a sense that the environment at the Vick School was harsh and insensitive, almost brutal, but not cruel. The absence of cruelty is evident in that, although individuals worked hard at Vick, in inferior positions and under tense and competitive conditions, the employer did not "feel" the experience of his trainees or take pleasure in it. If he sensed their unhappiness, that unhappiness did not affect his own imagination or influence his behavior.

("Spurious sympathy," Whyte notes, "did not conceal a strong preoccupation with results."[75])

These observations of the American workplace made by Tocqueville and Whyte present an interesting contrast to the experience of work in the society of the organization man. Work in postwar America was not cruel as opposed to brutal, but it was guided by the principle of fellow-feeling, which has a closer connection with cruelty than brutality. Fellow-feeling, like cruelty, requires that a person "feel" another person's feelings and be affected by them. Fellow-feeling, like cruelty, presumes that a special link has been established between separate imaginations, with the imaginative experience of one person strongly affecting the imaginative experience of the other.

In the society of the organization man, the "job-minded" entrepreneur was replaced with the "people-minded" manager.[76] The manager was not a person who simply directed physical activity, but one who was "in charge of people getting along together."[77] Business in the society of the organization man was not just about making money, but about building morale, helping workers fulfill themselves, and making workers "happy."[78] A worker's "sincerity" was viewed, at times, to be more important than his competence.[79] Personnel managers in the organization, guided by human-relations theories of management, made an effort to cross the divide that had separated the employer from the employee in Tocqueville's America and to become sensitive to the feelings and inner experiences of their workers. It was no longer just the worker's labor that was desired by business but also, according to Whyte, the worker's "soul,"[80] his psyche.[81] In Tocqueville's America, the employer was insensitive. In the society of the organization man, the employer was sensitive to the worker's feelings and attitudes, to what that person longed for or was depressed by.[82]

That the new link between employer and employee was ultimately designed to serve the old cause of profit does not change the revolution in spirit implied by the new situation. Both employer and employee in the society of the organization man felt that it was necessary to function in this new way and that the imaginative and emotional connections between employer and employee were altogether natural. These new connections correspond to the intimate ties forged between master and servant in aristocratic society described by Tocqueville.

In aristocratic society, the servant would dissolve a part of his identity into the identity of his master, and the relationship was unequal. The absorption of identity was so complete and the will to submit penetrated so deep into the servant's consciousness that the servant's experience of subjugation almost disappeared below the level of consciousness. In the society of the organization man, the commingling of imaginations occurred on a more democratic plane. The goal was to enhance the worker's "happiness" and "positive feelings," not to explicitly make him feel his dependence. But the absorption of identity was so complete for the organization man that it became possible again to cause the feeling of submission to sink below the level of consciousness. Through the "manipulation" of feelings, as opposed to the aristocratic method of using fear to instill reverence, the employer in the society of the organization man tried to make the worker happy, content, and fulfilled, even though in the world of raw power the worker was dutifully obeying some command. [83]

The experiences of the workplace in aristocratic society and the society of the organization man were very different from the experience of the workplace in Tocqueville's America. In Tocqueville's America, the workplace was harsh, brutal, and insensitive; the imagination of the employer was unaffected by the imaginations of his employees. He made no attempt to understand them or to "feel" them, let alone to act on that knowledge. There was no "bond of affection." [84] The feeling of detachment, which was rooted in the spirit of perseverance, contributed to a business climate that was harsh yet benign. The capitalist experience in nineteenth-century America was physically grueling, but it did not consume the soul of the worker as it did in aristocratic society. Whyte's observation, that business in the society of the organization man desired not just the labor of its workmen but also their souls perhaps made the capitalist experience less harsh than it was in Tocqueville's America, but it also made it more dangerous and more like the experience of the Old World. [85]

Why the Rise of Fellow-Feeling Contributed to Status-Consciousness

According to Riesman, Whyte, Mills, and Packard, the organization man was a member of some group, either at home or at work, in which he made a great effort to preserve harmony between members. At the same time, the organization man was extremely status-conscious, a quality that each of these authors believed to be an important new phenomenon in American society (or at least a phenomenon more conspicuous than before). The organization man tried to keep relations between peer group members smooth and harmonious and condemned any effort on the part of one to dominate the others. Yet he also took a perverse pleasure in another's misery and fall, for his status swelled in direct proportion to another person's feeling of decline. "Keeping up with the Joneses" was a way to insure harmony on the neighborhood block, but surpassing the Joneses would secretly fill one's soul with pride.

This is the same experience observed in the Old World, where the competition for status operated as a "zero-sum game." Two people may both improve their physical circumstances, but if one does so slightly more than the other, the imagination of the latter senses a miserable decline in status relative to the former, and the status of the former rises the same increment that the status of the latter falls. The organization man's obsession with status is not actually inconsistent with the spirit of fellow-feeling, for fellow-feeling is not the same as "friendly-feeling."[86] Fellow-feeling does not require people to like each other. It merely establishes the necessary psychological connections between people that set in motion the "zero-sum" competition of status. Once people's imaginations become interlocked, the quest for status can begin.

Fellow-feeling also explains the tendency of the society of the organization man to rank jobs according to relative status, a phenomenon observed by both Whyte and Packard. Moreover, it explains why, within that hierarchy, certain jobs were recognized as high-status positions. The new status hierarchy in jobs did not simply parallel the hierarchy in salaries for, as Packard notes, a low-paying white-collar position (e.g., a salesclerk) was believed to be higher in status than a well-paying blue-collar position (e.g., a factory laborer).[87] The spirit of fellow-feeling and its close connection with the old aristocratic spirit of reverence can help explain this new phenomenon.

In aristocratic society, the spirit of reverence caused those jobs in which a person could command others, dominate others, or stand out among others to be high in status; hence, the warrior occupied a high-status position. In the society of the organization man, the spirit of fellow-feeling caused those jobs that involved "dealing with people" and aiding interpersonal communication, or "manipulating" people and helping them to "adjust," to be higher in status. Thus, in the society of the organization man, the personnel director, the manager, the administrator, the service-provider, the counselor, and the public relations expert were high-status positions.[88] Those jobs were perceived to be somehow more important or worthwhile than others.

This, perhaps, explains why it is increasingly popular in America for jobs largely involving manual labor to be given fancy appellations. The fancy appellations have come into being because of the new status hierarchy in jobs. They emphasize, on purpose, those parts of the task that require a worker to deal with other people, in accordance with new value system. Dealing with other people is considered more worthy in a society based on fellow-feeling in much the same way that commanding other people is considered more worthy in a society based on reverence. Hence, in postwar America, tow-operators are called "roadside counselors."[89]

How Public Opinion in Tocqueville's America Differs from Fellow-Feeling in the Society of the Organization Man

The tendency of the organization man to dwell on the opinions and judgments of others brings to mind the oppressive experience of public opinion in Tocqueville's America. In both cases, it seems, a person's interior sense is being guided by pressure from without. Yet there is an important difference between public opinion and fellow-feeling that Max Scheler alludes to in his work *The Nature of Sympathy*. Public opinion, he argues, belongs to a distinct category of psychological experiences called "emotional infection." Emotional infection is different from fellow-feeling because it involves the transference of a general state of feeling into an individual and not the recognition of certain feelings by a particular individual. The individual who succumbs to public opinion, Scheler argues, is infected by an emotion that prevails in the atmosphere; it is a reaction that is almost involuntary and occurs almost below the level of consciousness. To be infected by a state of feeling does not presuppose any deep intimacy between persons or any heightened state of sensitivity towards a particular person's feelings. Scheler writes,

> Quite different again from these, is the case where there is no true appearance of fellow-feeling at all, although it is very frequently confused with this. . . . I have in mind the case of mere *emotional infection*. We all know how the cheerful atmosphere in a "pub" or at a party may "infect" the newcomers, who may even have been depressed beforehand, so that they are "swept up" into the prevailing gaiety. It is the same when laughter proves "catching", as can happen especially with children. . . . The same thing occurs when a group is infected by the mournful tone of one of its members. . . . Here there is neither a *directing* of feeling towards the other's joy or suffering, nor any participation in her experience. On the contrary, it is a characteristic of emotional infection that it occurs only as a transference of the *state* of feeling, and does *not* presuppose any sort of *knowledge* of the joy which others feel. Thus one may only notice afterwards that a mournful feeling, encountered in oneself, is traceable to infection from a group one has visited some hours before. There is nothing in the mournful feeling itself to point to this origin; only by inference from casual considerations does it become clear where it came from. For such contagion it is by no means necessary that any *emotional* experiences should have occurred in the other person[90] (his italics).

Scheler continues,

> The process of infection is an involuntary one. Especially characteristic is its tendency to return to its point of departure, so that the feelings concerned *gather*

momentum like an avalanche. The emotion caused by infection reproduces itself *again* by means of expression and imitation. . . . In all mass-excitement, even in the formation of "public opinion", it is above all this *reciprocal effect* of a self-generating infection which leads to the uprush of a common surge of emotion. . . .these processes of infection are not merely involuntary but operate "unconsciously" in the sense that we "get into" these states without realizing that this is how it comes about[91] (his italics).

Scheler's account of public opinion is quite compatible with Bryce and Tocqueville's discussion of that phenomenon as it occurred in nineteenth-century America. Bryce comments on the enormous power of public opinion in America and how it could change a person's state of mind by exerting tremendous power just below the level of conscious thought. He writes,

This peculiar gift which the Republic has shown, of quickly dissolving and assimilating the foreign bodies that are poured into her . . . is mainly due to the all-pervading force of opinion, which the newcomer, so soon as he has formed social and business relations with the natives, breathes in daily till it insensibly transmutes him.[92]

Public opinion is different from fellow-feeling (and reverence) because it does not require an intimate knowledge of a particular person's feelings in order to develop or spread, and this fact is touched on by Bryce when he compares the origin of public opinion in America with the experience of opinion in Europe. Bryce writes, "whereas in Europe it is patent who does make the beginning, in America a view often seems to arise spontaneously, and to be the work of many rather than of few. The individual counts for less, the mass counts for more."[93]

In aristocratic society and postwar America, a person formed deep and intimate bonds with other peer group members, and peer group opinion became the unique sum total of a particular set of imaginations. In Tocqueville's America, public opinion seemed "to pass into the category of the phenomena of nature, governed by far-reaching and inexorable laws whose character science has only imperfectly ascertained."[94] The deep bonds of affection in aristocratic society and the society of the organization man differ significantly from the invisible force in Tocqueville's America that subdued a person by wearing him down with the force and weight of an inanimate mass.[95]

It is not the "knowledge" of another person's feelings that generates public opinion or comprises the mechanism by which public opinion exerts tremendous force on a single person's imagination. The transmission of public opinion does not require a person to intuit, through radar, another person's feelings. Public opinion is a state of feeling that, almost through invisible force, somehow converts the mind. The person who succumbs to it is more a passive agent of a higher power than an active participant in another person's feelings.

In a way, public opinion, or "emotional infection," is a perfect form of communication between individuals who are detached and have not commingled their imaginations. Public opinion does not require a person to dwell on another person's feelings or to become sensitive to the feelings of particular individuals within a peer group in order to adjust. It does not require a person to gain knowledge or insight into another person's imagination. Public opinion is simply the transference of a state of feeling at the lowest level of consciousness. Thus, it was well suited to the unusual psychology of Tocqueville's American, who was prevented by the spirit of perseverance from building bridges to the imaginations of others. Public opinion was the mechanism by which detached, otherworldly persons could articulate a common understanding.

Why Conformism in Tocqueville's America Was Different from Conformism in the Society of the Organization Man

One reason that contemporary expressive individualists find little difference between the society of the organization man and Tocqueville's America is that in both societies, enormous pressure was placed on individuals to conform. The fact that fellow-feeling replaced public opinion as the operative mechanism by which individuals were made to fall in line is obscured by the intense hostility of expressive individualism towards any kind of conformism. Because individuals in both the society of the organization man and Tocqueville's America were made to conform, there appears, to the expressive individualist, to be little difference between the two societies. The two societies seem to possess a certain kinship because they suffer from this one great evil.

But the experiences of conformism in Tocqueville's America and in the society of the organization man are different. When the individual conforms under the pressure of public opinion, he or she conforms because a certain state of feeling prevalent in the atmosphere enters the mind and produces a conformational change in attitude. As a force, public opinion originates in no particular person, but rather assumes the form of a phenomenon of nature. The sheer weight of public opinion when brought to bear on a single individual leads to a kind of "fatalism"[96] in that person. The power of public opinion, tenacious yet invisible, eventually overwhelms the solitary individual and causes him to fall in line.

On the other hand, when the individual conforms in a society based on fellow-feeling, the individual "adjusts" himself voluntarily on the basis of particular knowledge gained by observing the emotions and actions of certain individuals. That experience of conformism, unlike conformism under public opinion, requires one to be sensitive to another person's feelings, to be, in fact, deeply aware of them, and to consciously incorporate those feelings into one's own imaginative experience in order to calculate the right response that will help one to get along.

Since conformism that results from the pressure of public opinion represents a transference of a state of feeling, it does not affect or consume the entire conscious personality of the individual. (It is, as Scheler argues, a behavioral response that is almost involuntary and subconscious). For that reason, Tocqueville's American could conform in accordance with public opinion, but nevertheless remain quirky, peculiar, distinctive, and individualistic. Conformism in a society based on fellow-feeling, however, consumes the entire person, for every conscious element of the psyche, every desire or mood or emotion, is tested against a knowledge of the imaginative content of other peer group members. That knowledge is collected through "sensitivity." In the case of fellow-feeling, the entire psyche, not just one's general outlook or mood, becomes subject to conformist pressure.

One can detect a difference in the types of conformism in Riesman's comparison of inner-directed and other-directed persons. Comparing the experience of the other-directed person with the individualist type who preceded him, Riesman says that all " 'knobby' or idiosyncratic qualities and vices are more or less eliminated or repressed" by the peer group of the other-directed person. [97] Discussing the differences between inner-directed children (i.e., Tocqueville's Americans) and other-directed children when they meet to discuss their hobbies, Riesman says of the inner-directed children,

> There is nothing anxious about such a meeting: no problem of maintaining marginal differentiation (difference, that is, but not too much) in taste such as we find in other-directed hobbyists. The child is not shaken in his own hobby by the fact that others have a different hobby; rather, he is confirmed in the idiosyncrasy which, within wide limits, is respected. [98]

The conformist in Tocqueville's America could remain quirky and different. The conformist in the society of the organization man had the rough edges of his or her personality shaved off. He or she became "well-rounded." [99]

Conformism in the society of the organization man was, unlike that in

Tocqueville's America, all-consuming and suffocating, which may have contributed to the expressive individualist rebellion against all conformism. It is perhaps no coincidence that such authors as Erving Goffman and Michel Foucault (although Foucault was writing in France) and the school of thought that they represent rose to prominence after the society of the organization man was established and not before. Their criticism of the pressures placed on individuals to conform was in response to the conformist experience of postwar America, not of Tocqueville's America. Conformism in postwar America required every element within the human personality to conform to a standard that was presumed to represent the "normal" or the "average." Whyte comments, for example, on the new personality tests that dominated the workplace in the society of the organization man and examined for "averageness."[100] Riesman notes the same new obsession with being "normal" among other-directed persons, and the demands made by the peer group that a member conform in all aspects of life.[101] Deviance of any kind was not tolerated.

That experience of conformism is different from the experience of conformism in Tocqueville's America. The former was so all-consuming, bringing much "misery to the deviate," that it could induce "nervous breakdowns" in peer group members.[102] Reprisals for failing to conform in the society of the organization man were common, Whyte notes.[103] The pressure to conform in nineteenth-century America, Bryce says, was clearly evident but, unlike in the society of the organization man, not overbearing. Reprisals for failing to conform rarely occurred.[104]

Works such as Goffman's *The Presentation of Self in Everyday Life* and Foucault's *Madness and Civilization* are motivated by intense hostility to the values of the organization man.[105] Their charge, that the line separating the "normal" from the "deviant," or the sane from the insane, is the result of an arbitrary political decision that comforts some but unfairly condemns others, is a direct criticism of the all-consuming experience of conformism in the society of the organization man. In the same vein, the experience of the white-collar employees of that era, who were manipulated in order to feel "happy" and "important" at work,[106] leads directly to Goffman's conclusion that society is omnipotent and can instill within individuals the very feeling of freedom. Society, Goffman argues, can essentially trick or manipulate people into believing that they are "free" by defining the experience of "freedom" for them and convincing them of this truth. Such criticism represents a rebellion against the experience of the organization man, his obsession with sameness and being average. But those are not necessarily the same values that prevailed in Tocqueville's America.

How Republican Principle in Tocqueville's America Was Replaced with the Consumer Culture of the Organization Man

Earlier, it was argued that republican principle in Tocqueville's America represented an otherworldly adaptation of Old World aristocratic manners. In aristocratic society, ceremony, gestures, and other forms of social display were fragmented and separate, but a concentrated and harmonious whole was achieved within the mental experience of Tocqueville's American. Republican principle provided a theoretical and unified basis for the arrangement of people in physical space. In Tocqueville's America, it was no longer the particular features of articles of clothing or methods of speaking that compelled people to set themselves properly but rather the force of a single axiom.

The consumer culture of postwar America signals a return to the experience of the Old World. In the consumer culture, people are grouped together according to specific tastes, choices, likes, and styles. Purchases like cars, food, furniture, and art are almost infinitely particular; they are not united by any common theme or underlying principle. They are simply an expression of the particular tastes and desires of the particular individuals who buy them.

Republican principle, by its universality, can organize any group of people. Its code of conduct can be applied at any place and at any time. The objects purchased in a consumer culture, on the other hand, correspond to the feelings, manners, and tastes of only a small number of people. All can embrace the democratic ideal, but in the consumer culture of postwar America, a slightly different color, a slightly different cut, or a slightly different model could take one person out of one peer group and plunge her into an entirely different one. Such differences could make two persons once comfortable with each other suddenly feel like strangers.

In an aristocratic system of manners, according to Tocqueville, "the rules of politeness form a complex system of legislation, which it is difficult to be perfectly master of."[107] In such a system, "ceremonial observances [are] infinitely varied according to different ranks."[108] In Tocqueville's America, the system of etiquette was not defined by a great variety of external phenomena but by a few democratic principles. Those principles were not specific to any rank, order, or class, nor did they present themselves in a great number of complex forms. As abstract notions, they could be applied to any person in any society.

This is perhaps one reason why Tocqueville's American was often uncomfortable while traveling through Europe, becoming lost and confused in that society's complex system of etiquette. In aristocratic society, the American was "like a man surrounded by traps,"[109] and he quickly became perplexed by the various rules of etiquette that "force[d] themselves upon his notice while [eluding] definition."[110] Tocqueville's American appreciated the rules and limits of social intercourse not by mastering an intricate code of signs and gestures but by contemplating a few simple democratic procedures. Traveling in the Old World, Tocqueville's American was like the person who tries to move about the world after suffering the loss of his or her senses, becoming annoyed and confused.

In postwar America, the old aristocratic system resurfaces, albeit in a new, democratic form. The society of the organization man was divided into numerous enclaves based not on wealth and power, but on tastes, habits, and consumption styles.[111] Cars, clothes, and posture, even the way one's dinner salad was prepared,[112] became the physical markers that distinguished people from one another. Just as a specific "style of life," such as "the privilege of wearing special costumes, of eating special dishes taboo to others, or of carrying arms,"[113] set apart groups of people in old aristocratic society, so did styles of life in the society of the organization man define the borders between different peer groups. In both societies, it was not one's class position or income that determined the nature of the peer group but, on the contrary, a much more intimate tie—the feeling among individuals that somehow "they belong[ed] together."[114]

Such a tie is very different from the one that connected manufacturers in Tocqueville's America. Of that group of men, Tocqueville writes, "To tell the truth, though there are rich men, the class of rich men does not exist; for these rich individuals have no feelings or purposes, no traditions or hopes, in common; they are individuals, therefore, but no definite class."[115]

In the peer groups of the Old World and postwar America, the connections between people were much more intimate; they were joined together not on the basis of income but rather according to a way of life. Each peer group articulated a particular set of attitudes and opinions that put a stamp on a particular population of individuals. In order to feel comfortable in such a society and to move easily from peer group to peer group, one would have to learn the codes and manners of each peer group. Tocqueville's American, with his universal democratic axioms, would probably have been as annoyed and confused traveling in the society of the organization man as he was traveling in old aristocratic society.[116]

The consumer culture of the organization man brings to mind the earthly City of Man that Augustine described in late antiquity. Once again, people were grouped together according to all that was visible, in this case by "type of home, automobile, clothing, and home furnishings."[117] The "snob appeal" of the house,"[118] the constant "sniffing out of other's tastes,"[119] the effort to differentiate between individuals on the basis of minor discrepancies in consumption preferences recall the ambition of the fourth-century African, which was to enjoy high status and hoard praise.[120] With the rise of the organization man, the interior sense of the postwar American became firmly anchored in the visible world.

The Society of the Organization Man as a Transitional Society

The culture of expressive individualism that took hold in America in the 1960s completes the transformation in American individualism. But for the purpose of understanding the American character, the real moment of revolutionary change occurred not during the tumultuous decade of the 1960s but during the "conservative" decade of the 1950s. The great psychological divide separating the America of today from Tocqueville's America was crossed during the society of the organization man. The subsequent rise of expressive individualism announced another change in the imaginative experience of the American individualist, but the basic structure of that experience was established during the immediate postwar period. Expressive individualism grew out of, and came to adorn, the established worldview of the organization man.

Many of the features that make the contemporary society of expressive individualism so much like past aristocratic society can already be discerned in the society of the organization man. The elements of "aristocraticism" that have blossomed fully in the society of expressive individualism are merely immature buds in the society of the organization man but nevertheless are quite evident.

For example, it was in the society of the organization man that the "politicization" of the family began. The rules governing the larger political world began to affect family relations in the society of the organization man just as they did in old aristocratic society. Family relations in the society of the organization man became stilted and forced as they had been in aristocratic society, and less natural (though more "equal") as parents and children tried to become sensitive to each other's feelings and parents tried to court the "good will" of their children.[121] In the new family, there was "a heightening of awareness of the self in relation to others,"[122] and parents employed the same "personnel" methods in raising children that were used to manipulate workers in business.[123]

It was in the society of the organization man that the tendency of American individualists to insert man-made institutions between man and the divine first became evident. Inspired by the new Social ethic, quasi-religious institutions began to appear in the civic life of America. Guided by a new "moral" imperative and conceived in religious purpose as opposed to base self-interest, social centers and "socially useful" programs, often sponsored by churches, began to appear in the suburbs. These centers were designed to make individuals "happier," to help them become "fulfilled." The new moral imperative of the church of the organization man, to "meet people" and "get along" with others, is very different from the moral imperative of the church of Tocqueville's American, which was to persevere in God.

These phenomena mark the dawn of the modern experience in Manicheism, Pelagianism, Donatism, Platonism, and pagan aristocracy. But if the evolution of American culture is, to some degree, an evolution in the experience of aristocracy, from aristocracy in the City of Man to the City of God and back to the City of Man, then some aspects of the organization man's character are rather confusing. The organization man seems more like the Old World peasant than the Old World aristocrat. Many of the similarities between the peer group of the organization man and the peasant peer group were mentioned above. This seems to conflict with the idea that American individualism has moved towards a unique cultural form derived mainly from aristocratic, not peasant, peer group behavior.

The contradiction can be explained by the fact that the society of the organization man was a transitional society. It was inherently unstable, lasting only ten years. It was almost "unnatural" that American individualists with their aristocratic heritage would find contentment in peasant-like peer groups. The psychological tension that Whyte, Riesman, and Mills observed within the organization man, that figure's growing recognition that one could be an external success yet an internal failure,[124] that conformism was stifling the "self"[125] and turning one into a "phony," testifies that within the mind of the organization man, imprisoned as it was in a peasant-like social system, the special aristocratic feature known as the "imperial self" was desperately trying to emerge.

In a way, the situation of the American individualist in the society of the organization man is the exact opposite of the current situation of some Russian democrats who have lived in collectives for the last half-century, but who are now asked to function in a market economy. With the collapse of communism, the appellation "democrat" has been affixed to their persons, but such people have a much longer tradition of functioning in the environment of peasant peer groups. For them, the new market economy is unsettling because it brings "individualism" and "competition." The market is potentially destructive, a threat to the "harmony" and "community" that have traditionally prevailed within the peer group. To them, the market economy seems "unnatural" and goes against their basic instincts.[126]

For the American individualist, life in the peasant-like social system of the organization man was life without "individualism" or "individuality." It was stifling, suffocating, unfree and, to the American character, almost unnatural. Within the mind of the organization man raged a mental struggle that, in a way, is the exact opposite of the struggle currently raging inside the minds of some Russian democrats. But in the case of the American individualist, the struggle represented natural aristocratic tendencies trying to reassert themselves, which they would soon do in the form of expressive individualism.

12

The Rise of the Imperial Self

The decade of the organization man soon gave way to a new era, one that stretches into the present. Starting in the 1960s, the expressive individualist revolt against the values of the organization man transformed American culture. It declared each person to be a sovereign "I," possessed of a sphere of power that was morally and legally unchallengeable. It attacked 1950s orthodoxy and proclaimed conformity, averageness, group-think, and normalcy to be evil, not good. It discovered in each man a hidden greatness *as man* and found within the self a key to happiness and salvation. In doing this, expressive individualism resurrected an idea buried long ago—the idea of an imperial self.

The imperial self need not have a domineering style. While the pagan aristocrats of late antiquity conquered people and held them in tutelage, it was not physical aggressiveness that made them imperial selves. The imperial self is less an expression of will than a state of belief, which is why passive citizens in a modern democracy can be linked to the violent aristocrats of late antiquity. The imperial self imagines that one is undisputed master within a carefully defined circle. Within that circle, the self, or the "I," is sovereign, and all forces challenging the self are imagined to come from beyond. What ancient and modern imperial selves do with that sovereignty differs—the ancient imperial self extends it to rule over others, the modern imperial self assumes a more defensive posture—but all imperial selves believe in an "I" that they endeavor to make impregnable.

The connection between the modern imperial self and the original aristocratic form observed by Augustine will be discussed in this chapter with Tocqueville's American in relief. The contrast is important, for although nineteenth-century Americans were highly individualistic and ambitious, they were not imperial selves. Tocqueville's American was bold and independent, yet possessed a degree of mental helplessness undetectable in both the Old World aristocrat and the contemporary expressive individualist. Tocqueville's American believed in freedom and "free will" but, unlike the imperial self, not necessarily that he held the issues of his life or that he had the power to spin out the thread of his mortal being.

The Imperial Self and the Aristocrat in the City of Man

Augustine's understanding of human psychology again provides a helpful starting point in making comparisons between the Old World aristocrat, Tocqueville's American, and the contemporary expressive individualist. It helps demonstrate how the belief in the imperial self was integrated into the psyches of the aristocrat and the expressive individualist, but not of Tocqueville's American.

Augustine understands the human will to be an "inner sense," something that interprets the other bodily senses, including the faculty of reason.[1] An element common to both man and beast, it is the spark initiating thought and action, but that itself is separate from thought and action. For example, it is the inner sense within the beast, Augustine writes, and not the sense of the eye that determines when the eye is not open and not seeing.[2]

Nietzsche makes a similar distinction between the power in the human will and the actions committed by the will. For Nietzsche, the "will to power" is associated with the "in-itself,"[3] with a discharge of strength found in all living things.[4] It is a force or surge in sensation, away or towards something, which is separate from the action that follows willing.[5] Nietzsche's "will to power" is rather like Augustine's "inner sense." It is "something complicated"[6] preceding the action that follows willing, like the beast's "inner sense" that judges the sense of the eye and precedes the eye's opening. For both Augustine and Nietzsche, the will and the bodily senses are separate, as are the will and the actions originating in the will.[7]

This similarity between Augustine and Nietzsche is surprising, given that the philosophies of the two men are practically antithetical. Nietzsche is the philosopher of aristocracy. He admires human greatness and condemns democracy and Christianity as belief systems of the weak, the envious, and the vindictive. Augustine is the philosopher of Christianity who strongly criticizes the belief system of pagan aristocrats in the first five books of *The City of God*. Yet this similarity between Nietzsche and Augustine on the question of "will" provides the key to understanding something very important about aristocracy. Within Nietzsche's robust description of the aristocratic personality lies a quality not really fundamental to aristocracy but only associated with its conventional expression. That quality is the belief in the imperial self. By focusing on the area of agreement between Augustine and Nietzsche, one can shear away the appendage Nietzsche confused with aristocratic nature and leave a residue more refined, more pure in spirit, and still deserving of Nietzsche's praise, but also compatible with Augustinian philosophy.

To put it in a slightly different way, Nietzsche greatly admired the aristocrat in the City of Man. As that figure was most certainly an imperial self, Nietzsche concluded that the imperial self was a timeless feature of aristocratic nature. But the imperial self is a feature observed only among aristocrats in the City of Man, not aristocrats in the City of God. One can be an aristocrat and not be an imperial self.

Before establishing the connection between Augustine and Nietzsche, the effort will be made to build a composite of the aristocratic imperial self within a framework accommodating the terminology of both philosophers and highlighting their points of agreement.

In *The City of God*, Augustine attacks a conception of the human will that comports with the personality of the aristocrat in the City of Man. Augustine attacks Cicero, an upper-class Roman, for the method he uses to resolve the conflict between free will and fate.[8] Cicero understands free will and fate to be mutually exclusive phenomena, with fate signifying foreknowledge of things to come and identified with the power of God. Cicero denies the existence of any knowledge of future events in order to safeguard the autonomy of the human will. He rejects an order of causes so as to preserve significance in human decision and action (more specifically, to preserve the "freedom of the human will.") Since God, if He is God, must have foreknowledge of events that occur, then God, according to Cicero, cannot exist. Cicero, says Augustine, makes men free by making them sacrilegious.[9]

The Cicero described by Augustine has an understanding of human will and "free will" that complements the personality of the aristocrat introduced in this book. Augustine's Cicero tries to preserve the "freedom of the human will," even at the cost of God's existence, which closely parallels the aristocratic urge to reject ideas of salvation that infringe on one's honor and dignity. There is something quite grand and magnificent, almost God-like, though incredibly pompous, in the way Augustine's Cicero and later aristocrats interpret the notion of "freedom of the will." The result is a category of human pride separate from the simple vanity omnipresent in human nature. It is a pride so stupendous, so outrageous, that it comes to define a specific character type.

The Greek term *hubris* touches on this imagined state of being, and it also is not to be confused with more conventional expressions of vanity. The aristocrat in a state of *hubris* was not simply proud, but an "overfed ass whom would bray and prance about," who had a mind "like a plant-filled garden that has run riot," that has "grown rank and luxuriant."[10] The spirit of the aristocrat soared towards heaven, his image of himself swelled, and his mind outstripped the physical limits imposed on his mortal body. The aristocrat challenged the power of God and truly believed that he was God-like, as Augustine's Cicero did to preserve human power and significance, to preserve his "free will." Confident and self-assured, the aristocrat radiated the light that marked the path before him. He was the agent of his own freedom and the source of the vital energy that propelled him forward. By any measure, this was not the imagined experience of a common self. This was the imagined experience of an *imperial* self.

Augustine observed such aristocrats in late antiquity who were moved to an outstanding show of virtue only by this overweening love of self. Of the aristocrats, Augustine writes, "Glory they most ardently loved: for it they wished to live, for it they did not hesitate to die. Every other desire was repressed by the strength of their passion for that one thing."[11] Such tremendous pride was even considered to be a virtue among the Roman aristocrats because illustrious things done for glory were seen to benefit the empire.[12] It was for hoarding glory, exerting mastery, and expressing dominance that the Roman aristocrat lived.

The imperial self detected in the musings of Augustine's Cicero and the sagas of the Homeric heroes brings to mind Tocqueville's aristocrat who lived many centuries later. Tocqueville's aristocrat possessed a strong belief in his own honor and dignity that weakened his dependence on an otherworldly giver of blessedness. His virtues were as grand as his vices, and he was as quick to forgive and be merciful as he was to indulge in his passions and be undisciplined in his lusts, the oscillation between states depending not on any pious faith but on a steady current of self-praise.

The imperial self of late antiquity brings to mind Bryce's aristocrat, who was arrogantly individualistic, who, like Augustine's Cicero, had a "strong consciousness of personal free will,"[13] who possessed a love of liberty deeply intertwined with a love of domination, and who, desirous of personal glory and the praise of others, accomplished many great things, never hesitating to die.

The imperial self of late antiquity brings to mind Nietzsche's aristocrat, who was exceptional and unaverage,[14] who possessed lofty attitudes and the will to dominate,[15] who was unique and great, and who raised himself above the masses.[16]

The doctrine of free will put forth by Augustine's Cicero resonates in the glory, honor, and power that aristocrats in history have desired for themselves. It was in the aristocrat that a love of liberty was joined to an obsession with glory, a love of independence was joined to a tremendous self-centeredness, and an urge to conquer was joined to a life lived in the mouths of admirers. It is in this way that the aristocrat in the City of Man was an imperial self.

Not only does a special aristocratic conception of "free will" emerge from these descriptions, but so also does a unique strain of aristocratic individualism. Tocqueville understood "individualism" to be part of the new American experience and did not comment on this older, imperial form. The spirit of detachment was central to Tocqueville's understanding of individualism, which is perhaps why he did not classify the arrogant, status-obsessed aristocrat as an individualist. But the aristocratic imperial self was a kind of individualist, one that exhibited a tremendous self-centeredness.

Unlike the individualism of Tocqueville's American, aristocratic individualism was expressed within the context of others, in a contest or struggle against others, not apart from others. Even the term *hubris* suggests the importance of the social context in which aristocratic individualism was practiced as "outrage," "insult," and "maltreat" are offered as secondary meanings in the translation of the word.[17] The translation suggests that the overweening pride of the imperial self was experienced relative to others, with fluctuations in status intrinsic to the practice of aristocratic individualism.

The individualism of Tocqueville's American conveys the opposite experience—a kind of inertness, or detachment from others—with the individualist less affected by judgments arising from another person's imagination. Individualists in Tocqueville's America did not, in order to fulfill the meaning of that philosophy, commit an outrage against or insult another person. When Tocqueville's American "opposed the love of freedom to the love of equality," he or she opposed freedom to an obsession with relative status. In becoming self-centered, he or she moved away from a dependence on worldly praise and concern for another's social position. The thrust of Tocquevillian individualism was in the opposite direction of aristocratic individualism, as the latter combined a love of liberty with a desire for admiration and praise.

Bryce, on the other hand, does comment on the unique strain of individualism found among aristocrats, and he actually associates that individualism with a kind of aristocratic belief in "freedom of the will."[18] Bryce writes,

> The most striking pictures of individualism that literature has preserved for us are those of the Homeric heroes, and of the even more terrible and self-reliant warriors of the Norse sagas, men like Ragnar Lodbrog and Egil son of Skallagrim, who did not regard even the gods, but trusted their own might and main.[19]

In the aristocratic individualism described by Bryce, one claims tremendous, almost God-like, powers for the self.

To finish building a composite of the aristocratic imperial self, it is important to recognize how that figure imagined the few limitations on his or her power. What was set against "free will" in the mind of the aristocrat was fate. In *The City of God*, Augustine describes the Stoics as opponents of Cicero. If Cicero argued in support of "free will," the Stoics argued that foreknowledge, or an order of causes, does exist, depriving the human will of any real power. This idea is expressed in Seneca's statement, "the Fates do lead the man that follows willing, but that man that is unwilling, him they drag."[20]

The positions of Cicero and the Stoics are united by a common under- standing of fate. Fate is a power that must reach everywhere if it does exist, steering the course of a man's life and eliminating personal freedom and independence. The competition between free will and fate is a competition between two powerful forces, between an imperial self who believes he holds the issues of his life and a force of destiny recognized to be under the control of God and that totally enfeebles the human will. Augustine's Cicero defends the imperial self against fate and rejects divination. Augustine's Seneca defends the gods against the imperial self and rejects free will.[21]

In Augustine's description of the conflict between Cicero and the Stoics, fate and the human will are understood to be two separate phenomena, each with its own source of power. In Greek literature, the conflict between the two gives way to a balance of power such that the free will of the imperial self is preserved, yet "threatened" by destiny. Fate is a power that lurks nearby and strikes when the gods are jealous. When it prevails, it does so because of its strength, not because of a deficiency or weakness in the human will. The synthesis of the two forces is evident in the work of Herodotus, who "tends to narrate events so that the force of destiny is never far from them," but who "insists that men act freely as well."[22] Since fate is believed to be separate from the human will, it is not the self who is blamed when disaster occurs but the gods, for the gods have wielded a power believed to be beyond the control of man.

Several important points emerge from the above discussion that relate to the modern imperial self.

First, there exists an imagined experience of "free will" and "individual- ism" that is singularly aristocratic. The aristocratic understanding of "free will" generates an imperial self because it rejects the existence of God in order to preserve human freedom. It is expressed through an aristocratic form of individualism that is practiced in the context of others, often to dominate others.

Second, the aristocratic belief in "free will" generates an "I," or a self, of truly imperial proportions. The aristocrat imagines moving through time with almost limitless powers. What is arrayed against the aristocrat's free will is fate. Fate confronts the imperial self as a completely external force, and the two fight on the battleground of a man's life. When the imperial self moves in a favorable direction, it is because the "I" of the imperial self has beaten back fate, because fate has proved to be a "weaker" force, and not because one part of the human will has successfully arrested an impulse arising from another part. When the imperial self moves in an unfavorable direction, it is because the "I" has been conquered by fate, because the will has been forced to conform to a predetermined order of things, and not because one is weak-willed or held in tutelage by the imagined fear, confusion, and wonder that arises from within.

Augustine and Nietzsche's Criticism of the Imperial Self

The belief in the imperial self is a prominent feature among aristocrats in the City of Man. It is not surprising that Augustine, the critic of conventional aristocracy, would attack it. But what is perhaps more interesting is that Nietzsche, the defender of conventional aristocracy, also attacks it.

Nietzsche's criticism of "free will" actually parallels Augustine's criticism of Cicero's doctrine. Nietzsche does not actually condemn Cicero by name or any doctrine of "free will" thought to be aristocratic. On the contrary, Nietzsche barely discriminates between aristocratic "free will" and Christian "free will," tending to associate "free will" with Christian doctrine. "Free will" is believed by Nietzsche to be little more than a preparatory stance for making one feel guilty, making it the mechanism of control in the Christian religion.[23] But Nietzsche does allude to a conception of "free will" similar to the one that I have associated with aristocrats, and his criticism of "free will" follows along Augustinian lines.

Nietzsche argues that the concept "free will" is erroneous because it identifies the "will" with the action that follows willing and identifies the "I" with only that aspect of the will that has commanded within the will.[24] For Nietzsche, the will is not "free" because there is always commanding and obeying within the will, and to demonstrate delight when exercising volition is merely to identify the "I" with that aspect of the will that has triumphed. It is like "the governing class [that] identifies itself with the successes of the commonwealth."[25] According to Nietzsche, the synthetic "I" derived from the notion of "free will" represents an attempt by the dominant element within the will to claim for itself, to actually usurp, the power in will. Those who advance the belief that the "I" and the power in will are one and the same, who in this way believe in themselves, belong to the "vain races."[26]

The individual who promulgates the belief in an "I" enjoys the feeling of power accompanying success in willing, but such feeling, according to Nietzsche, is deceptive and based on erroneous conclusions regarding the will.[27]

A similar idea is found in Augustine's criticism of Cicero's doctrine. Augustine argues, like Nietzsche, that to link the power in one's will to some artificial "I" is to ignore the special power central to willing. A difference between the two philosophers emerges as Nietzsche argues that the synthetic "I" wrongly takes credit for the "many souls"[28] within the human will that command and obey, while Augustine argues that the synthetic "I" wrongly takes credit for the power, or "inner sense," bestowed upon man by God. According to Augustine, the "free will" of Cicero ignores the power in willing, a power implanted by God. Still, like Nietzsche, Augustine argues that Cicero's doctrine of free will erroneously credits that aspect of the will that triumphs in willing to an "I," and mistakenly presumes the "I" to be whole, self-sufficient, and in control.

Nietzsche also criticizes the concept of "fate," or destiny. He says that in "unfree will," like "free will," the human will is incorrectly linked to actions merely expressing the will. The will is incorrectly presumed to be synonymous with the power behind willing. Nietzsche separates the power in willing from external events, from the "cause" and "effect" relationship established by natural science.[29] Nietzsche argues that there is no "causal connection" or "necessity" that can affect the power to will. The power to will has no rule of "law" and is not influenced by the course of events.[30] He says "unfree will" is a "mythology" and "in real life it is only a matter of strong and weak wills."[31] For Nietzsche, the will is not affected by fate, but rather the power to will is affected by the relative power in other wills. He concludes that the belief in "unfreedom of the will" is simply a mechanism used by persons who want to relieve themselves of responsibility, who "seek to lay the blame for themselves somewhere else."[32]

Nietzsche's criticism of "unfree will" parallels Augustine's attack on the Stoics. Augustine argues that God, who has foreknowledge of events, endowed man not with a will but with the power to will. And when a will is "not able to do what it wills," it is not oppressed by fate, but rather simply "overborne by a more powerful will."[33] Suffering wills are resolved in the *power* of God, not in "the will of men, or of angels, or of any created spirit."[34] Augustine insists that "if the name of fate is applied to anything at all," it is that "fate belongs to the weaker of two parties, will to the stronger, who has the other in his power," and "not that the freedom of our will is excluded by that order of causes which the Stoics call fate."[35]

Both Nietzsche, the philosopher of aristocracy, and Augustine, the Christian, criticize the most basic operating beliefs of the imperial self. Not only do they criticize the "free will" of the imperial self but also the imperial self's notion of destiny, or "unfree will." The entire imaginative system of the Old World aristocrat relating to the doctrine of the imperial self is repudiated by both Nietzsche and Augustine. This suggests that the aristocratic spirit admired by Nietzsche and the belief in the imperial self are not synonymous. The two can be separated.

Augustine helps separate the two by arguing the following:

Cicero's "free will" depends on God not existing because it is based on an erroneous concept of will, one that does not separate the power behind willing from will. The autonomy of Cicero's will was threatened by God because Cicero did not realize that God bestows not all wills (since some wills are evil and evil does not come from God), but all power in wills. Cicero feared God because he believed that the Christian God created human wills and not simply the power behind willing. He assumed that the will and the will's actions, not simply the power in will, must be determined by God. Because Cicero did not separate power from will, he feared the existence of God and fate on his will, and thus credited the God-given power to will to the commander within his will.

Augustine, by separating the power in will from willing, is able to resolve Cicero's dilemma. Augustine argues that man commits acts because God foreknew that man had the *power* within his will to commit such acts and that because He foreknew this, He did not foreknow nothing. [36] For Augustine, it is God, not the "I" or some unitary conception of the self, that takes credit for the power in man's will. In this way, God is tied to freedom of the will, though it is no longer "freedom of the will" as conceived by Augustine's Cicero. According to Augustine, God foreknew what would be in the *power* of man's will, which means that he foreknew something, and it would be contradictory to say that foreknowledge eliminates human power as that would mean that God foreknew nothing in the power of man's will when it was just asserted that He foreknew something. [37] By relying on the crucial element of power within will, implanted in man by God, Augustine enables man to "live well" (with power in his will) and "believe well" (in God's prescience of future things). [38]

By separating the power in will from will and making God responsible for such power, Augustine changes the entire imaginative experience of a person. No longer is God the external force threatening the self-sufficient, autonomous being. God now forms an integral part of the human will. The "I" of the imperial self is destroyed because the power in human will is credited to a higher force. God becomes the companion of man through life, present in every decision and every act, for He has foreknowledge of the power in man's will. At the same time, that foreknowledge does not preclude freedom of the will, though it is not "freedom of the will" as conceived by Augustine's Cicero. This is because foreknowledge is no longer a force external to the person and competitive with that person's freedom, but rather one that has been kneaded into the substance of the will. It is in this way that the Augustinian comes to lose the belief in an imperial self.

How the Imperial Self Disappeared from the Imagination of Tocqueville's American

The particular historical circumstances fixing the imagination of the Old World aristocrat were compatible with the belief in the imperial self. In revering the history of a human past, putting a special stamp on one's domain, and practicing manners as "a means of self-assertion,"[39] the aristocrat in the City of Man was a self-contained, self-sufficient, and self-assured "I" of truly imperial proportions. God, fate, nature, foreign worlds, and other rivals to power were competitors of the imperial self, but they could only attack the imperial self from without. At times they gained the upper hand, but never because of a loss of resisting power within the aristocrat or because the "I" of the aristocrat had lost confidence in its claim to total power.

For the aristocrat in the City of God, the imperial self is incompatible with the aristocratic spirit. This is because Christianity, public opinion, and republican principle—the essential components of the belief system of the aristocrat in the City of God—prevent an individual from ever claiming total power. The belief in an afterlife, the order of public opinion, and the rule of republican principle form an analog of the Old World that has been reflected onto the surface of the mind. But they signify more than this. They are expressions of superior force, operating very much like the divine force in Augustine's theology.

The power exerted by Christian (particularly Calvinist) ideas on the mind of the aristocrat in the City of God causes the belief in the imperial self to be erased. For the nineteenth-century Christian individualist, human action was not the outcome of a titanic struggle between the will of man and the power of God. Rather, all power within the human will was simply credited to God. All man's accomplishments were believed to be the work of an imagined higher power, not the work of an imagined "I."

Tocqueville's American imagined the idea of "free will" in a different way than the aristocrat in the City of Man. The Old World aristocrat claimed all achievements for himself and believed all accomplishments to be the products of his power, to be the magnificent creations of his will. For Tocqueville's American, achievements were gained for the glory of God. They were merely the fulfillment of what God Himself had promised to do.[40] By acting, even triumphing, the individualist simply learned for himself what God already foreknew, making each step forward in life an achievement of God, not man. Thus, Tocqueville's American, by his own energy and success, became a window through which he could discern his own state of election. If he could persevere, it was because he was destined to persevere, and if he could not persevere, it was because he was destined not to persevere and be one of the elect. Within man's great freedom of action stood the set determination of the will of God. It was in this way that Tocqueville's American was motivated to persevere in life, to push forward and drive on, for contained within his own energy and commitment was evidence that he had been chosen by God.

Tocqueville's American believed that he possessed real power in his will and that his actions were significant, but he understood that power to belong to God, not man, thus making him dependent on the grace of God. Instead of bringing glory to the self, accomplishments provided a more humble glimpse of a divine plan. In this way the belief in imperial self was eliminated. A new idea of "free will" emerged, one steeped in hope, not arrogance, in respect for a higher power, not a lust for praise.

The power of public opinion also makes the belief in the imperial self incompatible with aristocracy in the City of God. Public opinion corresponds to the Old World community. It makes possible the dimensionless community by allowing itself to be carried within the imagination of every citizen, independent of geographical location. But it also causes energy and resourcefulness to be divorced from the "habit of intellectual command and individual self-confidence" commonly observed among Old World aristocrats.[41]

Bryce describes the nineteenth-century American as a person who possessed vigor and ambition, but who lacked the arrogant presumption of correctness found in the conventional aristocrat. The American individualist was enterprising, but "the strong man's confidence and sense of individual force . . . have inevitably been lowered."[42] Just as the American yielded to divine force and credited the power in his will to God, so did he defer to the will of the majority and credit his thoughts to the opinions of others. The parallel between the belief in God and the power of public opinion is apt, as Bryce describes how public opinion in nineteenth-century America accrued almost divine power. Bryce says the "voice of the multitude" is like the "voice of fate,"[43] and through public opinion one feels the "insignificance which overwhelms us when at night we survey the host of heaven, and know that from even the nearest fixed star this planet of ours is invisible."[44] Public opinion "inspires a sort of awe, a sense of individual impotence, like that which man feels when he contemplates the majestic and eternal forces of the inanimate world."[45]

Just as Christian teaching insinuated the power of God into the will of Tocqueville's American, so was the power of public opinion woven "into the texture of every mind."[46] And just as divine force modified that person's understanding of "free will," causing him to credit the fruit of his labor to God and to accept fate as the will of God, so did the power of public opinion temper the arrogance of the individualist, causing him to believe in the rightness of the majority and accept the judgment of the majority as truth.

Bryce comments on the curious mixture of vigor and fatalism in the personality of the American individualist. American individualism, he writes, is "in many forms and directions so vigorous,"[47] with "explorers, settlers, and businessmen pushing great enterprises,"[48] but it is combined with a kind of "fatalistic temper," a "self-distrust, a despondency, a disposition to fall in line."[49] When the power of public opinion entered the mind of the individualist, it caused him to "submit thought as well as action to the encompassing power of numbers."[50] The American was as proud and ambitious as the Old World imperial self, but compared to this other figure, he lacked a certain spring of inward strength.

Bryce describes a similar state of mind following the loss of an election in America. He writes,

A man of convictions may insist that they are after the polling just what they were before. But the average man will repeat his arguments with less faith, less zeal, more of a secret fear that he may be wrong, than he did while the majority was still doubtful; and after every reassertion by the majority of its judgement, his knees grow feebler, till at last they refuse to carry him into combat.[51]

While public opinion did not immobilize the American, it caused a loss of energy within that figure's will, a drooping of the wings, a feeling of dismay arising from no clearly identifiable outside pressure. The American's resolve was not obliterated so much as it was melted like wax in the sun. A peculiar state of despondency followed from contemplating one's smallness in a very large, unformed universe. The power of public opinion led to a powerlessness of mind and will incompatible with the belief in an imperial self.

The order of republican principle is also incompatible with the belief in an imperial self. While manners were used by the Old World aristocrat to express power and achieve supremacy, in Tocqueville's American they reflected a willingness to dissolve the self into a higher order. When Tocqueville's American followed the rules of democracy by serving out supper dishes in order or by waiting respectfully in line at the butcher's shop, he or she was not defending personal sovereignty. Rather, he or she was admitting that in freedom one must yield. Republican principle in Tocqueville's America was not invoked as a shield against threats to one's "autonomy." Its purpose was just the opposite—to submerge the self within a grand design, a design in which everybody's position was carefully laid out just as in God's divine plan.

Republican principle in Tocqueville's America was not a declaration of the imperial self but a repudiation of it. Republican principle muted cries for personal recognition, that one be first. It caused Tocqueville's American to assert not his own power (not the power of some imagined "I"), but the rightness of some higher order. It attests to the incompatibility of a belief in the imperial self with aristocracy in the City of God.

The Resurrection of the Imperial Self

In Tocqueville's American, the belief in the imperial self was annulled by superior powers attaching themselves to the human will. Christianity, public opinion, and republican principle prevented the love of self in Tocqueville's American from assuming magnificent proportions. As the spirit of Tocqueville's America declined, those forces no longer operated on the American mind. The rise of the organization man announced the return of self-love to America, but more importantly, it set the stage for a return of self-love on an imperial scale.

The belief in equality and harmony, the fear of difference, and the obsession with relative status shaped the institutions of the organization man—his workplace, his suburban life, his university, his church, his friendships, and his politics—and those attitudes are rooted in a tremendous love of self. Rather than defend a higher order or ideal, they serve to defend self-esteem, to reassure the unsure, and to allow the individual to hoard praise. On the surface, the emphasis on sameness and equality suggests more a sacrifice of self than a love of self, implying a link with Tocqueville's America. But upon closer inspection, the love of self is quite evident.

It was because the organization man loved himself so much that his entire world was shaped to appease his vanity and prevent it from being threatened. Self-love animated the peer groups that closed themselves to strangers, the psychological tests that separated the normal from the deviate, the salesclerks who submerged their identities into the corporations they worked for, and the vacation trips that promised higher status. It carved American society into a honeycomb of enclaves, invested some jobs with more honor than others, demanded absolute conformity, and raised the psychological importance of trinkets sold in the marketplace (e.g., the need to "keep up with the Joneses.") If one could not be admired by society as a whole, one could be admired within the confines of a small peer group. If one could not be a success, one could at least be "normal." If one could not compete, one could win admiration by being a "team player." If one knew only how to "care" and give of one's feelings, then one was still deserving of honor. Every institution and social arrangement in the society of the organization man served to protect and further one's estimation of oneself, to flatter the self and bring it praise.

But the organization man was a transitional figure, lasting only ten to fifteen years. By the 1960s, the ideology of expressive individualism was dominant. From the perspective of world history, one can perhaps see the logic behind this train of events.

Tocqueville's American was not just any democrat or any individualist. He did not represent just another twist of liberal sensibilities. On the contrary, he belongs in a genealogy of aristocracy that extends back many centuries. Tocqueville's American is the carrier of aristocracy in the democratic age and can be linked to the Roman aristocrats of late antiquity just as firmly as he can to the philosophers of the Enlightenment. The major difference between Tocqueville's American and the aristocrats preceding him is that Tocqueville's American lacked the belief in the imperial self. Tocqueville's American was the first aristocrat in the City of God and thus represents an aberration in the long tradition of worldly aristocrats.

Seen in this light, the rapid decline of the organization man and equally rapid rise of the expressive individualist seem altogether natural. Tocqueville's America was followed by ten years of organization man society, but was preceded by more than fifteen hundred years of aristocracy. As the carrier of the aristocratic tradition, Tocqueville's American contained within him the "instincts" of worldly aristocrats, smothered as they were by Christianity, public opinion, and republican principle. Flashes of imperial behavior can even be observed in the philosophy and literature of nineteenth-century America. In a work titled *The Imperial Self*, Quentin Anderson describes the obsession with the self in the writings of Emerson and Whitman,[52] and Peter Shaw draws a line between those writings and 1960s expressive individualism.[53] If an ideology that lured Europe was Saint-Simonian socialism, attesting to a strong peasant tradition, the ideology that lured America was Emersonianism, attesting to an equally strong aristocratic tradition. Lying dormant like a recessive gene, the belief in the imperial self was hidden in the early American character, contained by powers and waiting to be expressed in a later generation of aristocrats. When those powers bearing down on the mind and will of Tocqueville's American became inoperative and the love of something above the self was replaced by a love of self, the stage was set in America for a return to aristocracy in its conventional form.

The imperial self returned to prominence in the first generation of worldly aristocrats that followed the aristocrat in the City of God—the generation of expressive individualists. In the mind of the organization man, one can literally see the imperial self struggling to free itself from its confines. The organization man was "trapped" in his job, sucked into the "rat race," hiding his "true self," and playing the "phony." He could barely control his "imperial" urges. A master self that had partially been liberated by the decline of Christianity, public opinion, and republican principle was desperately trying to make a complete break-out. With the expressive individualist revolt, it would finally do so. Like a spring artificially held taught, the aristocratic tendency in the American character was finally allowed to attain a relaxed state.

In this way, the triumph of expressive individualism represents the resurgence of an aristocratic tradition going back many centuries. Only now, instead of operating within the environment of reverence that guided the ancient imperial self, the modern imperial self operates within the environment of fellow-feeling established during the society of the organization man. The expressive individualist brings with him many of the ways of the organization man—the social ethic, the belief that some jobs are more honorable than others, the consumer culture, the search for "fulfillment"—and merely joins them to a belief in the imperial self. The organization man's emphasis on conformism has died away because it constitutes a direct threat to the imperial self. But much else remains. Expressive individualism resurrects an old ideal and ushers in a new age of aristocracy, but it does so according to a new spirit of human motivation. The movement of expressive individualism is inspired by ancient beliefs, yet the society of the organization man was its crucible.

How the Imperial Self of the Expressive Individualist Recalls the Imperial Self of the Old World Aristocrat

In demonstrating a link between the expressive individualist and the aristocrat, it is not enough to show that the new imperial self possesses, like his or her Old World counterpart, an arrogance and presumption of superiority over and above that commonly observed in human nature. The tie between the two character types can be more firmly established by showing how the imperial self is imagined similarly in expressive individualism and Old World aristocratic belief. Like the imperial self of late antiquity, the modern imperial self declares the self to be sovereign, with an imagined threat to his or her "free will" coming from the world beyond. The modern imperial self, like the ancient imperial self, believes that certain dangerous forces exist separately from the will of man, always lurking nearby. For the imperial self of Augustine's Cicero, the opposing force was fate, which was under the control of the gods. For the expressive individualist, the opposing force is "society."

The expressive individualist imagines two loci of power, one lying within the self and the other lying beyond. The empowered self is in command, and it is in this spirit that the expressive individualist defends autonomy, individuality, unrestricted rights, and infinite choice. At the same time, the expressive individualist believes that the self is potentially a "victim" of society. Society can be maliciously clever. It can trick the self and cause it to deviate from its "real" aspirations. Society can hold the self in a vise and prevent it from realizing all possibilities. Just as the gods in the writings of Herodotus can interfere with the "free will" of a mortal in subtle and insidious ways, so can society in the culture of expressive individualism interfere with the freedom of the modern imperial self.

Within this belief system are positions corresponding exactly to those of Cicero and Seneca in Augustine's *City of God*. Corresponding to Cicero's position is the rejection of society by the modern imperial self and the declaration that real autonomy and true freedom are possible because the power of society is insignificant. Corresponding to Seneca's position is the belief that individuals are incapable of freedom, that, to paraphrase Seneca, society drags the man who is unwilling. In a way, Erving Goffman functions as sort of a modern-day Seneca when he declares the idea of liberty a sham because society coerces the individual and prevents him or her from ever being truly free. Just as Seneca's gods tricked the hero into believing destiny was the product of man's will (even though it had already been predetermined), so does Goffman's society trick the modern imperial self into believing in freedom and autonomy (even though one is really molded by social pressure).

Even the ancient writer, Herodotus, has his counterpart in contemporary America. The journalist who reports a crime and says the offender's actions are not only a manifestation of free will but also a reflection of society's influence recalls Herodotus's description of the ancient Greek hero whose destiny was determined by both the free will of the person and the power of the gods. The proposition that the criminal can be simultaneously a free agent and a victim of society is made in the society of expressive individualism without fear of contradiction, just as the ancient historian declared the hero to be in control of his destiny yet subject to the whims of the gods. In both cases, the will of the sovereign self is occasionally influenced by a locus of power standing outside of the self.

This struggle between the modern imperial self and "society" can also be found in scholarship devoted to the study of expressive individualism. Arlie Hochschild describes how the modern self is forced to "deep act," to feign certain feelings that are demanded by conventions that prevent expression of one's "real" self.[54] While society applies pressure from the outside, Hochschild believes, there remains a core lying deep within the person that can be shielded from external force. That core represents the inner, or true," self.[55] Christopher Lasch describes how the external world of "society" (the world of "manipulation"[56]) bears down on an individual and how the individual must fight back with "assertiveness" training. Richard Merelman describes how the self can be threatened by society, how it is potentially a "social creation,"[57] and how it can be victimized by social pressure in its effort to gain autonomy.[58] C. Wright Mills finds the self in America to be threatened by commercial forces as it is encouraged to adopt a prepackaged personality, thus leaving less space for the "real" self.[59] Through this influence, Mills writes, one becomes self-alienated.[60]

Each of these authors describes the experience of the modern imperial self in a manner that closely parallels the experience of the ancient imperial self. The ancient imperial self also discerned the major threat to one's person to lie in a separate locus of power. The modern imperial self who is harassed by society recalls the ancient imperial self who was harassed by Seneca's gods. In each case there is an "I" presumed to be whole and sufficient and prevented from realizing its ambitions and full potential by a force beyond.

The Modern Imperial Self and "Honor" in the Culture of Expressive Individualism

The contemporary expressive individualist bears a strong resemblance to the aristocrat in the City of Man. The two character types share common attitudes toward work, family, religion, and personal reputation, and even a belief in the imperial self. But one facet of the old aristocrat's personality is not shared by the expressive individualist. The expressive individualist does not have the "honor" of the aristocrat in the City of Man.

The Old World aristocrat was competitive and ambitious and desirous of personal glory, but also in possession of great self-confidence and inner security. Deep within his mind were memories of experience and principles of education that bolstered his identity, independent of personal success or failure. They confirmed his own sense of value even when his value measured by others in the zero-sum game of status transiently declined. It is this high estimation of personal value that I equate with "honor."

Honor differs from simple pride by referring more to one's opinion of oneself than a concern for the judgments of others. It is true that another's opinion mattered greatly to the Old World aristocrat; he was extremely sensitive to personal slights and aggressively competed for status. But while status-consciousness may be connected with a vigorous defense of honor, it is not synonymous with it. Honor is a sentiment distinct and independent, representing in some ways even the antithesis of status-seeking behavior. To be status-conscious is to define and become aware of one's own value through a comparison with others. It does not suggest a defense of value so much as a search for value. Honor is something very different. It represents a natural, almost unthinking, recognition of value prior to comparison with others.

As aristocrats evolved through history, becoming, as Bendix notes, more self-controlled and less impulsive after the feudal era, the honor of the gentleman replaced the military prowess of the warrior as the highest value. [61] The aristocrat became less personally combative and physically aggressive. [62] According to Bendix, the aristocratic obsession with relative status remained, though now the zero-sum game of status was played out in court rather than on the battlefield. [63] Towards the end of the nineteenth century, however, a different kind of aristocrat emerges, one who almost voluntarily withdraws from the competition for status but who nevertheless retains a firm belief in his honor. Status-consciousness and great inner confidence, generally observed in tandem in the personality of the Old World aristocrat, begin to diverge. It is in this new figure that the difference between honor and simple pride is most glaring.

The divergence between the two feelings can sometimes be observed among characters in late nineteenth- and early twentieth-century fiction designed to portray aristocrats. In novels, they live idle lives not simply because they find labor for profit contemptible, but because they are self-sufficient and feel no compulsion to prove anything to anyone. Perhaps these later aristocrats who felt little urge to compete and triumph as the warrior-aristocrat once did, who lived in the world of dining clubs, cigarettes, and sexual nuance described by Ronald Firbank, Vita Sackville-West, E. F. Benson, and Evelyn Waugh, represent a decadent form of aristocracy. But there are other aristocratic characters drawn from the same period who, upon losing wealth and title, live contentedly in obscurity, sustained not by a love of vice but only by an inner confidence in who they are. [64]

Max Scheler discusses the special aristocratic characteristic that I am referring to, which he also distinguishes from simple pride and social competitiveness. Scheler writes, "The noble man experiences value prior to any comparison, the common man in and through a comparison. . . . The latter [the common man] arrives at value judgements by comparing himself to others and others to himself." [65] He continues,

The "noble person" has a completely naive and nonreflective awareness of his own value and of his fullness of being, an obscure conviction which enriches every conscious moment of his existence, as if he were autonomously rooted in the universe. This should not be mistaken for "pride." Quite on the contrary, pride results from an experienced diminution of this "naive" self-confidence. It is a way of "holding" on to one's value, of seizing and "preserving" it deliberately. The noble man's naive self-confidence, which is as natural to him as tension is to the muscles, permits him calmly to assimilate the merits of others in all the fullness of their substance and configuration.[66]

There was hidden within the Old World aristocrat a kind of fundamental certainty of identity independent of whether or not he or she emerged triumphant in the competition for status. While traditional aristocrats competed against each other and feared a decline in status, their ambition, haughtiness, and feelings of superiority should not be confused with their tremendous poise and self-confidence. The inner security of the aristocrat constitutes a distinct psychological element, one that can coexist in the human personality with status-consciousness and extreme sensitivity, but that nevertheless is separate. The status-consciousness of aristocrats is merely a reflection of the high degree of socialization of such persons and that high degree of socialization can be found among other character types, like the peasant and the organization man. Within their respective peer groups, the peasant and the organization man also desired the respect and good opinion of others. But only in the aristocrat did the distinct psychological element called "honor" exist, separate from vanity and the urge to compare oneself with others.

The distinction between the social competitiveness of the aristocrat and that figure's inner confidence is also alluded to by Tocqueville. Tocqueville refers to the aristocrat's honor as the system of rules adopted by the aristocratic class that confers glory or disgrace on a person, but applies only to the person of the aristocrat and not to the value of a particular action.[67] Honor in aristocratic society was "attached to a man's actions according to his condition" such that particular virtues and vices "belonged to the nobility rather than to the humble classes."[68] Tocqueville writes,

Thus some of the actions which were indifferent on the part of a man in humble life dishonored a noble; others changed their whole character according as the person aggrieved by them belonged or did not belong to the aristocracy.[69]

He continues,

Honor is easily mingled and identified in their minds with the idea of all that distinguishes their own position; it appears to them as the chief characteristic of their own rank; they apply its different rules with all the warmth of personal interest, and they may feel (if I may use the expression) a passion for complying with its dictates.[70]

The aristocrat vigorously defended his honor not to gain the admiration of others but to fulfill the meaning of his existence as a superior being. He had an awareness of his own value and special dignity, an awareness often observed in exhibitions of high-mindedness and self-restraint. Honor could require the aristocrat to be violent and vengeful, to be unforgiving of insults, yet at other times to be quiet and unpretending, to conquer one's passions, and to forget the self.[71] For Tocqueville's aristocrat, this inner confidence came from knowing that one was firmly ensconced in the highest class and was not in any way synonymous with pretentious displays of class privilege.

It was often in the smallest activities of life that the noble soul of the aristocrat felt and knew itself in its greatest depth. This is hinted at by H. Rider Haggard, who writes, "How true is the saying that the very highest in rank are always the most simple and kindly."[72] In describing a fictional character of aristocratic mien, Haggard notes her "sweet simplicity, and her kindly, genuine interest even in little things," which did not prevent her from being "queenly enough" during moments of great struggle.[73] It was not a proud, defiant, and overbearing nature that made the aristocrat noble but just the opposite. Another example of aristocratic honor is found in the true story of an English officer who puts a young recruit from a poor background at ease during a dinner party.[74] In this story, the recruit is offered ice to cool his champagne but, unfamiliar with such elegance, he hesitates and then puts the ice in his soup. While others around the table begin to chuckle, the English officer, when offered the ice, also puts it in his soup without breaking stride in his conversation or moving a muscle of his face. The recruit breathes freely, believing that he has conducted himself in the appropriate manner after all. Reverend Smythe Palmer, who reports the story, says, "That little act of delicate consideration for another's feelings was rightly characterized as an act distinctive of a true gentleman."

Just as "honor" is not the same as status-consciousness, neither is it synonymous with the aristocratic belief in the imperial self. That it remains a separate idea is demonstrated in the fact that the expressive individualist is also an imperial self, but one lacking in "honor."

Both the Old World aristocrat and the expressive individualist imagine that the will is unified under the command of a solitary "I," with all challenges to that state of control arising from beyond. The aristocrat, however, combined this tremendous egoism with honor, with feelings of sufficiency and completeness. No God or transcendent divinity was needed by the aristocrat to make the self whole. Nothing beyond the self was required to give meaning to his life. The very idea of a "mission in life," that a man should "have a purpose or seek to realize an ideal," was considered contemptible by the aristocrat, an insult to the very honor that so composed him.[75] It was in this way that the "value of aristocratic existence was self-contained"[76] and the Old World aristocrat displayed not only a belief in a sovereign "I" but honor's inner confidence. The expressive individualist also believes in the existence of a sovereign "I" and that only external forces threaten the self. But the expressive individualist lacks the aristocrat's inner confidence and fundamental certainty of identity, elements found in all Old World aristocrats (including both the feudal warrior and the decadent Edwardian). The expressive individualist senses a lack of completeness within. He is unsure of his own value; he is anxious about it, and that inner void compels him to search beyond the self for the piece that completes, for that which will make him whole and sufficient. It is in this way that the expressive individualist lacks honor.

The expressive individualist lacks this vital aristocratic feature to which he may attach his imperial self; he believes strongly in autonomy, but he feverishly searches beyond the self for "community," for a "mission in life," and for "meaning." Even the expressive individualist's quest for a loved one is guided by this purpose, becoming not just a way of gaining a little happiness, but rather of making the self whole and complete.[77] Thus, an important difference exists between the expressive individualist and the aristocrat in the City of Man, one that is unrelated to the fact that both are imperial selves.

The Imperial Self and "Community" in the Culture of Expressive Individualism

Both the Old World aristocrat and Tocqueville's American had honor, which leads to a second point—just as one can be an imperial self and not have honor, so can one have honor and not be an imperial self.

The honor of the Old World aristocrat was inseparable from membership in the highest class (in aristocracy).[78] Within that caste, the aristocrat and his fellows shared common experiences through the entire course of their lives. At a very early age, the aristocrat became familiar with the personalities of those who were destined to be his companions at school, partners at a club, fellow officers in the military, or associates in public service. Each new milestone in the life of the aristocrat was approached in the company of well-known persons, and each rite of passage, once passed, became a source of common reminiscences. These connections lent a certain firmness and solidity to the personality of the aristocrat. In nineteenth-century English fiction, for example, this sensibility was expressed in a meeting of aristocrats in some distant, war-torn land, where they would spend a moment conversing about a peer's hunting preserve or "who fagged for whom at Oxford." These characters exuded a certain natural confidence and, although they were complete strangers to one another, they were comfortable with each other (and with themselves) because they were members of a small aristocratic community. They came from England's "Ten Thousand First," or "the Upper Ten Thousand of this our English world," which was composed of those families in "Society" who were connected by family links or by association at school or university.[79] It was through membership in this highest stratum and close familiarity with its institutions that an aristocrat came to be aware of a certain completeness in his freestanding self and of a great value hidden within.

There were no fixed castes in Tocqueville's America and therefore no physical "community" in which to nourish honor. Yet the aristocrat in the City of God has a counterpart to the worldly aristocrat's closed community, and that is public opinion. Public opinion was a rather imperfect mechanism for instilling honor, due to its volatility, but it was able to penetrate deep into the psyche of Tocqueville's American and implant within that figure a sense of high value. In a different way, public opinion produced the same result as habitual interaction between members of an aristocratic peer group.

Tocqueville touches briefly on this phenomenon, writing,

> Some loose notions of the old aristocratic honor of Europe are still to be found scattered among the opinions of the Americans, but these traditional opinions are few in number. . . . They are like a religion which has still some temples left standing, though men have ceased to believe in it. But amidst these half-obliterated notions of exotic honor some new opinions have sprung up which constitute what may be termed in our days American honor.[80]

The special system of honor in nineteenth-century America was grounded in the commercial and industrial activity of the nation. It had a different basis than conventional aristocratic honor; that which was was "stigmatized as servile cupidity" in the Middle Ages (e.g., a love of money) became, in Tocqueville's America, "noble and praiseworthy ambition."[81] But when Tocqueville's American displayed courage in business, persevered in an enterprise, and made it "a matter of honor to live chastely"[82] not simply because he worried about another person's opinion but to defend the high values lying behind those opinions, he was apprehending the full value of his isolated self just as the aristocrat did when he defended his honor. The spirit suggests not an effort to look beyond the self for justification, but rather an effort to perfect and hallow an already abundant self through strong discipline.

Tocqueville says of public opinion that it

> very gently represses that love of wealth which promotes the commercial greatness and the prosperity of the nation, and especially condemns that laxity of morals which diverts the human mind from the pursuit of well-being and disturbs the internal order of domestic life which is necessary to success in business.[83]

Military bravery and the code of the gentlemen were sustained among aristocrats through a common upbringing, a common system of education, and a strong family tradition. Courage in business and order in domestic life were, in Tocqueville's America, sustained through public opinion. Public opinion instilled within the Americans the essential elements of honor—a moral code, a method of internal discipline and authority, an identity, a positive sense of self, and an understanding of one's great purpose. By internalizing those values synonymous with the noble life, Tocqueville's Americans could take the measure of themselves. For example, while traveling in a distant land, Tocqueville's American had a fair approximation of his own worth; he was only afraid of ranking himself too high or too low.[84] Perhaps the Old World aristocrat who traveled abroad naturally assumed that he ranked the highest, and therefore his poise and inner confidence were greater than that of the American. But public opinion was successful in convincing the American that certain marks of respect were due to him, that he also possessed great value. Tocqueville's Americans did not all attend the same schools or the same clubs but through public opinion they found security in right thinking and proper behavior, all while gaining an easy familiarity with one another.

The expressive individualist has neither the "community" of the Old World aristocrat nor the public opinion of Tocqueville's American. On the contrary, it is precisely "community" that he searches for. If the Old World aristocrat was locked into a community, the expressive individualist is locked out. This is why the modern imperial self comes to lack honor.

Although the ancient imperial self proclaimed the existence of a sovereign "I" and rejected divination, the social stratum called "aristocracy" remained intact. The imperial self's sacrilegiousness did not in any way endanger the physical community of aristocrats, and thus a source of common experiences and worldly memories went untouched. The ancient imperial self left intact the mechanism by which honor was instilled in aristocrats in the City of Man.

The modern imperial self also proclaims the existence of a sovereign "I" but does so by rejecting physical communities. The imperial self rejects society because it is potentially hostile and suffocating, because it demands conformity and prevents one from growing. The expressive individualist places great importance on "meeting people," on "finding that special someone," or on simulating those experiences in books and movies. But the expressive individualist also discerns the greatest threat to the self to be in a union of minds. Social bonds can be warm and cozy, but to the modern imperial self, they can also be like ropes cutting wrists.

On a small scale, this tension is commonly observed among expressive individualists who desire a relationship but fear commitment. The modern imperial self wants to form a deep and lasting tie with another but fears sacrificing independence and autonomy. On a larger scale, this tension underlies the expressive individualist's struggle between "individual" and "community." The expressive individualist fears the impact of society on his or her freedom, but at the same time hankers after society in order to fulfill some inner need. All-threatening society is occasionally transformed into "community;" a new mask is put on the same figure to make what was once very threatening now quite desirable. These conflicting impulses are understood to be a part of the "quest for community."[85]

Yet by wavering between rejecting and embracing physical communities, the modern imperial self destroys the very mechanism by which honor was nurtured and sustained in the personality of the ancient imperial self. And by rejecting public opinion and the conformism it engenders, the modern imperial self dismantles the democratic mechanism by which a slightly different understanding of honor was instilled in Tocqueville's American. The modern imperial self, by defining itself against the social order, is left without those instruments by which inner confidence, feelings of complete-ness, and a naive awareness of one's own excellence have been instilled in aristocratic forms throughout history. The modern imperial self poisons the source of honor at its roots.

For many Americans, the search for community has become a mission or purpose. But while many have searched for it, the community of expressive individualists has never actually been sighted on this continent. This is because such a community does not exist except in the minds of expressive individualists who are needy, who lack inner strength and vital plenitude, who are anxious and confused, and who lack honor. Operating almost like a homing instinct, the quest for community guides America's new aristocrats in the direction of a social form that centuries ago provided Old World aristocrats with a subconscious awareness of their own value. Yet once rejected, the expressive individualist cannot get it back. Because the modern imperial self defines the sovereign "I" against society, he or she is destined to spend a lifetime searching for ideals like "community," a "politics of meaning," or the "higher self." By destroying all sources of honor, the modern imperial self has come to lack the inner security possessed by both the Old World aristocrat and Tocqueville's American and is compelled to be forever looking for the piece that completes, that will make the self whole. Ironically, when expressive individualists proclaim their sovereignty and freedom, they are merely building their own tombs.

The Modern Imperial Self and the Lifestyle Enclave

One popular form of community in expressive individualist America is the lifestyle enclave. Common recreational and leisure interests bring people together so that they can enjoy each other's company and feel the warmth of "belonging." But the lifestyle enclave is not really an authentic community. It can not instill honor in its members, as the Old World aristocratic community once did.

The lifestyle enclave brings people together on the basis of just one interest and allows members to shield the bulk of their personalities from any socializing force. Members can escape the conformist pressure of the lifestyle enclave simply by not attending its meetings or events or by shifting their attention elsewhere. The situation was very different in the Old World aristocratic community. The aristocratic community provided a system so complete and detailed that it consumed the entire life of a person. It configured a person's mind from infancy so that all thought and action, not just a single interest, were touched by its influence. The lifestyle enclave has no such socializing power. It cannot capture the imaginations of its members so completely. The expressive individualist controls the impact of the lifestyle enclave on his or her personality like a faucet; it can be turned on and off or simply adjusted to meet the needs of the autonomous self.

This explains why the lifestyle enclave fails to perform the vital functions of the Old World aristocratic community. More specifically, it explains why the lifestyle enclave cannot instill honor in its members. Membership in the lifestyle enclave is voluntary. People pick and choose lifestyle enclaves according to their interests and do so with the power of conscious reason. The problem is that honor, nobility, and a firm knowledge of identity denote a naive and subconscious awareness of one's value; they describe a psychological posture that is reflexively maintained outside of the sphere of reason. The positive feeling towards the self that Scheler attributes to the "noble person" is best understood as something instinctive. It is not formulated on the plane of conscious reason, which is the level on which expressive individualists join lifestyle enclaves.

A system of honor, if it is to succeed, need not be logical or rational. It need only sway the will of its believer. A system of honor works by shackling the individual mind below the level of conscious thought. Its precepts and opinions prune and bend the imagination of an individual until he or she mouths its virtues reflexively, without hesitation. In order to accomplish this, a system of honor must penetrate into every crevice of a person's life and touch him or her at every moment of existence. The angles of a young child's character must be fretted and whittled away by a constant exposure to the injunctions of honor, and an adult must not even perceive that he or she has acquired the habit of obedience when following its dictates. A system of honor succeeds by gradually refining and modeling a person's imagination until obeying the rules of honor becomes the meaning of life itself. When that point is reached, when the person becomes smooth and round and polished, he or she is ready to become a part of the great edifice of civilized society.

This is how the Old World aristocratic community and the network of public opinion in Tocqueville's America instilled honor. Rather than appealing to conscious reason or asking people to deliberate thoughtfully, they concentrated all efforts on the nonrational parts of the human mind. Tocqueville reports that for aristocratic honor, the power its injunctions exerted over the mind grew more fantastic the further removed they were from the sphere of common reason.[86] A similar situation operated in public opinion. Public opinion exerted power on the mind by entering a portal below the level of conscious thought. In this way, the person was not persuaded so much as he or she was "infected." In both cases, the process was nonrational. Neither the Old World aristocratic community nor the network of public opinion in Tocqueville's America instilled honor by offering "choice." Instead, the "noble person" came into being after countless minute acts, judgments, and experiences steadily bombarded the mind and penetrated it, causing a certain disposition to be formed in much the way that a steady stream of water, over time, hollows out a rock.

The expressive individualist gains membership in a lifestyle enclave on a completely different level. Membership is voluntary, and the rules of the enclave are obeyed so long as interest in the particular enclave continues. This experience fails to effect the necessary psychological reaction that generates honor or a positive sense of self. Even those lifestyle enclaves that have rules that are as fantastic as those governing aristocratic communities cannot deliver the necessary psychological impact. The member of the lifestyle enclave always retains some distance. There remains a consciousness that any submission to a larger whole is voluntary, and any relationship entered into is nonbinding. Even when a bond is made in the spirit of fellow-feeling, when people have come to know each other through psychology,[87] a person remains aware that one can exit a group if its rules become oppressive to the autonomous self. The lifestyle enclave, unlike the aristocratic community and public opinion, has no pronounced effect on the subconscious of a person. It is joined through rational choice and on that plane it remains.

The Old World aristocratic community and the lifestyle enclave appear similar because both are filled with like-minded people. The difference between the two turns on the issue of honor. The aristocratic community was filled with people who moved about with confidence and ease and who demonstrated a consideration for others because they were comfortable with themselves. The lifestyle enclave is filled with expressive individualists who lack the aristocrat's inner confidence and who move about with fear and anxiety. The experience, for example, of the bohemian city artist dressed in black attending a wedding in a conservative, middle-class suburb, or of the retiree venturing into a nightclub for youth, yields an often characteristic response. The expressive individualist grows unsure and a bit rattled when entering a part of society that has a different value structure from the one he or she is used to. Unlike the Old World aristocrat who never doubted the value of his or her person, the expressive individualist turns wistful when venturing into a new setting (e.g., the urban professional visiting a country town, the educated and lapsed Catholic venturing into a sect of religious believers). The expressive individualist wonders if members of the new enclave enjoy a richer and fuller life, whether they are more complete and vibrant. In such cases, the expressive individualist may be sustained by musing, "Have not others done what I have done?" or by nervously mocking those values put forth by the new lifestyle enclave. And if the expressive individualist is considerate of others in the new enclave, it is not because of a tremendous inner confidence but rather a lack of confidence, because the expressive individualist fears that casting a negative judgment on others may expose him or her to a similar judgement in the future, which is threatening.

Hence, the aristocratic community and the lifestyle enclave differ even though both are homogeneous in their membership. The former serves as a crucible for making positive, self-confident, and secure individuals. The latter is often a retreat for the anxious and the confused.

The Modern Imperial Self, the "Career," and the "Calling"

The modern imperial self's lack of honor is also evident in the tremendous emphasis placed by expressive individualists on the "career" and the "calling." Like those who search for "community," the expressive individualists who aspire to work in a career or a calling feel the same urge to place themselves in the current of life, to make their lives valid and special. These expressive individualists lack self-sufficiency and rely on certain events and experiences to validate their existences.

This phenomenon can be observed independent of political affiliation. Those working in callings like the caring professions are often more "liberal" than careerists in law, business, and finance. The character of Brian Palmer in Robert Bellah's book, who strives for success, who sacrifices everything for "the job, the career, the company,"[88] may be more politically conservative than the social worker working in the environment of poverty and neglect. But among those who work in either a career or a calling, there can be seen a common desire to justify and complete the self, to make the self whole through a marriage to one's work.

This motive is not the same as ambition. Ambition is a longstanding feature of human nature, not a new imaginative experience. The desire to excel in something and ensure the memory of one's name is an age-old conceit. Nor is it the same as the desire for high status. If anything, it signifies an effort to validate the self independent of one's position in a status hierarchy. Nor is it like the Old World aristocrat's urge to "do one's duty." To do one's duty is to give physical expression to one's great inner value, to act in accordance with a high estimation of one's value, and not to acquire value. For the expressive individualist, the career and the calling are engaged in to reassure the self, to give the self an identity, and to prove to the self that one has value, which is held in doubt.

The Old World aristocrat was self-contained. He felt no urge to set out on a mission in life or to prove his worthiness as a human being by pursuing a career or a calling. The Old World aristocrat did not fear a negative judgment on his existence if all he accomplished in life was the preservation of his honor and dignity. There is evidence that the idea of a calling had greater significance in Tocqueville's America; Max Weber's study of nineteenth-century capitalism notes the importance of the calling in the Protestant tradition.[89] But even within the American experience there is an important difference between the "calling" of the expressive individualist and the "calling" of the nineteenth-century Protestant capitalist.

According to Weber, the Protestant capitalist believed that "the fulfillment of worldly duties is under all circumstances the only way to live acceptably to God."[90] Weber says that in the Protestant calling, an individual "saw more and more a special command of God to fulfill those particular duties which the Divine Will had imposed upon him."[91] It signified a surrender of one's self and one's life to the superior power of God, not an assertion of one's imperial being against God. The calling in Tocqueville's America was undertaken to glorify God, not to ennoble or justify the self independent of God.

This is why the idea of the calling in Tocqueville's America coexisted with a belief that all honest jobs are honorable. All labor, according to Weber's interpretation of Protestant teaching, is believed to represent the "will of God," and hence "every legitimate calling has exactly the same worth in the sight of God."[92] The calling in the Protestant tradition is not noble because a circle of human beings has attached a high value to it or because the task possesses inherent virtue. It is noble only because it is labor and because, "One may attain salvation in any walk of life; on the short pilgrimage of life there is no use in laying weight on the form of occupation."[93] In every work undertaken with this high aim, there lies an element of nobility, no matter how humble or unrecognized the work may be. The calling in nineteenth-century America capitalism encompassed virtually all forms of labor because it was undertaken to shed glory on God, not on the self.

For the expressive individualist, worldly activity in careers and callings is not engaged in as a service to God, but to bring honor to the self. It is to bring honor where honor is lacking, to reassure the self that one is vital because it is presumed that by engaging in activity judged positive and uplifting, one must be vital. The expressive individualist desires to work in a career or a calling, which is different from Weber's Protestant capitalist who simply desired to work because all labor was a calling. The "career" in business and the "calling" in social work, one "conservative" and the other "liberal," are entered into by the expressive individualist to justify the self, to bolster a self that secretly doubts whether it has positive value. The glory of the career and the calling in the society of expressive individualism conceals a fervent hope that the task, once engaged in, will provide the completing piece to an incomplete identity.

The only difference between the career and the calling in expressive individualist America is that the calling is invested with a particular kind of virtue. The calling combines the search for identity with the virtues of love, compassion, and caring, which are preeminent virtues in a society animated by the spirit of fellow-feeling. But while the career is not necessarily as virtuous as the calling, both the career and the calling represent a kind of holy mission, one that the old aristocrat would have scoffed at but that also would have been quite foreign to Weber's Protestant capitalist.

This is an important point that needs to be developed more thoroughly. The Old World aristocrat believed some jobs to be more honorable than others, but this is because a high estimation of his own value, reinforced by the rules of honor, caused him to be so discriminating. The aristocrat avoided those jobs that he considered dishonorable in order to preserve his dignity, to harbor and protect the great value that he discerned within himself. It was precisely because he was so self-contained and self-sufficient that the aristocrat scorned the idea of a calling and considered it an insult to his dignity. The aristocrat's status-consciousness was filtered through the spirit of reverence and those jobs considered most honorable were those where he could command and be revered by others. Yet this status-consciousness is separate from the particular psychological deficiency that might urge one to pursue a calling. A confusion about whether one has value is separate from the state of belief that causes some jobs in a society to be invested with greater honor than others.

The expressive individualist believes some jobs to be more honorable than others because what little status-consciousness he does possess is filtered through the spirit of fellow-feeling.[94] The result is the same as when status-consciousness was filtered through the spirit of reverence in old aristocratic society—the creation of a hierarchy in jobs that descended from the honorable to the dishonorable. But for the expressive individualist, unlike the Old World aristocrat, the most virtuous job in the hierarchy of occupations is a calling. This is because, for the expressive individualist, the belief in the imperial self is joined to a lack of coherent identity and a confused sense of self. The expressive individualist desires to work in a calling not simply because it constitutes the most honorable form of work, but because he hopes that by working at such a task, he will become more complete, more fulfilled, more worthwhile, and more noble. By working in the most honorable job in the society of expressive individualism, one tries to capture dignity for the self more than to protect dignity that is already a part of the self.

In this way, the expressive individualist stands as the mirror image of the Old World aristocrat. Both figures, unlike Tocqueville's American, create a spectrum of work ranging from the honorable to the dishonorable. But while the Old World aristocrat engages in only those tasks that are compatible with the rules of honor and complement his great dignity, the expressive individualist engages in only those tasks that are compatible with the virtues of compassion and fellow-feeling and that instill within the self a needed confidence. The honorable task for the expressive individualist is a calling because he or she, unlike the Old World aristocrat, needs a mission in life to feel complete and worthwhile.

The Modern Imperial Self and the "Self"

The search for "community," the effort to get "involved," the lifestyle enclave, the "career" and the "calling"—these are all aspects of life in contemporary America rooted in the expressive individualist's lack of honor. This lack of honor is also manifested in the expressive individualist's tendency to dissect the self and its feelings. In this pattern of behavior, the "I" of the modern imperial self begins to lose control over the very realm of conduct that the ancient imperial self confidently proclaimed to have absolute sovereignty. Through constant introspection, the "I" of the modern imperial self begins to lose control over one's person and feelings—in other words, of that domain that the ancient imperial self shielded from external force and declared to be his own. For the modern imperial self, the "self" soon becomes one more phenomenon, like "community" and the "calling," which is perceived to be somehow external to the "I." It becomes another ideal to be sought.

When the expressive individualist wonders who he is and what constitutes his "true" self, [95] when he mourns a separation between himself and his "feelings," or when he imagines a part of his own psyche to be lying somehow beyond (that he is self-alienated), he presumes that a part of the self exists beyond the controlling power of the "I." The expressive individualist perceives a disconnection between himself and these vital mental processes and, in doing so, functions as if he were partially dead. [96] There is no life or vitality in feelings that have been separated from the sense of the person; such feelings are merely a cluster of sensations or mental phenomena. Instead of being kneaded into the subconscious of a living person, they come to stand outside of the experience of the person.

The expressive individualist probes and inspects his feelings with all the power of reason, as if they formed a project in a lab. He pays great attention to his feelings, but in such a way that he transforms them into mere mechanical attachments of his body. They no longer form a part of his living "I," but rather constitute a separate "experience" that he hopes can be worked on in order to raise his mood and gain happiness.

This is the underlying basis for many of the efforts to "heighten one's feelings," to "induce feeling," and to "feel in a certain way."[97] In primal therapy, *est*, holistic medicine, psychotherapy, New Age mysticism, and even some new born-again religious movements, the self is treated as if it were an object external to the "I," one that can be hammered and chiseled and refined like so much lifeless plaster, all on the plane of conscious reason and rational choice. The effort to extirpate or recall certain memories,[98] to redefine some feelings while emphasizing others, all in order to build a "better" self or a "higher" self, is urged forward by an inner desire to fill a void, complete an identity, and convince the self that one is "really" living.

This effort is done not so much to maintain existing life, as the rules of honor and the codes of good breeding served the aristocrat. The aristocrat's rules of honor shaped attitudes, convictions, and behavior without a direct appeal to reason or choice. They affected the subconscious of a living organism and determined the instincts and reflexes of an individual whose feelings had not yet been rationally disconnected from his person. For the expressive individualist, the effort to create a higher self or find a true self represents more an effort to rescue life that is declining, to smooth over and adjust feelings that a person imagines to be distant and that, when properly adjusted and fine-tuned, he hopes to rationally incorporate back into the self.

This phenomenon is apparent, for example, in the vacation experience of the expressive individualist. For the organization man, the vacation was designed to elevate in that person's mind one's position in the status hierarchy. For the expressive individualist, the vacation is designed to satisfy the inner needs of the imperial self. Whether it be trekking in Nepal, biking in Italy, boating in Alaska, or touring the wine country, the vacation of the expressive individualist is arranged so as to set just the right tone, to capture just the right mood and feeling, and to allow that person's body to go through the same motions as the ideal person whom the expressive individualist believes to really have a life. By venturing into the same conditions, the expressive individualist on vacation hopes to experience certain feelings, trigger certain sensations, and elevate certain moods so that he can say, "I am living for this is what living is supposed to be." The "I" of the expressive individualist, his inner sense, detects the change in those feelings as if they were being measured on a galvanometer, and he infers from them whether or not he is really "experiencing life."

In the final analysis, the modern imperial self implodes. It begins to feed even on itself in its feverish quest for completeness. Therapy and vacation, like "community" and "career," do not solve the problem of identity or the fear of negative value but rather thrive on those deficiencies. They are all activities pursued "rationally," through "choice," and therefore are carried forth on a psychological plane lying far above the subconscious where honor, true positive feeling, and a dim awareness of one's own vital value are sustained. The expressive individualist, with his tremendous power of reason, concentrates much attention on himself and on the authenticity of the fleeting present moment in which he lives. But in this way, he loses control over the essentials of his person. The "I," the commander in his will, begins to disintegrate into a series of confused and shifting impulses; "I believe," in the society of expressive individualism, is transformed into "one feels."[99]

How the Expressive Individualist Is the Aristocrat's *Ressentiment* Opposite

The history of the aristocratic spirit traced from the City of Man to the City of God and then back to the City of Man helps to explain how the contemporary expressive individualist in the earthly city stands in relation to the Old World aristocrat who occupied a similar position centuries ago.

The expressive individualist, like the Tocquevillian American who came before him, is an "individualist." He feels detached from others, with no great tradition bonding him to anything or anyone, and much of life is traveled alone. But the sense of detachment in the expressive individualist originates in a different spirit than that which caused a related feeling in Tocqueville's American. In Tocqueville's American, a feeling of detachment was firmly rooted in the spirit of perseverance that animated him. His mind was telescoped forward into imagined distant time such that those who crossed his path during the present barely signified against the distant horizon. For the expressive individualist, the feeling of detachment originates in a completely different source of energy. It is caused by a reanimation of the idea of the imperial self, which forms part of a belief system that predates Tocqueville's America. Detachment in the expressive individualist arises when the age-old idea of an imperial self is filtered through the new spirit of fellow-feeling, such that the imperial self rebels against "society."

But if the expressive individualist who lives in the City of Man is a new kind of imperial self, he or she is not an aristocrat. On the contrary, the expressive individualist forms the aristocrat's direct *ressentiment* opposite, and to understood this point it is helpful to look at the values of expressive individualism in relation to socialist values.

Socialism constitutes a rebellion against the external world of aristocracy, against material inequality. The peasant and the socialist have little conception of the aristocratic spirit; all they see is the facade of the aristocrat—his wealth, his possessions, and his splendor—and it is because of their resentment against all that is visible in aristocratic society that the peasant and socialist invert the aristocratic value structure. Socialist values are configured in a particular way; they attempt to level the physical world of aristocratic society and make the distribution of wealth more equal. The socialist argues that the highest value is material equality and the greatest evil is the desire to achieve wealth above all others. Anger, impotence, and an obsessive concern with material things combine to create a new value structure, and the socialist who embraces these new values carries none of the aristocratic tradition within him, only the bitter image of the wealthy aristocrat.

Expressive individualism constitutes a rebellion within the aristocratic tradition because the expressive individualist inverts not the physical world of aristocratic society but rather a pattern of thought lying within the mind of the aristocrat. The expressive individualist carries within his own imagination the aristocratic belief in the imperial self; that belief is a part of his personality, of his experience. The anger of the expressive individualist is directed towards a different facet of aristocratic life, and his self-deception assumes a different form. He does not so much resent the splendor of the aristocrat's physical environment, as did the peasant who lacked wealth, but the aristocrat's inner confidence and positive sense of self. The expressive individualist does not lack money so much as he lacks "honor," and it is a mixture of anger and impotence, anger at this deficiency within himself and impotence in his effort to change it, that gives rise to the new value structure.

This is why in the society of expressive individualism, the highest value is not material equality, as it is in socialist society, but "sincerity." The socialist vigorously promotes material equality because he is sensitive about his low position in the status hierarchy; by making equality the highest value, the socialist intercepts any negative judgement on his existence that comes his way. The expressive individualist vigorously promotes "authenticity,"[100] "tolerance," and "diversity" because he is sensitive about his confusion over identity, about his failure to comprehend who he really is and why his life is worthwhile. "Authenticity" and "sincerity" are virtues because they defend the value of the person who has only his feelings to offer, nothing else. "Tolerance" and "diversity" are virtues that flow not from a tremendous self-confidence, not from a spiritual enthusiasm that overflows into magnanimity, but from anxiety and fear, from an effort to shield one's fragile identity. They do not reveal generous strength but confusion and weakness. By making these virtues the highest ones, the expressive individualist intercepts any negative judgement on his existence that comes his way. They defend the imperial self who lacks an awareness of his own value.

In the same spirit, both "liberals" and "conservatives" in the society of expressive individualism support the quest for community, the young person's search for a career or a calling, the feverish efforts to join a lifestyle enclave and get involved, and the urge to remake the self and achieve the higher self. Such actions are believed to be in the service of high and noble aims. The old aristocrat would have judged them contemptible, not because they are emblematic of democratic values but because they suggest a certain lack within the person, that the person must search beyond himself or herself to acquire value. These values have arisen in America because of a widespread lack of honor. The search for value and the activities associated with it are not judged contemptible by expressive individualist America but actually believed to represent positive, life-affirming behavior. In this way, the expressive individualist engages in self-deception and the new values act like a narcotic. They ease the pain of living without honor, just as socialist values ease the pain of living without splendor.

Therefore, both the socialist and the expressive individualist posit value structures steeped in resentment, but with an important difference. The socialist inverts the material world of aristocratic society and creates a world without splendor, which he calls good. The expressive individualist inverts the internal world of the aristocrat, the mind of the "noble person," and creates a world without honor, which he calls good. Both constitute *ressentiment* forms, but while the socialist rebels against the experience of aristocracy, the expressive individualist rebels within the experience of aristocracy, and because he lies firmly within that tradition, his fall is a comparatively greater one.

Conclusion

The experience of America brings to mind the words of the ancient writer who said there is no new thing under the sun and that, with certain variations, it is the same thing over and over again.[1] The sun goes up, the sun comes down, the wind heads north, the wind heads south and, for man, all is vanity. In a way, this is what the transformation in American culture is all about. The struggle in America is not a struggle between "postmoderns" and "moderns," but between a love of self and a love of something beyond the self. It is a struggle between the earthly city and the heavenly city, a struggle that Augustine says has been raging since the dawn of time and will continue to rage for all time. The mortal forms of Augustine and his competitors have long since been reduced to dust, but their animating spirits have been passed down through the ages and, although they inhabit different bodies, their expressions are the same.

This is what is so interesting about the culture wars of America. They recall the ideological struggles of late antiquity. Although the combatants have new names, they evoke the names of much older ones. The Tocquevillian American is the Augustinian. It is he who preaches the love of something beyond the self over the love of self. It is he who appears hard, stiff, unjust, and intolerant to those who defend the love of self, and the criticism leveled against Augustine fifteen centuries ago can often be heard leveled against this other person. Julian, the disciple of Pelagius, wrote of Augustine's ideas,

> You ask me why I would not consent to the idea that there is a sin that is a part of human nature? I answer: it is improbable, it is untrue; it is unjust and impious; it makes it seem as if the Devil were the maker of men. It violates and destroys the freedom of the will. . . . by saying that men are so incapable of virtue, that in the very wombs of their mothers they are filled with bygone sins. You imagine so great a power in such a sin, that not only can it blot out the

new-born innocence of nature but, forever afterwards, will force a man throughout his life into every form of viciousness.[2]

This is how the ideology of Tocqueville's America appears to many
expressive individualists today. It does not allow the human will to be its own
master. It does not allow for the possibility of the "higher self." It does not
allow people to "find themselves." It does not allow "choice." It is strict,
harsh, and unyielding in its pronouncements, and it looks for the worst in
man, not the best. These were some of the accusations hurled at Augustine
in late antiquity by the Platonists, the Manicheans, the Pelagians, the
Donatists, and the pagan aristocrats, and they are hurled just as frequently at
those now speaking for the Tocquevillian American position.

The source of these accusations is the movement of expressive individualism, now the dominant ideology in the United States. Expressive individualism encompasses a wide spectrum of ideas, some of them contradictory,
which draw from the anti-Augustinian sects of late antiquity. What unites all
expressive individualists is what united the Manichean, the Donatist, the
Pelagian, the Platonist, and the pagan aristocrat many centuries ago—an
extreme love of self. There are different expressive individualist types in
America and each has a distinctive personality. The "master of the universe"
businessman is cold and calculating. The suburbanite living in a private
enclave is discriminating and fearful. The ex-hippie is carefree and impulsive.
The radical environmentalist is rugged and wholesome. The caring professional is passionate and expressive. But all of these people are ardent and
busy while they exert their vain powers to construct their coming lives. All of
them are committed to the fulfillment of some special vision that has
life moving forward on the highest plane of expectations and themselves
as stupendous.

At the time Tocqueville visited America, the continuity in the human
experience was less clear. If anything, America seemed to represent a radical
break with past, and the rise of American democracy implied that there
might be something new under the sun after all. But one senses while reading
Tocqueville that this is not the whole story. In his great admiration for
the Americans, one feels that Tocqueville, the aristocrat, peered into the
imagination of the nineteenth-century American democrat and saw something of himself, a certain familiar effect radiating from the lamp of the spirit
within. Tocqueville was well acquainted with the proper manners and
appearance of the aristocrat, but he also had insight into the intangible spirit
flickering within the aristocratic mind. He used that insight to look beyond
the nineteenth-century American's humble existence, unimpressive facade,
and coarse manners and discover something honorable and noble in that

figure, even though he did not know precisely where such nobility stood in relation to his own aristocratic experience.

One of the purposes of this book is to confirm Tocqueville's suspicions that something aristocratic was housed in mind of the early American. This book carries the effort further, arguing that what Tocqueville saw in the imagination of the American was the conventional aristocratic world reflected into the City of God. What Tocqueville observed and was sympathetic to in the American individualist was the entire physical world of aristocratic society transposed into the mental space of a single person.

Christianity, public opinion, and republican principle each represent a different aspect of the Old World that was shifted into the internal world of the mind. It was through this momentous shift inward that the aristocratic spirit was sustained in the democratic age. If the external world in democratic society was hostile to traditional forms of aristocracy, the internal world of the imagination could still receive and house them.

Christianity, public opinion, and republican principle served two other purposes in Tocqueville's America. They caused the mind of the early American individualist to be fixed and ordered even when the surrounding world could not be. And they caused the old aristocratic belief in the imperial self to be filtered out when aristocratic society was shifted into the mind of Tocqueville's American. They are what caused Tocqueville's American to radiate the same vital energy and power of person as the Old World aristocrat, but without the Old World aristocrat's tremendous egoism and presumption of superiority.

Tocqueville's America and the contemporary society of expressive individualism each occupy a place on the long timeline of aristocracy. Each shares, in its own way, common ground with aristocracy in the City of Man. Tocqueville's American emitted a definite aristocratic spirit even though the society in which he lived differed significantly from the Old World. Tocqueville's American was an aristocrat, but from the perspective of the City of Man, he did not look like one. The earthly city has certain fixed notions of how an aristocrat should appear, and Tocqueville's American, with his democratic character and humble posture, does not fit them.

Ironically, the expressive individualist looks more like the conventional aristocrat in the City of Man. He shares more character traits with the conventional aristocrat, including attitudes toward work, religion, family, and personal reputation. The expressive individualist also believes in the idea of the "imperial self." But those traits in the expressive individualist represent only shades of aristocratic behavior, and he himself is only a *ressentiment* image of the aristocrat. This is because the expressive individualist lacks the honor of the Old World aristocrat. Even though the expressive individualist resembles the Old World aristocrat in ways that Tocqueville's American does not, and the society of expressive individualism reveals a high degree of aristocraticism in its institutions, the expressive individualist lies on the other side of that great divide separating the aristocratic spirit from the spirit of *ressentiment*. The personalities of Tocqueville's American and the Old World aristocrat intersect at fewer points, but those common areas are sufficient to keep both figures on the same side of the great divide.

Expressive Individualism and Fellow-Feeling

In some ways, the American society of expressive individualism does represent something new. The contemporary expressive individualist lives in a society animated by the third, and perhaps final, variant of human motivation that has given life to people.

The first variant, the spirit of reverence, animated people for countless generations. It is with reverence that both the aristocrat and the peasant pondered the measureless years of a deity's existence or the everlastingness of family and blood. Every institution in the Old World was impregnated with history, the walls of every temple echoed voices from the past, and in every ritual was the reflection of a lost presence. Inhabitants of the Old World revered the past because they were awed by it, and it was in that milieu that the aristocratic doctrine of the imperial self was expressed and an extreme love of self was nourished.

The spirit of perseverance constitutes the second major variant of human motivation, and it distinguishes Tocqueville's America from all that had come before it. I speak of perseverance in a higher and wider sense, towards some distant end in imagined future time. The belief in an afterlife had a profound effect on the conduct of Tocqueville's American in actual time. Unlike the Old World aristocrat, Tocqueville's American oriented his little hour of existence towards the future rather than the past, and this new way of thinking sent ripples through the rest of his imagination and ultimately beyond, into the institutions of his external world. The new belief system is responsible for the gulf observed by Tocqueville between America and Old World. But from an Augustinian perspective, that gulf separates two societies not according to the degree of aristocracy but according to the spirit of human love. The Old World was an aristocratic society animated by self-love. Tocqueville's America was an aristocratic society animated by a love of something beyond the self.

The spirit of fellow-feeling is the third important variant of human motivation, making its appearance in the American society of the organization man. It produces effects on institutions and human relationships similar to those caused by the spirit of reverence, and it is for this reason that some of the attitudes and institutions in expressive individualist society reveal a high degree of aristocraticism. It is in this milieu that the old aristocratic belief in the imperial self has resurfaced, which had lain dormant among the Americans for nearly two centuries. The spirit of fellow-feeling signals the dawn of a new experience in aristocracy and the continuation of a form that has existed for centuries. It signals a return to an extreme love of self, but to a love of self configured somewhat differently from that which ruled the past.

Expressive Individualism and the Break with Tocqueville's America

The rise of expressive individualism also suggests that a break has occurred within the American experience. The transformation from Tocqueville's America to the contemporary society of expressive individualism is as dramatic and revolutionary as the transformation from Old World aristocratic society to Tocqueville's America. This is because it represents a change from Tocqueville's America back to aristocracy, albeit aristocracy in a new, "inverted form. While the second transformation is different, it covers the same distance as the first. Perhaps more institutions from Tocqueville's America will "peep out"[3] in expressive individualist America than Old World institutions did in Tocqueville's America, but the spirit of the age is vastly different from the one preceding it. That is a sufficient basis for upheaval.

The distinctions I have drawn between the animating spirits of the Old World, nineteenth-century America, and contemporary America find support in Tocqueville's commentary on the American Constitution. At one point, Tocqueville writes that the Constitution of the United States "resembles those fine creations of human industry which ensure wealth and renown to their inventors, but which are profitless in other hands."[4] He makes a distinction between the letter of the law and the all-important spirit resonating within it when he says,

> The Mexicans were desirous of establishing a federal system, and they took the Federal Constitution of their neighbors, the Anglo-Americans, as their model and copied it almost entirely. But although they had borrowed the letter of the law, they could not carry over the spirit that gives it life.[5]

This concept is particularly relevant to the change that seems to be occurring in contemporary American politics. The recent electoral failure of welfare-state liberalism and the rise of antigovernment conservatism suggest that a return to an earlier pattern of life is occurring. The growing popularity of libertarian themes has encouraged activists who have long argued that the welfare state represents a desertion of America's founding principles. Their solutions to current problems adopt, in many ways, the letter of nineteenth-century laws and institutions, including traditional family values, the work ethic, and limited government.

But it will prove difficult, if not impossible, to enliven the tradition that once reigned. Tocqueville warned aging aristocrats that it would not be possible to reinstitute conventional aristocratic forms in the new age of equality. In the same way, contemporary conservatives should be warned that figures from Tocqueville's America will not return to dominance. The individualist who, when faced with a crisis, would not just stand with his arms folded waiting for government to come to his aid but would actively join with others to attempt a solution, will not return to dominance. He has been replaced by someone who dreams of leaving such concerns to others so that he may have time to explore himself more fully. In the age of the imperial self, the person who would submerge his ego and his feelings in the calm pleasantries of domestic order will not return to dominance. He has been replaced by someone who will not hesitate to sacrifice all for "fulfill-ment" and "personal growth." The union of two expressive individualists through marriage will not be made stronger through a simple repeal of no-fault divorce laws, and no state intervention will make the tie of marriage as deeply respected as it was in Tocqueville's America.[6] Marriage has become simply another lifestyle to be "tried out" for awhile. The public association, once composed of strangers who recognized each other's independence in their effort to promote a common undertaking, will not return to dominance. It has been replaced by a politicized enclave that expects individual judgment and independence of mind to be sacrificed to the collective will of the like-minded. In enclaves like the feminist movement, the politicized minority, and extreme anti-abortion groups, free persons are obeying the leaders of their cause with servility, and individual thoughts are submitted to the control of others so that all will "follow the same track" towards the same end.[7]

All this has come to pass in America through the deep process of feeling and for this reason cannot so easily be reversed. While the letter of the institutions of Tocqueville's America can be legislated back into existence by conservatives, the spirit quickening them cannot, and conservatives in the society of expressive individualism who try to recapture the ideals of Tocque-ville's America in this manner will produce a result no better than the Mexicans observed by Tocqueville, who tried to copy the American federal system of government but met with little success.

The change in the imagination of the contemporary American individualist, even in the imagination of the contemporary conservative, can be surmised from Tocqueville's observation of the old American individualist. He writes,

> But if an American were condemned to confine his activity to his own affairs, he would be robbed of one half of his existence; he would feel an immense void in the life which he is accustomed to lead, and his wretchedness would be unbearable.[8]

Many conservatives in the new society of expressive individualism have withdrawn from public life, but they experience no such wretchedness in their imaginations. They believe private life beckons with the promise of tremendous excitement and adventure. Many conservatives, particularly those living in the suburbs, do not aspire to public life. They want government services to be privatized because they want greater efficiency, not because they want to participate. They want to avoid taxation. They want to be left alone.

In a way, the Republican Party may actually be the true heir to the movement of expressive individualism in America. Liberal Democrats emphasize loving, caring, helping, and sharing, and these are expressive individualist ideals, but the doctrine of the imperial self in some of its most hardcore manifestations has definitely found a home in the Republican Party. Government is a threat to the imperial self, and while there is a culturally conservative strand in the Republican Party that is prominent and calls for federal involvement on certain social issues, the recent Republican victory based on the "Contract With America" promises to decrease government interference in the lives of Americans. When Speaker Newt Gingrich says that he wants to cut taxes and reduce federal regulations in order to give the average person more time and money to pursue the lifestyle of his or her choice, he belongs squarely in the tradition of expressive individualism and the doctrine of the imperial self. The Republican Party is offering a conservative variant of expressive individualism that includes tremendous new freedom and choice in business, health care, schools, personal finance, lifestyle, and gun ownership, one that is immensely popular.

The new spirit of human motivation in expressive individualism permeates other activities of American life and does so to great effect. The notion of "dealignment" has recently been used to describe the decline of political parties in the United States. Americans voters are not as loyal to political parties as they once were and will now vote "for the person," not just the party. Associated with this new attitude is an ominous cynicism towards all political institutions. Yet the new outlook does not reflect a decline of politics so much as a change in political behavior. Political loyalties are now filtered through the medium of expressive individualism and, for this reason, the ties that bind a partisan to an organization are necessarily weakened. In a culture dominated by the idea of the imperial self, it cannot be expected that loyalty to political parties would be on the same level as that of the status-obsessed, group-oriented organization man of the 1950s. What has occurred in America is not a decline of political parties so much as a transformation in their role in accordance with the tenets of expressive individualism.

The spirit of expressive individualism may even have repercussions for tax policy in the United States. The increase in the marginal tax rate, from 31 percent to 39.6 percent, may not increase government receipts as much as expected. Republicans argue that this is because people will adjust their behavior by working less as every extra dollar they earn above a certain level is taxed more. But this is true largely when wealthy persons are expressive individualists, perhaps something that conservatives do not want to admit. The Tocquevillian American would have worked no matter what the tax rate was because, to him, labor was a calling, and he justified himself to God when he committed himself to his occupation. The organization man would have worked no matter what the tax rate was because, to him, relative status was essential, and every increase in salary (as well as every consumer product that he could buy with that extra pay) was a positive move in the competitive game for status. But some expressive individualists feel no such internal compulsion to work. They are concerned with lifestyle and "quality time," about exploring themselves and their feelings. For this reason some expressive individualists, unlike Tocqueville's American and the organization man, are extremely sensitive to marginal tax rates. Above a certain rate, they will not work because they do not feel compelled to work.

The movement of expressive individualism not only separates contemporary America from an earlier America, but also opens up a new rift between America and Europe. The belief in the imperial self is practiced in the United States in its purest form; it merely colors the experience of Western Europe and, to a lesser extent, Eastern Europe. For this reason, certain extreme political movements spawned by the ideology of expressive individualism, such as "power" feminism and aggressive gay rights activism on the left and "empowerment" libertarianism on the right, may not gain the same level of influence in Western Europe and, especially, Eastern Europe as they have in America. A dichotomy between East and West that was first observed by Tocqueville still exists, but on a slightly different plane.[9] Expressive individualism and socialism rather than democracy and feudalism now denote the two extremes.

Feminism, for example, is an important political movement in Europe, but it is filtered through the dominant ideology of that society, which differs from the dominant ideology of America. It is shaped by a socialist philosophy and thus emphasizes protection against discrimination in the workplace and a more equal distribution of wealth between the sexes. Feminism in America has a definite socialist component to it, and it calls attention to the material status of women, but its emphasis changes when it is filtered through the ideology of expressive individualism. Feminism begins to emphasize more the empowerment of women and brings criticism to bear not just on the workplace, where money is made, but on institutions like the family, the church, and the school. It preaches not simply equality, but autonomy. It is not merely interested in who owns the means of production but in the relationship between the sexes in all areas of civil society.

Many years ago, Werner Sombart wrote a book titled *Why is There No Socialism in the United States?* in which he tries to explain why socialism is an important political movement in Europe but not in America.[10] His observation that a gap exists between America and Europe on this issue is consistent with my position that an important difference exists between American and European culture. It is quite plausible that a few decades from now, an author reflecting on the past may be able to write an essay titled, "Why Is There No 'Power' Feminism in Europe?" showing once again the important differences between America and Europe.

Life in Expressive Individualist Society

The contemporary society of expressive individualism is, in one sense, a variation on a very old theme. It is not the first time that men and women have tried to build theories of human happiness in ways that stroke their pride. The expressive individualist believes that the supreme good lies somewhere within the human grasp and, like the pompous minds of late antiquity, he expects to find it. Thus, he is carried forth by some wind of doctrine until purity and completeness are found in a theory of "self-improvement" or "empowerment." Whether it be religion, community, therapy, a relationship, nature, literature, or the arts, something fashionable enraptures him, especially when it is filled with pictures of his own desires, his own challenges, and his own loves. The expressive individualist embraces whatever allows him to ponder the richness of the world while meditating on his own greatness. Even the command to humble thyself does not necessarily threaten such conceit, as the expressive individualist is quite capable of finding glory in humility, even glory in misery. But gradually the effect dissipates and the expressive individualist moves on. The ideal becomes tiresome or oppressive; it no longer makes him "feel good." In this spirit, the expressive individualist embarks on another search for the supreme good, with pride waving him on.

In *The City of God*, Augustine criticizes this tremendous conceit, writing,

> Salvation, such as it shall be in the world to come, shall itself be our final happiness. And this happiness these philosophers refuse to believe in, because they do not see it, and attempt to fabricate for themselves a happiness in this life, based upon a virtue which is as deceitful as it is proud.[11]

The supreme good has never been, and will never be, within anyone's grasp. In a single breath, Augustine could deliver up a list of evils requiring a person to travel no further than himself to find. Augustine recognized that it was very hard, perhaps the hardest thing of all, for a person to give up the search for the supreme good, to admit that what little happiness one has received comes from a higher power, that blessedness does not exist in this life or in oneself but only in the world to come. It means admitting that one is dependent. It means admitting that one cannot soar higher. It means sacrificing one's pride.

In another sense, however, the society of expressive individualism represents a very new and novel experiment. It is not new because the chance of finding the supreme good has suddenly increased. The chance of that is still zero. It is new because the effort to find the supreme good is now being made in a different context. In the period of late antiquity in which Augustine lived, the force of tradition swirled around the mind of every peasant, every laborer, every aristocrat, every minister, and even every philosopher. In Roman Africa, there was a cycle of life undergirded by some constancy. Certain sights and sounds barely changed. There were the same established families living in the great country houses, the same churches and village fountains standing firm, and the same people rubbing shoulders in the streets. One could see young date-pickers scrambling up the palm trunks or hawkers at the pepper markets performing duties unchanged for centuries. In the external world of Roman Africa, the past was writ large. Small bits of life had an enduring quality, and as they distracted the imagination of the viewer, perhaps they had a small psychological benefit. Nothing in the earthly city lasts, said Augustine, but some things do last more than others, and those repetitive images stored in the great abyss of the human psyche may have been called up from time to time during moments of confusion or unhappiness to give a modicum of relief. Perhaps even the philosophers of the age surreptitiously crept through the back doors of their academies and renegade churches to find something more pleasant and comforting in age-old custom.

Compared to America, where everything changes with great speed and towns receive a new face every decade, the earthly city of antiquity seems almost continuing. Americans search for the supreme good in an environment that differs considerably from the provincial towns of Roman Africa. People in America are constantly uprooting, and the closeness of the population is not like that found in Thagaste, the African town where Augustine grew up. Even Augustine, reports Peter Brown, "hardly ever spent a moment of his life without some friend, even some blood-relative, close by him."[12] The situation is different in expressive individualist America, where loneliness and feelings of isolation are great problems. It is in this environment that the search for the supreme good is now being carried out, making the stakes higher. Without the faith and hope that once carried Tocqueville's American through difficult moments, there is now nothing left to fall back on.

In his or her strenuous hour of life, the expressive individualist carries the same burdens of human nature that men and women of past ages carried. But to reach the same point of rest, he or she treads a new and difficult way. The life of the expressive individualist is filled with visions of personal excellence and great deeds, yet there is something irrevocably amiss and lost in his or her lot. The expressive individualist boasts of living a "full" life but one wonders, is it truly life?

Notes

Introduction

1. Alexis de Tocqueville, *Democracy in America*, vol. 2, Henry Reeve, trans., Phillips Bradley, ed. (New York: Vintage Classics, Random House, 1990), 136–139.

2. Tocqueville, *Democracy in America*, vol. 2, 98.

3. Description of Wall Street investment bankers during the 1980s in Thomas Wolfe, *The Bonfire of the Vanities* (New York: Farrar-Straus-Giroux, 1987).

4. Quoted in Geoffrey Willis, *Saint Augustine and the Donatist Controversy* (London: SPCK, 1950), 91.

5. Augustine, *Confessions*, John Ryan, trans. (New York: Doubleday, 1960), V, iii, 5.

6. Augustine, *The City of God*, Marcus Dods, trans. (New York: Random House, 1950) X, 28.

7. Augustine, *City of God*, II, 15.

8. Reinhard Bendix, *Kings or People: Power and the Mandate to Rule* (Berkeley: University of California Press, 1978), 204, 205, 232.

9. John Kautsky, *The Politics of Aristocratic Empires* (Chapel Hill: The University of North Carolina Press, 1982), 16.

10. Augustine, *City of God*, V, 17–19.

11. Augustine, *City of God*, V, 14.

12. Reinhard Bendix, *Kings or People: Power and the Mandate to Rule*, 231.

13. Augustine, *City of God*, V, 12, 13. John Kautsky, *The Politics of Aristocratic Empires*, 197, 216.

14. John Kautsky, *The Politics of Aristocratic Empires*, 177, 184.

Chapter 1, Expressive Individualism, Manicheism, and the "Higher Self"

1. Peter Brown, *Augustine of Hippo* (Berkeley: University of California Press, 1967), 46.

2. Brown, *Augustine of Hippo*, 52.

3. Brown, *Augustine of Hippo*, 47.

4. Brown, *Augustine of Hippo*, 47.

5. Brown, *Augustine of Hippo*, 50.

6. Brown, *Augustine of Hippo*, 52.

7. Brown, *Augustine of Hippo*, 52.

8. Brown, *Augustine of Hippo*, 52.

9. Augustine, *Confessions*, V, x, 18.

10. Augustine, *Confessions*, III, vi, 10.

11. Augustine, *Confessions*, III, vi, 10.

12. Stanley Hopper, "The Anti-Manichean Writings," in A *Companion to the Study of Saint Augustine*, Roy Battenhouse, ed. (New York: Oxford University Press, 1955), 154.

13. Hopper, "The Anti-Manichean Writings," 156.

14. Augustine, *Confessions*, IV, xiv, 23.

15. Augustine, *Confessions*, III, vii, 12.

16. Brown, *Augustine of Hippo*, 50.

17. Augustine, *Confessions*, V, x, 18.

18. Quoted in Hopper, "The Anti-Manichean Writings," 159.

19. Augustine, *Confessions*, V, x, 20.

20. Augustine, *Confessions*, V, x, 20.

21. Hopper, "The Anti-Manichean Writings," 159.

22. Quoted in Hopper, "The Anti-Manichean Writings," 160.

23. This is not to say that all efforts to transform human behavioral traits or improve the self are rooted in Manicheism. A person can have certain destructive tendencies within his personality ameliorated. For example, the fear of flying or of enclosed spaces can be eased. But there is an important distinction to be made between trying to alter a few subconscious reflexes and hoping that one's entire lifetime psychological experience can be reformulated so as to yield a new self. The former represents an effort to trick the mind on to a new axis. The latter is based on a religion that appeals to conscious reason and posits two natures to exist within a single mind.

24. Brown, *Augustine of Hippo*, 156.

25. Quoted in Brown, *Augustine of Hippo*, 150.

26. Augustine, *Confessions*, IV, xvi, 31.

27. Hopper, "The Anti-Manichean Writings," 161.

28. Hopper, "The Anti-Manichean Writings," 161.

29. Augustine, *The Catholic and Manichaean Ways of Life*, Donald Gallagher and Idella Gallagher, trans. (Washington, D.C.: The Catholic University of America Press, 1966), II, xiii, 29.

30. Augustine, *The Catholic and Manichaean Ways of Life*, II, xiii, 29.

31. Augustine, *The Catholic and Manichaean Ways of Life*, II, xvi, 39.

32. Augustine, *The Catholic and Manichaean Ways of Life*, II, xvi, 39.

33. Augustine, *The Catholic and Manichaean Ways of Life*, II, xvi, 39.

34. Augustine, *The Catholic and Manichaean Ways of Life*, II, xvi, 46, 48.

35. Augustine, *The Catholic and Manichaean Ways of Life*, II, xvi, 39. The example of the amusement park is inserted directly into Augustine's criticism of Manicheism.

36. Augustine, *The Catholic and Manichaean Ways of Life*, II, xvi, 43.

37. For an interesting discussion of this point, see Robert Paehlke, *Environmentalism and the Future of Progressive Politics* (New Haven: Yale University Press, 1989).

38. Lawrence Friedman, *The Republic of Choice* (Cambridge: Harvard University Press, 1990), 74. Friedman says that in the new American culture, "choice" is primary and "security" is secondary. Robert Bellah et. al., *Habits of the Heart* (New York: Harper and Row, 1985), 150. Bellah calls this new phenomenon "bureaucratic individualism."

39. Tocqueville, *Democracy in America*, vol. 1, 304.

40. Tocqueville, *Democracy in America*, vol. 1, 304.

41. Tocqueville, *Democracy in America*, vol. 1, 304.

42. Tocqueville, *Democracy in America*, vol. 2, 208.

43. Tocqueville, *Democracy in America*, vol. 2, 208.

44. Tocqueville, *Democracy in America*, vol. 2, 208.

45. Tocqueville, *Democracy in America*, vol. 2, 208.

46. Tocqueville, *Democracy in America*, vol. 2, 200.

47. Tocqueville, *Democracy in America*, vol. 2, 200.

48. Tocqueville, *Democracy in America*, vol. 2, 202.

49. Tocqueville, *Democracy in America*, vol. 2, 202.

50. Tocqueville, *Democracy in America*, vol. 2, 203.

51. Tocqueville, *Democracy in America*, vol. 2, 128–130, "Of the Taste for Physical Well-Being in America."

52. Tocqueville, *Democracy in America*, vol. 2, 131.

53. Tocqueville, *Democracy in America*, vol. 2, 44.

54. Augustine, *City of God*, II, 7.

55. Augustine, *City of God*, V, 13.

56. Augustine, *City of God*, II, 20.

57. Augustine, *Confessions*, IV, vi, 11.

58. Augustine, *Confessions*, III, ii, 4.

59. Augustine, *Confessions*, III, ii, 4.

60. Augustine, *Confessions*, III, ii, 4.

61. Augustine, "On the Trinity," in *Basic Writings of Saint Augustine*, Whitney Oates, ed. (New York: Random House, 1948), VIII, 7.

62. John Kautsky, *The Politics of Aristocratic Empires* (Chapel Hill: The University of North Carolina Press, 1982), 187–197. The author describes the antiutilitarian attitude that aristocrats demonstrate towards objects of consumption.

63. Tocqueville, *Democracy in America*, vol. 2, 132.

Chapter 2, The Expressive Individualist, the Donatists, and the Honor of Work

1. For an excellent study of the Donatist movement, see Geoffrey Willis, *Saint Augustine and the Donatist Controversy* (London: SPCK, 1950).

2. Willis, *Saint Augustine and the Donatist Controversy*, 154.

3. Augustine quoted in Willis, *Saint Augustine and the Donatist Controversy*, 155.

4. Willis, *Saint Augustine and the Donatist Controversy*, xii.

5. Willis, *Saint Augustine and the Donatist Controversy*, 40.

6. Tocqueville, *Democracy in America*, vol. 1, 207.

7. Tocqueville, *Democracy in America*, vol. 1, 207.

8. Bellah, *Habits of the Heart*, 66.

9. Tocqueville, *Democracy in America*, vol. 2, 153.

10. Tocqueville, *Democracy in America*, vol. 2, 153.

11. Tocqueville, *Democracy in America*, vol. 2, 152. See also Kautsky *The Politics of Aristocratic Empires*, 177–87.

12. Tocqueville, *Democracy in America*, vol. 2, 152.

13. Max Weber, *The Protestant Ethic and the Spirit of Capitalism*, Talcott Parsons, trans. (New York: Charles Scribner's Sons, 1958), chap. 3.

14. Tocqueville, *Democracy in America*, vol. 2, 153.

15. Bellah, *Habits of the Heart*, 66.

16. Bellah, *Habits of the Heart*, 70.

17. Bellah, *Habits of the Heart*, 70.

18. Tocqueville, *Democracy in America*, vol. 2, 232.

19. Tocqueville, *Democracy in America*, vol. 2, 153.

Chapter 3, Christianity, Public Opinion, and Republican Principle in the Imagination of Tocqueville's American

1. Tocqueville, *Democracy in America*, vol. 2, 257.

2. Tocqueville, *Democracy in America*, vol. 2, 20.

3. Tocqueville, *Democracy in America*, vol. 2, 22.

4. Tocqueville, *Democracy in America*, vol. 1, 307.

5. Tocqueville, *Democracy in America*, vol. 2, 27.

6. Tocqueville, *Democracy in America*, vol. 2, 27.

7. Tocqueville, *Democracy in America*, vol. 2, 27.

8. Tocqueville, *Democracy in America*, vol. 2, 27.

9. Tocqueville, *Democracy in America*, vol. 1, 264.

10. Tocqueville, *Democracy in America*, vol. 2, 83.

11. Tocqueville, *Democracy in America*, vol. 1, 263.

12. Tocqueville, *Democracy in America*, vol. 1, 166.

13. Tocqueville, *Democracy in America*, vol. 1, 245.

14. Tocqueville, *Democracy in America*, vol. 1, 318.

15. *The Federalist* (Cambridge, Mass: Belknap Press of Harvard University Press, 1961).

16. Tocqueville, *Democracy in America*, vol. 1, 87.

17. Augustine, *City of God*, VIII, 5.

18. Augustine, *City of God*, VIII, 8.

19. Robert Cushman, "Faith and Reason," in *A Companion to the Study of Saint Augustine*, Roy Battenhouse, ed. (New York: Oxford University Press, 1969), 290.

20. Robert Cushman, "Faith and Reason," 289.

21. Augustine, *City of God*, X, 29.

22. Cushman, "Faith and Reason," 300.

23. Augustine quoted in Cushman, "Faith and Reason," 299.

24. Cushman, "Faith and Reason," 310.

25. Cushman, "Faith and Reason," 299.

26. For a description of the love of order among the nineteenth-century Americans, see Tocqueville, *Democracy in America*, vol. 1, 297.

Chapter 4, Pelagianism in the Society of Expressive Individualism

1. Augustine, "On the Grace of Christ and on Original Sin," in *Basic Writings of Saint Augustine*, Whitney Oates, ed. (New York: Random House, 1948), V.

2. Augustine, "On the Grace of Christ and on Original Sin." The view of Coelestius, a figure associated with the Pelagian movement.

3. Augustine, "On the Grace of Christ and on Original Sin," XXI.

4. Brown, *Augustine of Hippo*, 346.

5. Augustine, "On the Grace of Christ and on Original Sin," VII.

6. Quoted in Paul Lehmann, "The Anti-Pelagian Writings," in *A Companion to the Study of St. Augustine*, Roy Battenhouse, ed. (New York: Oxford University Press, 1969), 208.

7. C. Randolph Ross, *Common Sense Christianity* (New York: Occam Publishers, 1989), 152.

8. Augustine, "On the Spirit and the Letter," in *Basic Writings of Saint Augustine*, IV.

9. Greg Anderson, *The 22 Laws of Wellness* (San Francisco: HarperCollins, 1995), 232.

10. Anderson, *The 22 Laws of Wellness*, 233

11. Paul Lehmann, "The Anti-Pelagian Writings," 209.

12. Augustine, "On Nature and Grace," in *Saint Augustine: Four Anti-Pelagian Writings*, John Mourant and William Collinge, trans. (Washington, D.C.: Catholic University of America Press, 1992), 49 (57).

13. Bellah, *Habits of the Heart*, 229.

14. Bellah, *Habits of the Heart*, 229.

15. James Fowler, *Stages of Faith* (San Francisco: Harper San Francisco, 1981), 196.

16. Ross, *Common Sense Christianity*, 150.

17. Ross, *Common Sense Christianity*, 153.

18. Bellah, *Habits of the Heart*, 236.

19. Bellah, *Habits of the Heart*, 229.

20. Bellah, *Habits of the Heart*, 229.

21. Ross, *Common Sense Christianity*, 154.

22. Ross, *Common Sense Christianity*, 155.

23. Brown, *Augustine of Hippo*, 382.

24. Augustine, "On Nature and Grace," in *Basic Writings of Saint Augustine*, XX.

25. Augustine, "On Nature and Grace," in *Basic Writings of Saint Augustine*, XX.

26. Ross, *Common Sense Christianity*, 223.

27. Augustine, "On the Grace of Christ and on Original Sin," XXVI.

28. Augustine, "On the Grace of Christ and on Original Sin," XXVI.

29. Augustine, "On Nature and Grace," in *Basic Writings of Saint Augustine*, LV.

30. Augustine, "On Nature and Grace," in *Basic Writings of Saint Augustine*, LVII.

31. Paul Lehmann, "The Anti-Pelagian Writings," 218.

32. Augustine, "On Nature and Grace," in *Basic Writings of Saint Augustine*, LVII.

33. Augustine, "On the Spirit and the Letter," LIII.

34. Bellah, *Habits of the Heart*, 230.

35. Bellah, *Habits of the Heart*, 64, 234.

36. Bellah, *Habits of the Heart*, 231.

37. Augustine quoted in Paul Lehmann in "The Anti-Pelagian Writings," 224.

38. Augustine quoted in Paul Lehmann, "The Anti-Pelagian Writings," 215.

39. Augustine, *Against Julian*, Matthew Schumacher, trans. (New York: Fathers of the Church, 1957).

40. Pelagius quoted in Brown, *Augustine of Hippo*, 366.

41. Bellah, *Habits of the Heart*, 100.

42. Bellah, *Habits of the Heart*, 99.

43. Bellah, *Habits of the Heart*, 100.

44. Bellah, *Habits of the Heart*, 100.

45. Bellah, *Habits of the Heart*, 99.

46. Bellah, *Habits of the Heart*, 122.

47. Bellah, *Habits of the Heart*, 124.

48. Bellah, *Habits of the Heart*, 122.

49. Bellah, *Habits of the Heart*, 223.

50. Tocqueville, *Democracy in America*, vol. 1, 325.

51. Tocqueville, *Democracy in America*, vol. 2, 125.

52. Tocqueville, *Democracy in America*, vol. 2, 125.

53. Tocqueville, *Democracy in America*, vol. 2, 126.

54. Augustine, *On Christian Doctrine*, D. W. Robertson, Jr., trans. (New York: Macmillan Publishing Company, 1958), I, xxix, 30.

55. Tocqueville, *Democracy in America*, vol. 2, 126.

56. Tocqueville, *Democracy in America*, vol. 2, 126.

57. Augustine, *City of God*, XIV, 28.

58. Augustine, *City of God*, V, 14.

59. Augustine, *City of God*, XIX, 13.

60. Augustine, *City of God*, XIX, 13.
61. Tocqueville, *Democracy in America*, vol. 2, 72.
62. Tocqueville, *Democracy in America*, vol. 2, 126.
63. Tocqueville, *Democracy in America*, vol. 2, 27.
64. Tocqueville, *Democracy in America*, vol. 1, 313.
65. Tocqueville, *Democracy in America*, vol. 1, 313.
66. Tocqueville, *Democracy in America*, vol. 1, 313.
67. Tocqueville, *Democracy in America*, vol. 1, 312.
68. Tocqueville, *Democracy in America*, vol. 1, 26.
69. Tocqueville, *Democracy in America*, vol. 1, 26.
70. Tocqueville, *Democracy in America*, vol. 1, 121.

Chapter 5, Donatism in the Society of Expressive Individualism

1. Geoffrey Willis, *Saint Augustine and the Donatist Controversy* (London: SPCK, 1950), 115.
2. Tocqueville, *Democracy in America*, vol. 2, 216.
3. Tocqueville, *Democracy in America*, vol. 2, 163.
4. Tocqueville, *Democracy in America*, vol. 2, 163.
5. Willis, *Saint Augustine and the Donatist Controversy*, 101.
6. James Bryce, *The American Commonwealth* (New York: The Macmillan Company, 1911), vol. 2, 353.
7. Tocqueville, *Democracy in America*, vol. 1, 264.
8. Tocqueville, *Democracy in America*, vol. 1, 263.
9. Bellah, *Habits of the Heart* and Richard Sennett, *The Uses of Disorder* (New York: Knopf, 1970).
10. Tocqueville, *Democracy in America*, vol. 1, 170.
11. Tocqueville, *Democracy in America*, vol. 1, 170.
12. James Bryce, *The American Commonwealth*, vol. 2, 828.
13. James Bryce, *The American Commonwealth*, vol. 2, 828.
14. James Bryce, *The American Commonwealth*, vol. 2, 828.
15. James Bryce, *The American Commonwealth*, vol. 2, 818.
16. Bellah, *Habits of the Heart*, 72.
17. Sennett, *The Uses of Disorder*, 34, 35.
18. Sennett, *The Uses of Disorder*, 12.
19. Willis, *Saint Augustine and the Donatist Controversy*, xii.
20. Bellah, *Habits of the Heart*, 73.
21. Tocqueville, *Democracy in America*, vol. 2, 215.
22. Tocqueville, *Democracy in America*, vol. 2, 216.
23. Tocqueville, *Democracy in America*, vol. 2, 105, 216.
24. Tocqueville, *Democracy in America*, vol. 2, 103.
25. Sennett, *The Uses of Disorder*, 73.
26. Tocqueville, *Democracy in America*, vol. 1, 243.

27. Tocqueville, *Democracy in America*, vol. 1, 250.
28. Tocqueville, *Democracy in America*, vol. 1, 250.
29. Tocqueville, *Democracy in America*, vol. 1, 303.
30. Tocqueville, *Democracy in America*, vol. 2, 228.
31. Bellah, *Habits of the Heart*, 73.
32. Tocqueville, *Democracy in America*, vol. 2, 103.
33. Tocqueville, *Democracy in America*, vol. 2, 102.
34. Max Weber, *The City*, Don Martindale and Gertrud Neuwirth, trans. (New York: The Free Press, 1958), 97.
35. Augustine, *City of God*, XVIV, 17.
36. Tocqueville, *Democracy in America*, vol. 1, 211.
37. James Bryce, *The American Commonwealth*, vol. 2, 825.
38. James Bryce, *The American Commonwealth*, vol. 2, 826.
39. James Bryce, *The American Commonwealth*, vol. 2, 828.
40. Tocqueville, *Democracy in America*, vol. 2, 72.
41. Tocqueville, *Democracy in America*, vol. 1, 211.
42. Tocqueville, *Democracy in America*, vol. 1, 243.
43. Bellah, *Habits of the Heart*, 153–54, 333.
44. Bellah, *Habits of the Heart*, 153.
45. Bellah, *Habits of the Heart*, 153.
46. Herbert Gans, *The Urban Villagers* (New York: The Free Press, 1962).
47. Augustine, *City of God*, XXII, 22, 23.

Chapter 6, Platonism in the Society of Expressive Individualism

1. Charles Cochrane, *Christianity and Classical Culture* (New York: Oxford University Press, 1944), 400–406.
2. Charles Cochrane, *Christianity and Classical Culture*, 409.
3. Charles Cochrane, *Christianity and Classical Culture*, 404–407.
4. Augustine, *City of God*, VIII, 5. Augustine, "On the Trinity," in *Basic Writings of Saint Augustine*, Whitney Oates, ed. (New York: Random House, 1948), X, x, 15.
5. Cochrane, *Christianity and Classical Culture*, 407.
6. Cochrane, *Christianity and Classical Culture*, 408.
7. Augustine quoted in Cochrane, *Christianity and Classical Culture*, 409.
8. Cochrane, *Christianity and Classical Culture*, 409.
9. Cochrane, *Christianity and Classical Culture*, 412.
10. Lawrence Friedman, *The Republic of Choice* (Cambridge: Harvard University Press, 1990), 17.
11. Friedman, *The Republic of Choice*, 17.
12. Tocqueville, *Democracy in America*, vol. 2, 192.
13. Tocqueville, *Democracy in America*, vol. 2, 194.

14. Tocqueville, *Democracy in America*, vol. 2, 194.

15. Tocqueville, *Democracy in America*, vol. 2, 197.

16. Tocqueville, *Democracy in America*, vol. 2, 196.

17. Tocqueville, *Democracy in America*, vol. 2, 195.

18. Tocqueville, *Democracy in America*, vol. 2, 195.

19. Tocqueville, *Democracy in America*, vol. 2, 197.

20. Tocqueville, *Democracy in America*, vol. 2, 197.

21. This phenomenon is described by Christopher Lasch in "Hillary Clinton, Childsaver," *Harper's Magazine* 285, no. 1709 (October 1992): 75.

22. Bellah, *Habits of the Heart*, 16.

23. Tocqueville, *Democracy in America*, vol. 2, 196.

24. Bellah, *Habits of the Heart*, 108.

25. Bellah, *Habits of the Heart*, 123.

26. Tocqueville, *Democracy in America*, vol. 2, 197.

27. Bellah, *Habits of the Heart*, 123.

28. Richard Sennett, *The Fall of Public Man* (New York: W. W. Norton and Company. 1976), 92.

29. For example, in Lasch's article, "Hillary Clinton, Childsaver," the author reports on Hillary Clinton's article, "Children's Rights: A Legal Perspective," in which Clinton defends children against the charge of incompetence. Clinton argues that children should be able to represent themselves in disputes because, like other individuals, they are the best judge of their own interests. Lasch, "Hillary Clinton, Childsaver," 75–76.

30. Philippe Aries, *Centuries of Childhood*, Robert Baldick, trans. (New York: Vintage Books, 1965).

31. Richard Sennett, *The Fall of Public Man*, 92.

32. Sennett, *The Fall of Public Man*, 92.

33. Sennett, *The Fall of Public Man*, 93.

34. Sennett, *The Fall of Public Man*, 93.

35. Sennett quoting Philippe Aries in *The Fall of Public Man*, 92.

36. Sennett, *The Fall of Public Man*, 94.

37. Sennett, *The Fall of Public Man*, 93.

38. Sennett, *The Fall of Public Man*, 93.

39. Sennett, *The Fall of Public Man*, 95.

40. Neil Postman, *The Disappearance of Childhood*, (New York: Delacorte Press, 1982). Postman also notes a blurring of the division between childhood and adulthood in contemporary America. However, he attributes the change to the influence of television (84) and to a reduced demand for "adult" skills, such as writing, in a picture-oriented information economy. He does not see it as part of a more profound world historical change, in which the culture of America is returning to Old World thought and practice.

41. Sennett, *The Fall of Public Man*, 95.

Chapter 7, The Expressive Individualist and Self-Esteem

1. Tocqueville, *Democracy in America*, vol. 2, 233.
2. Robert C. Post, "The Social Foundations of Defamation Law: Reputation and the Constitution," *California Law Review*, 74, 691–751.
3. Post, "The Social Foundations of Defamation Law," 693.
4. Post, "The Social Foundations of Defamation Law," 694.
5. Post, "The Social Foundations of Defamation Law," 694.
6. Post, "The Social Foundations of Defamation Law," 697.
7. Post, "The Social Foundations of Defamation Law," 696.
8. Post, "The Social Foundations of Defamation Law," 699.
9. Post, "The Social Foundations of Defamation Law," 701.
10. Post, "The Social Foundations of Defamation Law," 709.
11. Post, "The Social Foundations of Defamation Law," 716.
12. Post, "The Social Foundations of Defamation Law," 710.
13. Post, "The Social Foundations of Defamation Law," 711.
14. Post, "The Social Foundations of Defamation Law," 715.

Chapter 8, The Expressive Individualist and the Spirit of *Ressentiment*

1. Max Scheler, *Ressentiment*, William Holdheim, trans. (New York: The Free Press of Glencoe, 1961).
2. Nietzsche, *Beyond Good and Evil*, Walter Kaufmann, trans. (New York: Vintage Books, 1989), V, 199.
3. Tocqueville, *Democracy in America*, vol. 2, 158.
4. Tocqueville, *Democracy in America*, vol. 1, 276, 278.
5. Tocqueville, *Democracy in America*, vol. 1, 421.
6. Tocqueville, *Democracy in America*, vol. 2, 97.
7. Tocqueville, *Democracy in America*, vol. 2, 105.
8. Tocqueville, *Democracy in America*, vol. 2, 138.
9. Nietzsche, *Beyond Good and Evil*, V, 199.
10. Nietzsche, *Beyond Good and Evil*, V, 199.
11. Tocqueville, *Democracy in America*, vol. 2, 333.
12. Nietzsche, *Beyond Good and Evil*, IX, 260.
13. Nietzsche, *Beyond Good and Evil*, V, 199.
14. Nietzsche, *Beyond Good and Evil*, V, 188.
15. Nietzsche, *Beyond Good and Evil*, V, 188.
16. Nietzsche, *Beyond Good and Evil*, IX, 260.
17. Nietzsche, *Beyond Good and Evil*, IX, 287.
18. Nietzsche, *Beyond Good and Evil*, IX, 265.
19. Tocqueville, *Democracy in America*, vol. 2, 226.
20. Tocqueville, *Democracy in America*, vol. 2, 237.

21. Tocqueville, *Democracy in America*, vol. 2, 237.

22. Tocqueville, *Democracy in America*, vol. 1, 426.

23. Tocqueville, *Democracy in America*, vol. 1, 426.

24. Tocqueville, *Democracy in America*, vol. 1, 424.

25. Theodore Roosevelt, "The Strenuous Life," in *The Man in the Arena*, John Allen Gable, ed. (New York: The Theodore Roosevelt Association, 1987), 28.

26. Roosevelt, "The Strenuous Life," 29.

27. Nietzsche, *Beyond Good and Evil*, IX, 265.

28. Nietzsche, *Beyond Good and Evil*, IX, 265.

29. Tocqueville, *Democracy in America*, vol. 1, 325.

30. Nietzsche, *Beyond Good and Evil*, IX, 287.

Chapter 9, The Creation of the Aristocrat in the City of God

1. Augustine, *Confessions*, X, viii, 12.

2. Augustine, *Confessions*, X, viii, 12.

3. Augustine, *Confessions*, X, xiv, 21.

4. Augustine, *Confessions*, XI, xv, 18.

5. Augustine, *Confessions*, XI, xv, 18.

6. Charles Taylor, *Sources of the Self* (Cambridge, Mass: Harvard University Press, 1989), 152.

7. Taylor, *Sources of the Self*, 153.

8. Tocqueville, *Democracy in America*, vol. 2, 150.

9. Tocqueville, *Democracy in America*, vol. 2, 151.

10. Tocqueville, *Democracy in America*, vol. 2, 151.

11. For a discussion of the life-giving effects of time and history on the human psyche, see Nietzsche, "On the Uses and Disadvantages of History for Life," in *Untimely Meditations*, R. J. Hollingdale, trans. (Cambridge: Cambridge University Press, 1983).

12. Bryce, *The American Commonwealth*, vol. 2, 899–900.

13. Bryce, *The American Commonwealth*, vol. 2, 900.

14. Bryce, *The American Commonwealth*, vol. 2, 900.

15. Edmund Burke, *Reflections on the Revolution in France*, Conor Cruise O'Brien, ed. (London: Penguin Books, 1968), 135.

16. Tocqueville, *Democracy in America*, vol. 2, 228.

17. Frances Trollope, *Domestic Manners of the Americans* (New York: Vintage Books, 1949), 25, 233.

18. Yehoshua Arieli, *Individualism and Nationalism in American Ideology* (Cambridge: Harvard University Press, 1964), 193.

19. Arieli, *Individualism and Nationalism in American Ideology*, 193, 201.

20. Arieli, *Individualism and Nationalism in American Ideology*, 232.

21. For a discussion of the peasant peer group, see Herbert Gans, *The Urban Villagers* (New York: The Free Press, 1962), Robert Redfield, *Little Community and*

Peasant Society and Culture (Chicago: The University of Chicago Press, 1956), Daniel Lerner, *The Passing of Traditional Society* (Glencoe, Illinois: The Free Press, 1958), John Kautsky, *The Politics of Aristocratic Empires.*

22. Karen Brison notes the extreme sensitivity of people in traditional society towards "gossip," in *Just Talk* (Berkeley: University of California Press, 1992).

23. Tocqueville, *Democracy in America*, vol. 2, 233.

24. James Bryce, *The American Commonwealth*, vol. 2, 649.

25. H. Rider Haggard, *Allan Quartermain* (London: Longmans, Green, and Co., 1887), 210.

26. Josiah Ober, *Mass and Elite in Democratic Athens* (Princeton: Princeton University Press, 1989), 84.

27. Kautsky, *The Politics of Aristocratic Empires*, 212

28. Wayne Rebhorn, "The Crisis of the Aristocracy in *Julius Caesar*," *Renaissance Quarterly* XLIII, no. 1 (1990): 84.

29. Rebhorn, "The Crisis of the Aristocracy in *Julius Caesar*," 84.

30. Rebhorn, "The Crisis of the Aristocracy in *Julius Caesar*," 84.

31. Rebhorn, "The Crisis of the Aristocracy in *Julius Caesar*," 87.

32. Rebhorn, "The Crisis of the Aristocracy in *Julius Caesar*," 79.

33. Kautsky, *The Politics of Aristocratic Empires*, 297.

34. Kautsky, *The Politics of Aristocratic Empires*, 297.

35. Leszek Kolakowski, *Main Currents of Marxism* (Oxford: Clarendon Press, 1978), vol. 1, 231.

36. Kolakowski, *Main Currents of Marxism*, vol. 1, 184,189.

37. Arieli, *Individualism and Nationalism in American Ideology*, 227.

38. Arieli, *Individualism and Nationalism in American Ideology*, 230.

39. For actual reference to the idea of the "imperial self" in contemporary American culture, see Richard John Neuhaus, *The Naked Public Square* (Michigan: W. B. Eerdmans Pub. Co.,1984).

Chapter 10, Tocqueville's American as an Aristocrat in the City of God

1. Augustine, *City of God*, XVIV,17.

2. Tocqueville, *Democracy in America*, vol. 2, 33–34.

3. Augustine, *City of God*, X, 31.

4. Augustine, *City of God*, X, 31.

5. Augustine, *City of God*, XIV, 10.

6. Augustine, *City of God*, XIV, 17.

7. Tocqueville, *Democracy in America*, vol. 2, 126.

8. Nietzsche, "On the Uses and Disadvantages of History for Life," in *Untimely Meditations*, R. J. Hollingdale, trans. (Cambridge: Cambridge University Press, 1983).

9. Nietzsche, "On the Uses and Disadvantages of History for Life," 73.

10. Tocqueville, *Democracy in America*, vol. 2, 4.

11. Tocqueville, *Democracy in America*, vol. 2, 34.

12. Tocqueville argues that the American Indian culture was warrior-aristocratic just like the culture of feudal Europe, saying that "however strange it may seem, it is in the forests of the New World, and not among the Europeans who people its coasts, that the ancient prejudices of Europe still exist." (*Democracy in America*, vol. 1, 344).

13. My description of the warrior-aristocratic culture of the Zulu nation is derived from the work of H. Rider Haggard, the English novelist. About the accuracy of his observations, one authority notes, "Rider Haggard did a great service for South Africa by accurately portraying the Zulu character, and no one has ever succeeded in doing better. . . [His tales] are a perfect mirror of the Zulu as he was before he was touched by civilization." (Quoted in Morton Cohen, *Rider Haggard: His Life and Works* (New York: Walker and Company, 1960), 228.)

14. Nietzsche, *The Will to Power*, Walter Kaufmann, trans. (New York: Vintage Books, 1967), 14.

15. Augustine, *City of God*, X, 32.

16. Augustine, *City of God*, X, 29.

17. Augustine, *City of God*, X, 29.

18. Augustine, *City of God*, X, 29.

19. Augustine, *City of God*, X, 30.

20. Augustine, *City of God*, X, 30.

21. Augustine, *City of God*, XXII, 22.

22. Augustine, "On the Gift of Perseverance," in *Saint Augustine: Four Anti-Pelagian Writings*, John Mourant and William Collinge, trans. (Washington, D.C.: Catholic University of America Press 1992), XIV, 61.

23. Tocqueville, *Democracy in America*, vol. 2, 127.

24. Tocqueville, *Democracy in America*, vol. 2, 143.

25. Tocqueville, *Democracy in America*, vol. 1, 325.

26. Tocqueville, *Democracy in America*, vol. 2, 146.

27. Anthony Trollope, *North America* (New York: Alfred A. Knopf, 1951), 278.

28. Trollope, *North America*, 281.

29. Trollope, *North America*, 278.

30. Trollope, *North America*, 281.

31. Trollope, *North America*, 281.

32. Tocqueville, *The Old Regime and the French Revolution*, Stuart Gilbert, trans. (Garden City, New York: Doubleday Anchor Books, 1955), 118.

33. Weber quoted in Reinhard Bendix, *Max Weber* (New York: Anchor Books, 1960), 94. Bendix also says on the same page that "neither lords nor peasants have a desire for 'salvation' or a clear idea concerning the fate from which they should want to be saved."

34. For a discussion of the intimate connection between fear and reverence, see Edmund Burke, "A Philosophical Enquiry into the Origin of our Ideas of the Sublime and Beautiful," *The Works of Edmund Burke* (London: C. and J. Rivington, 1826), vol. 1.

35. It is important to make a distinction between real reverence and nostalgia. A kind of reverence for the past can be observed among American individualists, but it differs considerably from Old World reverence. Nostalgia is an indication of interest in the past and a kind of respect for it, but it is not like the all-consuming worship of tradition found in real reverence. It is not charged with the same holy purpose because it is not grounded in a fear of that which came before. In a way, it is based on just the opposite feeling—a kind of condescending love for that which seems harmless and adorable. Nietzsche himself alludes to the different spirits in which people can revere, noting that a worship of tradition can degenerate into "a thirst for novelty," where elements from the past simply become "bibliographical minutiae" to be "gobbled down." (Nietzsche, "On the Uses and Disadvantages of History for Life," 75). Both the Old World aristocrat and the American individualist can revere, but it is not the same kind of reverence, even while both are revering.

36. It is possible to persevere in the pursuit of someone, but the reason for persevering is generally explained by other phenomena, such as a reverence or hatred for the person being pursued. The "spirit of perseverance" is a different phenomenon and does not presuppose a mixing together of imaginations. It is independent of the special chemistry that exists between human beings and causes one to pursue or avoid another.

37. Tocqueville, *Democracy in America*, vol. 2, 179.

38. Tocqueville, *Democracy in America*, vol. 2, 180.

39. Tocqueville, *Democracy in America*, vol. 2, 178.

40. Tocqueville, *Democracy in America*, vol. 2, 179.

41. Tocqueville, Democracy in America, vol. 2, 179. Bryce also comments on the lack of reverence in American society, writing, "The feeling of the American public towards the very rich is, so far as a stranger can judge, one of curiosity and wonder rather than of respect. There is less snobbishness shown towards them than in England. They are admired as a famous runner or a jockey is admired, but do not seem to receive either flattery or social deference." *The American Commonwealth*, vol. 2, 817.

42. Augustine, "On the Gift of Perseverance," Introduction.

Chapter 11, The Fall of the Aristocrat in the City of God and the Rise of the "Organization Man"

1. William Whyte Jr., *The Organization Man* (New York: Doubleday, 1956). In this book, the "organization man" is synonymous with the "status-seeker" (Packard), the "other-directed" person (Riesman), and the "white collar" man (Mills).

2. Tocqueville, *Democracy in America*, vol. 2, 150.

3. Tocqueville, *Democracy in America*, vol. 2, 151.

4. Tocqueville, *Democracy in America*, vol. 2, 215.

5. David Riesman, *The Lonely Crowd* (New Haven: Yale University Press, 1950), 49, 264.

6. Riesman, *The Lonely Crowd*, Introduction.

7. Whyte, *The Organization Man*, 69.

8. Whyte, *The Organization Man*, Chapter 25.

9. Whyte, *The Organization Man* , 7.

10. Whyte, *The Organization Man*, 399.

11. Tocqueville, *Democracy in America*, vol. 2, 216.

12. Whyte, *The Organization Man*, 345–46.

13. C. Wright Mills, *White Collar* (New York: Oxford University Press, 1953), 239.

14. Mills, *White Collar*, 257.

15. Mills, *White Collar*, 258–259.

16. Riesman, *The Lonely Crowd*, 71.

17. Riesman, *The Lonely Crowd*, 71.

18. Weber, *The Protestant Ethic and the Spirit of Capitalism*, 153.

19. Riesman, *The Lonely Crowd*, 80.

20. Riesman, *The Lonely Crowd*, 80.

21. Whyte, *The Organization Man*, 150.

22. Whyte, *The Organization Man*, 200.

23. Whyte, *The Organization Man*, 136.

24. Whyte, *The Organization Man*, 164.

25. Riesman, *The Lonely Crowd*, 64.

26. Whyte, *The Organization Man*, 346.

27. Riesman, *The Lonely Crowd*, 83.

28. Whyte, *The Organization Man*, 389.

29. Whyte, *The Organization Man*, 395.

30. Gans, *The Urban Villagers*, 81, 85.

31. Vance Packard, *The Status-Seekers* (New York: David McKay Company, 1959), 46.

32. Whyte, *The Organization Man*, 358, 363, 378.

33. The similarities between the organization man in his "honeycomb" and the European peasant can also be detected in Bryce's observations of European peasant life. He writes, "The Swiss peasant, with all his manly independence, has in many cantons a touch of instinctive reverence for the old families; or perhaps, in some other cantons, a touch of jealousy which makes him desire to exclude their members from office, because he feels that they still think themselves better than he is. Nothing like this is possible in America. . . ." Bryce, *The American Commonwealth*, vol. 2, 818.

34. Tocqueville, *Democracy in America*, vol. 2, 180.

35. Tocqueville, *Democracy in America*, vol. 1, 242.

36. Tocqueville, *Democracy in America*, vol. 2, 180.

37. Christopher Lasch, for a different reason, also notes the tendency of the narcissist in the contemporary society of expressive individualism to dissolve his or her identity into the identity of another (e.g., in the celebrity culture). He does not, however, link this new phenomenon with the old experience of the *lackey*. Christopher Lasch, *The Culture of Narcissism* (New York: W. W. Norton and Co., 1979), 85.

38. Tocqueville, *Democracy in America*, vol. 2, 317.
39. Tocqueville, *Democracy in America*, vol. 2, 318.
40. Whyte, *The Organization Man*, 363.
41. Whyte, *The Organization Man*, 73.
42. Tocqueville, *Democracy in America*, vol. 2, 318.
43. Riesman, *The Lonely Crowd*, 26.
44. Augustine, *Confessions*, VI, viii, 13.
45. Riesman, *The Lonely Crowd*, 39.
46. Whyte, *The Organization Man*, 437.
47. Riesman, *The Lonely Crowd*, 16.
48. Riesman, *The Lonely Crowd*, 120.
49. Riesman, *The Lonely Crowd*, 120.
50. Riesman, *The Lonely Crowd*, 120, 196.
51. Riesman, *The Lonely Crowd*, 144.
52. Whyte, *The Organization Man*, 124. See also Mills, *White Collar*, 214.
53. Whyte, *The Organization Man*, 5.
54. Whyte, *The Organization Man*, 178.
55. Whyte, *The Organization Man*, 18.
56. Whyte, *The Organization Man*, 7.
57. Whyte, *The Organization Man*, 418.
58. Whyte, *The Organization Man*, 392, 419, 413.
59. Whyte, *The Organization Man*, 411, 421.
60. Max Scheler, *The Nature of Sympathy* (London: Routledge and Kegan Paul, 1954), 14.
61. Scheler says that a relationship based on reverence is an example of "emotional identification," which he distinguishes from "fellow-feeling." Moreover, he ties "emotional identification" more closely to "emotional infection," or public opinion, which seems to contradict my argument that public opinion in Tocqueville's America was radically different from both aristocratic reverence and contemporary fellow-feeling. This contradiction can be resolved by noting that both fellow-feeling and emotional identification stand for experiences between particular individuals; public opinion is a mass phenomenon. This similarity is hardly noted by Scheler, whose purpose in writing was not to show the common ground between emotional identification and fellow-feeling. In my study, this common ground is important, for I want to show how both reverence and fellow-feeling, unlike public opinion, create bonds of intimacy between persons.
62. Scheler, *The Nature of Sympathy*, 15.
63. Whyte, *The Organization Man*, 434. Riesman, *The Lonely Crowd*, 160.
64. Riesman, *The Lonely Crowd*, 286.
65. Mills, *White Collar*, 263.
66. Riesman, *The Lonely Crowd*, 48, 50.
67. Scheler, *The Nature of Sympathy*, 14.
68. Scheler, *The Nature of Sympathy*, 14.
69. Tocqueville, *Democracy in America*, vol. 2, 161.

70. Tocqueville, *Democracy in America*, vol. 2, 161.
71. Whyte, *The Organization Man,*124.
72. Whyte, *The Organization Man*, 127.
73. Whyte, *The Organization Man*, 126.
74. Whyte, *The Organization Man*, 127.
75. Whyte, *The Organization Man*, 129.
76. Whyte, *The Organization Man*, 84, Riesman, *The Lonely Crowd*, 130.
77. Whyte, *The Organization Man*, 135.
78. Whyte, *The Organization Man*, 136, 214.
79. Riesman, *The Lonely Crowd*, 211.
80. Whyte, *The Organization Man*, 440.
81. Whyte, *The Organization Man*, 221.
82. Whyte, *The Organization Man*, 353.
83. Mills, *White Collar*, 10–14.
84. Tocqueville, *Democracy in America*, vol. 1, 99.
85. The spirit of fellow-feeling in the workplace is not synonymous with economic "corporatism." In a corporatist arrangement, a worker forms a stronger bond with managers in his own company than he does with workers in parallel industries, hence the argument that corporatism deforms class-consciousness. But such a bond need not be structured on the basis of fellow-feeling; detached individualists can also bond together in a corporatist arrangement, just as organization men can bond together according to class. Corporatist bonds can be established on the basis of self-interest (through impersonal contract), and their existence does not necessarily mean that the imaginations of employers and employees have fused, which is what occurs in fellow-feeling.
86. Scheler, *The Nature of Sympathy*, 14.
87. Packard, *The Status-Seekers*, 36.
88. Whyte, *The Organization Man*, 80–82, Riesman, *The Lonely Crowd*, 134.
89. The way such people are described by the Automobile Association of America.
90. Scheler, *The Nature of Sympathy*, 15.
91. Scheler, *The Nature of Sympathy*, 16.
92. Bryce, *The American Commonwealth*, vol. 2, 370.
93. Bryce, *The American Commonwealth*, vol. 2, 326.
94. Bryce, *The American Commonwealth*, vol. 2, 351.
95. For the relevant discussion in Tocqueville's *Democracy in America*, see vol. 1, 263.
96. Bryce, *The American Commonwealth*, vol. 2, 347.
97. Riesman, *The Lonely Crowd*, 71.
98. Riesman, *The Lonely Crowd*, 68.
99. Whyte, *The Organization Man*, 305.
100. Whyte, *The Organization Man*, 203, 216, 401.
101. Riesman, *The Lonely Crowd*, 77, 397.
102. Whyte, *The Organization Man*, 397.
103. Whyte, *The Organization Man*, 396.

104. Bryce, *The American Commonwealth*, vol. 2, 342.

105. Erving Goffman, *The Presentation of Self in Everyday Life* (New York: Doubleday Anchor, 1959). Michel Foucault, *Madness and Civilization: A History of Insanity in the Age of Reason*, Richard Howard, trans. (London: Tavistock, 1977).

106. Mills, *White Collar*, 264.

107. Tocqueville, *Democracy in America*, vol. 2, 171.

108. Tocqueville, *Democracy in America*, vol. 2, 173.

109. Tocqueville, *Democracy in America*, vol. 2, 173.

110. Tocqueville, *Democracy in America*, vol. 2, 173.

111. Whyte, *The Organization Man*, 153.

112. Whyte, *The Organization Man*, 153.

113. Weber, quoted in Bendix, *Max Weber* (New York: Anchor Books, 1960), 86.

114. Bendix, *Max Weber*, 87.

115. Tocqueville, *Democracy in America*, vol. 2, 160.

116. The great confusion that Americans once displayed while touring Europe, noted by both Tocqueville and Bryce, is now rarely seen. A common consumer and entertainment culture unites the two continents. While touring, Americans quickly search out those peer groups most like the ones they belong to at home. Training in "consumer culture" has given contemporary Americans a mastery over codes of etiquette, taste, and lifestyle that Tocqueville's Americans did not have, enabling them to function quite comfortably in European society.

117. Packard, *The Status-Seekers*, 57.

118. Packard, *The Status-Seekers*, 64.

119. Whyte, *The Organization Man*, 73.

120. Brown, *Augustine of Hippo*, 32.

121. Riesman, *The Lonely Crowd*, 48, 53.

122. Riesman, *The Lonely Crowd*, 49.

123. Riesman, *The Lonely Crowd*, 52.

124. Mills, *White Collar*, 282.

125. Whyte, *The Organization Man*, 160.

126. Laurie Hays, "A Taste of Capitalism at Russian Collective Brings Chaos and Strife," *Wall Street Journal*, 27 November 1992, 1.

Chapter 12, The Rise of the Imperial Self

1. Augustine, *On Free Choice of the Will* (Washington, D.C: Catholic University of America Press, 1968), II, v, 47.

2. Augustine, *On Free Choice of the Will*, 47.

3. Nietzsche, *Beyond Good and Evil*, I, 21.

4. Nietzsche, *Beyond Good and Evil*, I, 13.

5. Nietzsche, *Beyond Good and Evil*, I, 19.

6. Nietzsche, *Beyond Good and Evil*, I, 19.

7. Nietzsche, *Beyond Good and Evil*, I, 19.

8. Augustine, *The City of God*, V, 9.

9. Augustine, *The City of God*, V, 9.

10. *Greek-English Lexicon*, Henry Liddel and Robert Scott, eds. (Oxford: Clarendon Press, 1968), 1841.

11. Augustine, *The City of God*, V, 12.

12. Augustine, *The City of God*, V, 13.

13. Bryce, *The American Commonwealth*, vol. 2, 348.

14. Nietzsche, *The Will to Power*, Walter Kaufmann, trans. (New York: Random House, 1967), II, 317.

15. Nietzsche, *The Will to Power*, IV, 936.

16. Nietzsche, *The Will to Power*, III, 752 and IV, 926.

17. *Greek-English Lexicon*, 1841. The following passages from classical texts help to illustrate this point:

"But if no *hubris* were there in addition to the things actually done, I would never have come to court, but in fact it is not because of the hurt arising from the blows, but because of the indignity and the dishonoring that I have come to make him pay." (Isocrates 20.5).

"For it is not the blow itself which arouses the anger, but the dishonour, and it is not actually getting hit which is so terrible for free people, though that's bad enough, but that it's done in *hubris*." (Demosthenes 21.72).

". . . he did *hubris* against me and I got my head smashed." (Lysias 3.40).

"He is the most *hubristic* of them all . . . hitting me viciously," (Aristophanes, *Wasps*, 1303).

"You thought he struck out of *hubris* and not because of the wine," (Demosthenes 21.180).

18. Bryce, *The American Commonwealth*, vol. 2, 348.

19. Bryce, *The American Commonwealth*, vol. 2, 347.

20. Augustine, *The City of God*, V, 8.

21. Brent Shaw also notes that Cicero and the Stoics shared common assumptions. Shaw writes, "Even men who overtly proclaimed their adherence to other philosophies (such as Cicero who claimed allegiance to the moderate views of the Academy) essentially operated, whether consciously or not, within the wider penumbra of Stoic thought." Brent Shaw, "The Divine Economy: Stoicism as Ideology," *Latomus* , no. 44, 1: 17.

22. Charles Beye, *Ancient Greek Literature and Society* (Ithaca: Cornell University Press, 1987), 214.

23. Nietzsche, *Twilight of the Idols*, Walter Kaufmann, trans. (London: Penguin Books, 1990), "The Four Great Errors," 7.

24. Nietzsche, *Beyond Good and Evil*, I, 19.

25. Nietzsche, *Beyond Good and Evil*, I, 19.

26. Nietzsche, *Beyond Good and Evil*, I, 21.

27. Nietzsche, *Beyond Good and Evil*, I, 19.

28. Nietzsche, *Beyond Good and Evil*, I, 19.

29. Nietzsche, *Beyond Good and Evil*, I, 21.

30. Nietzsche, *Beyond Good and Evil*, I, 21.
31. Nietzsche, *Beyond Good and Evil*, I, 21.
32. Nietzsche, *Beyond Good and Evil*, I, 21.
33. Augustine, *The City of God*, V, 10.
34. Augustine, *The City of God*, V, 10.
35. Augustine, *The City of God*, V, 10.
36. Augustine, *The City of God*, V, 10.
37. Augustine, *The City of God*, V, 10.
38. Augustine, *The City of God*, V, 10.
39. Reinhard Bendix, *Kings or People: Power and the Mandate to Rule* (Berkeley: University of California Press, 1978), 230.
40. See Max Weber, *The Protestant Ethic and the Spirit of Capitalism*, Talcott Parsons, trans. (New York: Charles Scribner's Sons, 1958).
41. Bryce, *The American Commonwealth*, vol. 2, 348.
42. Bryce, *The American Commonwealth*, vol. 2, 349.
43. Bryce, *The American Commonwealth*, vol. 2, 355.
44. Bryce, *The American Commonwealth*, vol. 2, 349.
45. Bryce, *The American Commonwealth*, vol. 2, 351.
46. Bryce, *The American Commonwealth*, vol. 2, 350.
47. Bryce, *The American Commonwealth*, vol. 2, 352.
48. Bryce, *The American Commonwealth*, vol. 2, 353.
49. Bryce, *The American Commonwealth*, vol. 2, 353.
50. Bryce, *The American Commonwealth*, vol. 2, 351.
51. Bryce, *The American Commonwealth*, vol. 2, 351.
52. Quentin Anderson, *The Imperial Self* (New York: Knopf, 1971), 21.
53. Peter Shaw, "The Imperial Self," *Sewanee Review*, vol. 93 (Spring 1985): 265–72.
54. Arlie Hochschild, *The Managed Heart* (Berkeley: University of California Press, 1983), 34, 43, 82–83.
55. Hochschild, *The Managed Heart*, 34.
56. Christopher Lasch, *The Culture of Narcissism* (New York: W. W. Norton and Co., 1979), 65.
57. Richard Merelman, *Making Something of Ourselves* (Berkeley: University of California Press, 1984), 24.
58. Merelman, *Making Something of Ourselves*, 240.
59. C. Wright Mills, *White Collar* (New York: Oxford University Press, 1953), 182.
60. Mills, *White Collar*, 184.
61. Bendix, *Kings or People*, 232.
62. Bendix, *Kings or People*, 232. Tocqueville also describes how feudal aristocracy "placed military courage foremost among virtues, but that notions of aristocratic honor vary among societies." *Democracy in America*, Volume 2, 233.
63. Bendix, *Kings or People*, 232.
64. For example, see the novels of John Buchan. See also a history of Russian

aristocrats after the 1917 Revolution in Alex Shoumatoff, *Russian Blood* (New York: Vintage Books,1982).

65. Max Scheler, *Ressentiment*, William Holdheim, trans. (New York: The Free Press of Glencoe, 1961), 55.

66. Scheler, *Ressentiment*, 54.

67. Scheler, *Ressentiment*, 231.

68. Scheler, *Ressentiment*, 232.

69. Scheler, *Ressentiment*, 231.

70. Scheler, *Ressentiment*, 240.

71. Scheler, *Ressentiment*, 232.

72. H. Rider Haggard, *Allan Quartermain* (London: Longmans, Green, and Co., 1887), XV.

73 Description of Princess Nyleptha in H. Rider Haggard, *Allan Quartermain*, XV.

74. Reverend Smythe Palmer, *The Perfect Gentleman*, quoted in Jennie Reekie, *The London Ritz Book of Etiquette* (New York: William Morrow and Co., 1991), 16–17.

75. Max Weber, quoted in Bendix, *Kings or People*, 230.

76. Bendix, *Kings or People*, 230.

77. Marriage for expressive individualists is a union of two people seeking completeness through one another. Marriage for Old World aristocrats was a union of property.

78. Kautsky also makes this point, writing, "Honor is inherently possessed by the aristocrat, not as an individual but as a member of the aristocracy." Kautsky, *The Politics of Aristocratic Empires*, 170.

79. Anthony Trollope, *Can You Forgive Her?* (Oxford: Oxford University Press, 1982), Chapter 1. Also see commentary by Hermione Lee in Anthony Trollope, *The Duke's Children* (Oxford: Oxford University Press, 1982), 651.

80. Tocqueville, *Democracy in America*, vol. 2, 235.

81. Tocqueville, *Democracy in America*, vol. 2, 236.

82. Tocqueville, *Democracy in America*, vol. 2, 237.

83. Tocqueville, *Democracy in America*, vol. 2, 237.

84. Tocqueville, *Democracy in America*, vol. 2, 173.

85. Robert Nisbet, *Community and Power* (New York: Oxford University Press, 1953).

86. Tocqueville, *Democracy in America*, vol. 2, 240.

87. Philip Rieff, *The Triumph of the Therapeutic* (New York: Harper and Row, 1966), 22.

88. Bellah, *Habits of the Heart*, 5, 6.

89. Max Weber, "Luther's Concept of the Calling," *The Protestant Ethic and the Spirit of Capitalism*.

90. Weber, *The Protestant Ethic and the Spirit of Capitalism*, 81.

91. Weber, *The Protestant Ethic and the Spirit of Capitalism*, 85.

92. Weber, *The Protestant Ethic and the Spirit of Capitalism*, 81.

93. Weber, *The Protestant Ethic and the Spirit of Capitalism*, 84.

94. The expressive individualist adopts the hierarchy in jobs that was established during the era of the organization man.

95. Hochschild, *The Managed Heart*, 194.

96. Max Scheler associates the "death" of the self with the spirit of *ressentiment*. In Max Scheler, *Ressentiment*.

97. Hochschild, *The Managed Heart*, 38, 47, 61.

98. Peter Clecak, *America's Quest for the Ideal Self* (New York: Oxford University Press, 1983), 49.

99. Philip Rieff, *The Triumph of the Therapeutic* (New York: Harper and Row, 1966), 25.

100. Merelman, *Making Something of Ourselves*, 103.

Conclusion

1. *Ecclesiastes* 1:9.

2. Brown, *Augustine of Hippo*, 387.

3. Tocqueville, *Democracy in America*, vol. 1, 45.

4. Tocqueville, *Democracy in America*, vol. 1, 167.

5. Tocqueville, *Democracy in America*, vol. 1, 167.

6. Michigan, for example, is considering reform of no-fault divorce laws because of the tremendous rise in the number of divorces over the last two decades. In Dana Milbank, "No-Fault Divorce Law Is Assailed in Michigan, and Debate Heats Up," *Wall Street Journal*, 5 January 1996, 1. Tocqueville says of marriage in nineteenth century America, "There is certainly no country in the world where the tie of marriage is more respected than in America or where conjugal happiness is more highly or worthily appreciated." *Democracy in America*, vol. 1, 304.

7. Tocqueville notes how political association in the Old World often assumed a military style and that members would submit thought and will to a group's leaders even while protesting the tyranny of their government. *Democracy in America*, vol. 1, 198.

8. Tocqueville, *Democracy in America*, vol. 1, 250.

9. Of the difference between East and West, Tocqueville writes, "The Anglo-American relies upon personal interest to accomplish his ends and gives free scope to the unguided strength and common sense of the people; the Russian centers all the authority of society in a single arm." *Democracy in America*, vol. 1, 434.

10. Werner Sombart, *Why is there no socialism in the United States?* Patricia M. Hocking and C.T. Husbands, trans. (White Plains, New York: International Arts and Sciences Press, 1976).

11. Augustine, *City of God*, XIX, 4.

12. Brown, *Augustine of Hippo*, 32.

Bibliography

Anderson, Gregg. *The 22 Laws of Wellness*. San Francisco: HarperCollins, 1995.

Anderson, Quentin. *The Imperial Self*. New York: Knopf, 1971.

Arieli, Yehoshua. *Individualism and Nationalism in American Ideology*. Cambridge, Mass.: Harvard University Press, 1964.

Aries, Philippe. *Centuries of Childhood*, Translated by Robert Baldick. New York: Vintage Books, 1965.

Armstrong, A. Hilary. *St. Augustine and Christian Platonism*. Villanova: Villanova University Press, 1967.

Augustine. *The City of God*. Translated by Marcus Dods. New York: Random House, 1950.

———. *The Confessions*. Translated by John Ryan. New York: Doubleday, 1960.

———. *Four Anti-Pelagian Writings*. Translated by John Mourant and William Collinge. Washington, D.C.: Catholic University of America Press, 1992.

———. *On Free Choice of the Will*. Washington, D.C.: Catholic University of America Press, 1968.

Basic Writings of Saint Augustine. 2 vols. Edited by Whitney Oates. New York: Random House, 1948.

Bell, Daniel. *The Coming of Post-Industrial Society*. New York: Basic Books, 1976.

———. *The Cultural Contradictions of Capitalism*. New York: Basic Books, 1976.

Bellah, Robert et. al. *Habits of the Heart*. New York: Harper & Row, 1985.

Bendix, Reinhard. *Kings or People: Power and the Mandate to Rule*. Berkeley: University of California Press, 1978.

———. *Max Weber*. New York: Anchor Books, 1960.

Beye, Charles. *Ancient Greek Literature and Society*. Ithaca: Cornell University Press, 1987.

Brandon, Nathaniel. *The Psychology of Self-Esteem*. Los Angeles: Nash, 1969.

Brison, Karen. *Just Talk*. Berkeley: University of California Press, 1992.

Brown, Peter. *Augustine of Hippo*. Berkeley: University of California Press, 1967.

Bryce, James. *The American Commonwealth*. 2 vols. New York: The Macmillan Company, 1911.

Buchan, John. *The Free Fishers*. London: Hodder and Stoughton, 1934.

———. *Pilgrim's Way*. Boston: Houghton Mifflin Company, 1940.

Burke, Edmund. "A Philosophical Enquiry into the Origins of Our Ideas of the

Sublime and Beautiful." In *The Works of Edmund Burke*. Vol. 1. London: C. and J. Rivington, 1826.

———. *Reflections on the Revolution in France*. Edited by Conor Cruise O'Brien. London: Penguin Books, 1968.

Callahan, John. *Augustine and the Greek Philosophers*. Villanova: Villanova University Press, 1967.

Clecak, Peter. *America's Quest for the Ideal Self*. New York: Oxford University Press, 1983.

Cochrane, Charles. *Christianity and Classical Culture*. London: Oxford University Press, 1944.

Cohen, Morton. *Rider Haggard: His Life and Works*. New York: Walker and Company, 1960.

A Companion to the Study of St. Augustine. Edited by Roy Battenhouse. New York: Oxford University Press, 1969.

The Cultural of Consumption. Edited by R. W. Fox and T. J. Jackson Lears. New York: Pantheon Books, 1983.

Dahrendorf, Ralf. *Society and Democracy in Germany*. New York: Anchor Books, 1969.

Dickens, Charles. *American Notes*. New York: Charles Scribner's Sons, 1924.

———. *Martin Chuzzlewit*. New York: Charles Scribner's Sons, 1924.

Ellis, Albert. *Anger: How to Live With and Without It*. Secaucus, New Jersey: Citadel Press, 1977.

Ellis, Albert and Robert Harper. *A New Guide to Practical Loving*. Englewood Cliffs, New Jersey: Prentice-Hall, 1975.

The Federalist. Cambridge, Mass.: Belknap Press of Harvard University Press, 1966.

Fischer, Claude. "Toward a Subcultural Theory of Urbanism." *American Journal of Sociology* 80, no. 6 (May 1975): 1319–1341.

Foucault, Michel. *Madness and Civilization: A History of Insanity in the Age of Reason*. Translated by Richard Howard. London: Tavistock, 1977.

Fowler, James. *Stages of Faith*. San Francisco: Harpers San Francisco, 1981.

Friedman, Lawrence. *The Republic of Choice*. Cambridge: Harvard University Press, 1990.

Gans, Herbert. *The Urban Villagers*. New York: The Free Press, 1962.

Gerschenkron, Alexander. *Bread and Democracy in Germany*. Berkeley: University of California Press, 1943.

Giddens, Anthony. *Capitalism and Modern Social Theory*. London: Cambridge University Press, 1971.

Glynn, Eugene David. "Television and the American Character—A Psychiatrist Looks at Television." In *Television's Impact on American Culture*, edited by William Elliot. East Lansing: University of Michigan Press, 1956.

Goffman, Erving. *The Presentation of Self in Everyday Life*. New York: Doubleday Anchor, 1959.

Greek-English Lexicon. Compiled by Henry Liddel and Robert Scott. Oxford: Clarendon Press, 1968.

Haggard, H. Rider. *Allan Quartermain*. London: Longmans, Green, and Co., 1887.

Hartz, Louis. *The Liberal Tradition in America*. New York: Harcourt Brace and World, Inc., 1955.

Hayek, Friedrich. *The Road to Serfdom*. Chicago: The University of Chicago Press, 1944.

Hays, Laurie, "A Taste of Capitalism at Russian Collective Brings Chaos and Strife." In *Wall Street Journal*, 27 November 1992, 1.

Hekman, Susan. *Weber, The Ideal Type, and Contemporary Social Theory*. Notre Dame: University of Notre Dame Press, 1983.

Hochschild, Arlie. *The Managed Heart*. Berkeley: University of California Press, 1983.

Kautsky, John. *The Politics of Aristocratic Empires*. Chapel Hill: The University of North Carolina Press, 1982.

Kolakowski, Leszek. *Main Currents of Marxism*. 3 vols. Oxford: Clarendon Press, 1978.

Lasch, Christopher. *The Culture of Narcissism*. New York: W. W. Norton and Co., 1979.

―――. "Hillary Clinton, Childsaver." *Harper's Magazine* 285, no. 1709 (October 1992).

Laski, Harold. *American Democracy*. New York: Viking Press, 1948.

Leiby, James. *A History of Social Welfare and Social Work in the United States*. New York: Columbia University Press, 1968.

Lerner, Daniel. *The Passing of Traditional Society*. Glencoe, Illinois: The Free Press, 1958.

Lyons, John. *The Invention of the Self*. Carbondale, Illinois: Southern Illinois University Press, 1978.

The Man in the Arena. Edited by John Allen Gable. New York: The Theodore Roosevelt Association, 1987.

Merelman, Richard. *Making Something of Ourselves*. Berkeley: University of California Press, 1984.

Milbank, Dana, "No-Fault Divorce Law Is Assailed in Michigan, And Debate Heats Up." In *Wall Street Journal*, 5 January 1996, 1.

Mills, C. Wright. *White Collar*. New York: Oxford University Press, 1953.

Molnar, Thomas. *The Emerging Atlantic Culture*. New Brunswick, New Jersey: Transaction Publishers, 1994.

Moore, Barrington Jr. *Social Origins of Dictatorship and Democracy*. Boston: Beacon Press, 1966.

Neuhaus, Richard John. *The Naked Public Square*. Grand Rapids, Michigan: W. B. Eerdmans Publishing Co., 1984.

The New Class? Edited by B. Bruce-Briggs. New Brunswick, New Jersey: Transaction Books, 1979.

Nietzsche, Friedrich. *The Anti-Christ*. Translated by Walter Kaufmann. London: Penguin Books, 1990.

―――. *Beyond Good and Evil*. Translated by Walter Kaufmann. New York: Random House, 1966.

———. *The Birth of Tragedy.* Translated by Walter Kaufmann. New York: Vintage Books, 1967.

———. *Thus Spoke Zarathustra.* Translated by Walter Kaufmann. New York: Penguin Books, 1954.

———. *Twilight of the Idols.* Translated by Walter Kaufmann. London: Penguin Books, 1990.

———. *Untimely Meditations.* Translated by R. J. Hollingdale. Cambridge: Cambridge University Press, 1983.

———. *The Will to Power.* Translated by Walter Kaufmann. New York: Random House, 1967.

Nisbet, Robert. *Community and Power.* New York: Oxford University Press, 1953.

Ober, Josiah. *Mass and Elite in Democratic Athens.* Princeton: Princeton University Press, 1989.

Packard, Vance. *The Status-Seekers.* New York: David McKay Company, 1959.

Postman, Neil. *The Disappearance of Childhood.* New York: Delacorte Press, 1982.

Rawls, John. *A Theory of Justice.* Cambridge: Harvard University Press, 1971.

Rebhorn, Wayne. "The Crisis of Aristocracy in *Julius Caesar.*" *Renaissance Quarterly* 43, no. 1, 1990.

Redfield, Robert. *Little Community and Peasant Society and Culture.* Chicago: The University of Chicago Press, 1956.

Reekie, Jennie. *The London Ritz Book of Etiquette.* New York: William Morrow and Co., 1991.

Rieff, Philip. *The Triumph of the Therapeutic.* New York: Harper and Row, 1966.

Riesman, David. *The Lonely Crowd.* New Haven: Yale University Press, 1950.

Robbins, Anthony. *Unlimited Power.* New York: Fawcett Columbine, 1986.

Ross, C. Randolph. *Common Sense Christianity.* New York: Occaam Publishers, 1989.

Sandel, Michael. "The Procedural Republic and the Unencumbered Self." *Political Theory* 12, no. 1 (February 1984): 81–96.

Scheler, Max. *The Nature of Sympathy.* London: Routledge and Kegan Paul, 1954.

———. *Ressentiment.* Translated by William Holdheim. New York: The Free Press of Glencoe, 1961.

———. "Shame and Feelings of Modesty." In *Person and Self-Value,* edited by M. S. Frings. Dordrecht: Kluwer Academic Publishers, 1987.

Sennett, Richard. *The Fall of Public Man.* (New York: W. W. Norton and Company, 1976.

———. *The Uses of Disorder.* New York: Knopf, 1970.

Shaw, Brent. "The Divine Economy: Stoicism as Ideology." *Latomus* 44, section 1.

Shaw, Peter. "The Imperial Self." *Sewanee Review* 93 (Spring 1985): 265–72.

Shoumatoff, Alex. *Russian Blood.* New York: Vintage Books, 1982.

Sombart, Werner. *Why Is There No Socialism in America?* Translated by Patricia M. Hocking and C. T. Husbands. White Plains, New York: International Arts and Science Press, 1976.

Strauss, Leo. *Liberalism Ancient and Modern.* Ithaca: Cornell University Press, 1968.

———. *Studies in Platonic Political Philosophy*. Chicago: University of Chicago Press, 1983.

Sylver, Marshall. *Passion, Profit, and Power*. New York: Simon and Schuster, 1995.

Taylor, Charles. *Sources of the Self*. Cambridge: Harvard University Press, 1989.

Tocqueville, Alexis de. *Democracy in America*. 2 vols. Translated by Henry Reeve. New York: Vintage Books, 1990.

———. *The Old Regime and the French Revolution*. Translated by Stuart Gilbert. New York: Doubleday Anchor Books, 1955.

Trollope, Anthony. *The Duke's Children*. Oxford: Oxford University Press, 1982.

———. *North America*. New York: Alfred Knopf, 1951.

———. *Phineas Finn*. New York: Dodd, Mead and Company, 1921.

———. *The Warden*. New York: Random House, 1936.

Trollope, Frances. *Domestic Manners of the Americans* New York: Vintage Books, 1949.

Turner, Ralph. "The Real Self: From Institution to Impulse." *American Journal of Sociology* 81, no. 5.

Unger, Roberto. *Knowledge and Politics*. New York: The Free Press, 1975.

Veroff, Joseph. *The Inner American: A Self-Portrait from 1957 to 1976*. New York: Basic Books, 1981.

Walzer, Michael. *Spheres of Justice*. New York: Basic Books, 1983.

Weber, Max. *The City*. Translated by Don Martindale and Gertrud Neuwirth. New York: The Free Press, 1958.

———. *The Protestant Ethic and the Spirit of Capitalism*. Translated by Talcott Parsons. New York: Charles Scribner's Sons, 1958.

———. "The Protestant Sects and the Spirit of Capitalism." In *From Max Weber: Essays in Sociology*. Translated by H. H. Gerth and C. Wright Mills. New York: Oxford University Press, 1949.

Whyte, William Jr. *The Organization Man*. New York: Doubleday, 1956.

Wiebe, Robert. *The Search for Order, 1877–1920*. New York: Hill and Wang, 1967.

Willis, Geoffrey. *Saint Augustine and the Donatist Controversy*. London: SPCK, 1950.

Wills, Garry. *Inventing America: Jefferson's Declaration of Independence*. New York: Doubleday, 1978.

Wirth, Louis. "Urbanism as a Way of Life." *American Journal of Sociology* 44, no. 1 (July 1938).

Wolfe, Thomas. *The Bonfire of the Vanities*. New York: Farrar-Straus-Giroux, 1987.

Index

Abrams, Jeremiah, 5
administrative despotism, 68, 147–48
Anderson, Greg, 41
Anderson, Quentin, 184
Arieli, Yehoshua, 118
Aries, Philippe, 83
aristocracy, xv–xvii, 143, 168; attitude
    towards religion in, 55, 57; attitude
    towards work in, 24–27; and castes, 60,
    69–70; childhood in, 82–86; and the
    experience of pleasure, 15–16, 18; fam-
    ily in, 80–82; and honor, 187–191; and
    the idea of peace, 122; and the impor-
    tance of status, 114–17, 134; and religi-
    osity, 96–100; and reputation, 87–90;
    and tradition, 105
aristocrat in the City of God, xvii, 101,
    103, 113, 120–28, 136–37, 139–40,
    149, 173, 180, 181, 183, 184, 185, 192
aristocrat in the City of Man, xvi, xvii, 87,
    90, 91, 97, 103, 113, 120–28, 136–37,
    149, 173, 177, 180, 187, 191, 193, 209
aristocraticism, 94, 95, 167, 211
Augustine, *Against Julian*, 48; *City of
    God*, 34, 53–54, 56, 116, 130, 172,
    173, 176, 186, 216; *Confessions*, 9,
    101–2, 149; criticism of aristocrats, xv,
    16, 174; criticism of Cicero, 173; criti-
    cism of the Donatists, xv, 21, 59, 64,
    65; criticism of Manicheism, xv, 7–13;

criticism of the Pelagians, xv, 42, 44,
    45–47; criticism of the Platonists, xv,
    35, 75–76, 122, 130–31; criticism of
    the Stoics, 178; and the invisible
    church of God, 60, 74; and the limita-
    tions of reason, 35; as a Manichee, 3,
    6, 7; *On Christian Doctrine*, 53; *On
    the Gift of Perseverance*, 131; praise of
    the Platonists, 34

Bellah, Robert, 14, 14n38, 26, 41, 50, 51,
    52–53, 62, 65, 67, 68, 73, 198
Bendix, Reinhard, xvi, 188
Bradshaw, John, 5
Brown, Peter, 217
Bryce, James, 61, 62, 71, 87–88, 106,
    107–8, 109, 115, 137n41, 145n33,
    161, 164, 174, 175, 181–82
Buchan, John, 115–16

calling, 24–27, 197–200
career, 24–27, 197–200
caring professions, 26, 54–55, 57, 86, 198
Children's Defense Fund, 84
Christianity, afterworld in, 125, 128–33,
    138, 139–40; and Europe, 56, 131–32;
    and expressive individualism, 40–51;
    and power over the American mind,
    30–31, 56, 180–81; and principle of
    utility, 55–56; respect for work in, 25,

247